AF893184

From the Edge

Latinidad

Transnational Cultures in the United States

This series publishes books that deepen and expand our understanding of Latina/o populations, especially in the context of their transnational relationships within the Americas. Focusing on borders and boundary-crossings, broadly conceived, the series is committed to publishing scholarship in history, film and media, literary and cultural studies, public policy, economics, sociology, and anthropology. Inspired by interdisciplinary approaches, methods, and theories developed out of the study of transborder lives, cultures, and experiences, the titles enrich our understanding of transnational dynamics.

Matt Garcia, Series Editor, School of Historical, Philosophical, and Religious Studies and Director of Comparative Border Studies, Arizona State University

For a list of titles in the series, see the last page of the book.

From the Edge

Chicana/o Border Literature and the Politics of Print

ALLISON E. FAGAN

Rutgers University Press
New Brunswick, New Jersey, and London

Library of Congress Cataloging-in-Publication Data

Names: Fagan, Allison E., 1982– author.
Title: From the edge : Chicana/o border literature and the politics of print / Allison E. Fagan.
Description: New Brunswick, New Jersey : Rutgers University Press, [2016] | Series: Transnational cultures in the United States | Includes bibliographical references and index.
Identifiers: LCCN 2015037352| ISBN 9780813583808 (hardcover : alk. paper) | ISBN 9780813583792 (pbk. : alk. paper) | ISBN 9780813583853 (e-book (epub)) | ISBN 9780813583907 (e-book (web pdf))
Subjects: LCSH: American literature—Mexican American authors—History and criticism. | Mexican Americans—Books and reading. | Authors and readers—United States. | Mexican Americans in literature.
Classification: LCC PS153.M4 F34 2016 | DDC 810.9/86872—dc23
LC record available at http://lccn.loc.gov/2015037352

A British Cataloging-in-Publication record for this book is available from the British Library.

Visit our website: http://rutgerspress.rutgers.edu

Manufactured in the United States of America

For my parents, Mike and Cindy

Contents

Preface

This book is the culmination of years of thinking about and living on the edges of texts. Though it took me years to figure it out, from my high school days reading *The House on Mango Street* to my undergraduate studies at Saint Xavier University in Chicago through my dissertation at Loyola University in Chicago, I have been compelled to examine the material borders of literature for signs and clues to how they were made. But I have also been compelled by a simple love of stories, and of reading and writing and the opportunity to make it my life. The Chicana/o novels and stories I have been fortunate to spend the past several years with have been great company and great inspiration, and I'm so grateful to have been welcomed into their worlds.

This book began as my dissertation, which in turn began as a series of discussions in a class on transnational and border literatures taught by Paul Jay at Loyola University in the summer of 2006. Paul would later chair my dissertation committee, and I have benefited immensely from his guidance and his enthusiasm for this literature that has made a home in my heart. Fellow committee members Steven Jones and Suzanne Bost were also instrumental in challenging my ideas about textual scholarship and Chicana/o literature, respectively; Suzanne in particular has been a model not only of scholarship but also of generosity and thoughtfulness, and her encouragement has meant the world to me. Loyola was a wonderful place to live and work. I was fortunate to work with and also wish to thank Badia Ahad, Pamela Caughie,

Suzanne Gossett, Joyce Wexler, Harveen Mann, Jack Kerkering, and, perhaps most important, Moe Taylor for their guidance and support.

Likewise, at James Madison University (JMU) in Harrisonburg, Virginia, I have had the good fortune of working with dedicated mentors, including Mark Parker and Dabney Bankert, who have been tireless in their efforts to encourage my research and writing. The writing group that has welcomed me at JMU—Siân White, Dawn Goode, and Mollie Godfrey—has also read various drafts with sensitivity, offering important insights as well as some good laughs, and the JMU English department faculty as a whole has offered encouragement in ways large and small. My gratitude goes to Matt Rebhorn, Mary Thompson, Brooks Hefner, Maria Odette Canivell, and Erica Cavanaugh, in particular, who have all been exceedingly kind and supportive, and to Rose Gray, who has never failed to have an answer to one of my questions.

Researching this book involved visits to archives and conversations with authors, and the Graduate Program at Loyola was instrumental in funding travel to research the archives of Ana Castillo. I thank in particular Sal Güereña at the University of California, Santa Barbara, for his assistance with Ana Castillo's archives, as well as Margarita Cota-Cárdenas and Richard Yañez for their generosity with their time. Earlier versions of chapters 1 and 2 have appeared in *MELUS* and the *Journal of Modern Literature*, respectively; I am grateful to the editors and readers of those versions for their insights and suggestions for revision. I have presented portions of this book at various conferences, and I am thankful for all of the feedback I've received while participating on panels hosted at the Modern Language Association, the American Studies Association, and the Latina/o Literary Theory and Criticism Conference. The anonymous manuscript readers offered penetrating insights and significant guidance. The entire staff with which I have been involved at Rutgers University Press has been accommodating and supportive, and I am grateful to Leslie Mitchner for finding this book worth reading.

Beyond the scope of writing this book, teachers, family, and friends whose names are too many to list have supported me at every turn, and without them I would not have believed I could make this book a reality. Just some of their names include Jeanne Garritano and George Grenchik, two passionate elementary school teachers at Saint Victor School in Calumet City, Illinois; Karolyn Steele, the most fabulous high school English teacher there has ever been; and Nelson Hathcock, who did me the great kindness of helping me believe graduate school was possible, even when others suggested it was not. My cohort at Loyola, which included Natalie Kalich, Julia Daniel, Erin Holliday Karre, Adam Augustyn, and Lacey Conley, should be the envy of all graduate school cohorts: they have become my best friends, and they gave me room to grow. My sisters and brothers, Stacy, Kelly, Bonnie, Kyle, and Randy, who have always laughed at my vocabulary, challenged me to write clearly and engagingly. My husband, Brian, and my dog, Marty, have been nearly equal in their loyal support and joy in my happiness. My daughter, Riley, has given me new incentive to make her proud. And my parents, to whom this book is dedicated, deserve so much more than a line on a page, but it's a start.

From the Edge

Introduction

In 1981, Chicana writers Gloria Anzaldúa and Cherríe Moraga published *This Bridge Called My Back: Writings by Radical Women of Color*, an anthology of essays now considered one of the foundational texts of U.S. Third World feminism. They describe their intentions for the book as follows: "We want to express to all women—especially to white middle-class women—the experiences which divide us as feminists" (xxiii). The often ambivalent way in which the writers included in this anthology discuss serving as a bridge between the theories of white feminists and the lived experiences of women of color reflects a reluctant embrace of the border spaces that characterize their lives. Significantly, such ambivalence is made material in the story of their anthology's struggle to stay in print. A close look at the opening pages of the book, particularly the 1983 edition, reveals evidence of the conflict and tensions surrounding the material text. One of the first pages of the second edition reads, in fine print halfway down the page:

> When Persephone Press, Inc., a white women's press of Watertown, Massachusetts and the original publishers of *Bridge*, ceased operation in the Spring of 1983, this book had already gone out of print. After many months of negotiations, the co-editors were finally able to retrieve control of their book, whereupon Kitchen Table: Women of Color Press of New York agreed to republish it. The following, then, is the second edition of *This Bridge Called My Back*, conceived of and produced entirely by women of color.

Before readers have even read the introduction, they are presented with hints of conflict; Kayann Short explains, "There is a story here, and like all tales of struggle, it speaks of power, pain, and loss. Yet there is also pride in the words 'conceived of and produced entirely by women of color,' and a final sense of restitution, celebration, and homecoming" (3). That narrative of restitution only continues for Anzaldúa and Moraga's anthology: in 2002, after years of being out of print, Norma Alarcón's Third Woman Press brought out a third edition, which again went out of print in 2008. After a seven-year lapse, State University of New York Press brought out a fourth edition with even further expanded material in March 2015. The story of Anzaldúa and Moraga's efforts to keep their book in print is told from the very textual margins of a collection that details the struggles for survival of women of color, reminding readers that the book they hold in front of them is part of that struggle.

In many works of border literature, particularly those authored by Chicana/o authors like Anzaldúa and Moraga, the margins or borders of the material text serve to underscore the narratives of struggle—for autonomy, civil rights, history, identity—their writers set out to tell. Textual margins, also defined as "paratexts" and "bibliographic codes," include those material elements that make up the border between the story and the world—cover pages, prefaces, glossaries, introductions, bibliographies, typography, and even the white space of the margins—and shape our understanding of those texts. The brief publishing history supplied at the opening of *This Bridge Called My Back* appears in the textual margins along with multiple forewords, prefaces, and other epigraphic materials and conditions our understanding of and expectations for the text it precedes. Sometimes the writers themselves speak from the textual margins, as when Moraga and Anzaldúa describe "retriev[ing] control of their book," though in each of its versions and editions they can never entirely control how or where it is marketed, sold, read, or reviewed. Just as often, the borders between the text and the world serve as sites in which publishers and readers manipulate the meanings of narratives, selecting attractive cover pages or literally filling the margins with their own words.

The literal borders of the text function as a space where the interests and desires of authors, publishers, editors, reviewers, and readers contest for control over its meaning, and in works of Chicana/o U.S.-Mexico border literature, they serve as a site from which to explore the instability common to border identity and the social lives of texts. By "social lives" I mean to invoke the work of social text theorists like D. F. McKenzie and Jerome McGann to describe the circulations throughout and interactions with the world of texts in various forms, constructed by the competing discourses, intentions, and expectations of authors, publishers, editors, critics, and readers. The social life of *This Bridge Called My Back* is constituted by the forces of Anzaldúa and Moraga; their contributors; Persephone Press, Kitchen Table Press, Third

Woman Press and State University of New York Press; readers; and the critics who cite the anthology to advance any number of arguments as well as the political climates of the 1980s, 1990s, and early 2000s. The anthology, like all border texts, demands that we read and understand its contents in the context of this complex social life.

Perhaps because Chicana/o literary studies has often privileged performance and orality in Mexican American border traditions—from border *corridos* to El Teatro Campesino—discussions of the role and uses of the material text have yet to surface in the work of border theorists, though Kirsten Silva Gruesz's work in the field of nineteenth-century Latina/o print culture has been positively groundbreaking.[1] Likewise, though textual scholars recognize that the borders of the text invisibly control, alter, and subvert the intentions of authors and their texts, such a relationship for border writers functions differently from the relationship of more canonical or central writers and identities to their respective textual margins. Racism, sexism, classism, and nationalism permeate the history of American publishing, leading to an imbalance of power that complicates any relationship between a border author and editor, publisher, and audience. This difference has only recently been attended to in book history and demands further attention.

In drawing together border literary scholarship and textual materialism, or what Bill Brown calls "a mode of analytic objectification that focuses on the physical properties of an embodied text" (25), this book negotiates the border in many senses, both material and metaphorical, so it is worth pausing to define the border and its meanings. Throughout, I employ and study the terminology of the border in ways that account for its use in Chicana/o literature and elsewhere to suggest both a physical, lived space and a sometimes problematic metaphor for identity by asking how a textual materialist concern for borders might intersect with, rather than conflate or erase, those definitions. What follows is a survey of the border as geographic space and place, as metaphor, and as a material textual element.

Making Metaphors out of the Material Border

When we call together a genre of literature that employs the U.S.-Mexico border as a setting, invokes the U.S.-Mexico border as a place that shapes characters' lives, or that was simply written while living in these spaces, under the umbrella of border literature, we grant that similar geographic realities might shape narrative in similar ways. But even to suggest that such literature is interested in or located on the U.S.-Mexico border is to assign a stability or sameness that misleads. Culturally and geographically, the border of Matamoros/Brownsville is not the same as the border of El Paso/Juárez, Nogales/Sonora, or Columbus/Puerto Palomas, to say nothing of narrative representations of such places. In turn, historians of the U.S.-Mexico border have highlighted the seemingly haphazard and fitful negotiations of these national boundary lines drawn as a result of the repeated conquests of contested territory, telling the story of a border always in the process of becoming.[2] Even the 1848 Treaty of Guadalupe Hidalgo, which signaled the end of the U.S.-Mexican War and the loss of more than half of Mexico's territory to the United States, failed to nail down the boundary: it required the supplementation of the Gadsden Purchase five years later to iron out the details, and its provisions are debated even today.

This border is one that soldiers, surveyors, cartographers, politicians, and historians alike have sought to fix in place while the land and our experience of it resists such fixing. This is, in part, no metaphor: the border literally moves. It crosses and zigzags each landscape differently, in some places marked, in others unmarked. The Río Grande moves, and we move our fences—or sometimes, the river itself—to accommodate its movements, to preserve the boundaries of nations. But we can't neglect the ways the border and its conflicts also move with people, whether with migrant workers who make their way north and back south again season after season, as so eloquently depicted in Tomás Rivera's *. . . y no se lo tragó la tierra* (1971), or in the minds of soldiers including Ulysses S. Grant, who saw the Civil War as "the outgrowth of the Mexican War." Grant calls upon karmic justice as he links U.S.-Mexican border disputes to the question of slavery, claiming, "Nations, like individuals, are punished for their transgressions. We got our punishment in the most sanguinary and expensive war of modern times" (478). By extension, he also suggests that the changing boundaries of the American Southwest are mapped onto the changing boundaries of the North and South in the American Civil War, altering the angle from which we view those histories and geographies. Even the famous Chicano civil rights chant "We didn't cross the border, the border crossed us" suggests that this kind of paradoxical mobility is an essential characteristic of the national boundary.[3]

The simultaneous desire and inability to fix the U.S.-Mexico border in place is perhaps what entices writers of all kinds to draw on the term in its more metaphoric senses. What we can't permanently root in geography, we locate in metaphor. Mary Pat Brady has referred to this characteristic as the "fungibility of borders," or the ability of borders "to slip outside of the material and the metaphoric and also to lay hold to both" ("Fungibility" 178). Certainly one of the founding texts of border theorizing, Gloria Anzaldúa's *Borderlands / La Frontera: The New Mestiza*, suggests such mixing: while the author's focus is explicitly on "the Texas–U.S., Southwest–Mexican border," Anzaldúa's text expands "borderlands" to include "the psychological borderlands, the sexual borderlands and the spiritual borderlands," even in her preface. In the invocation of "borderlands" in lieu of a singular "border," Anzaldúa highlights the linguistic indeterminacy of *la frontera*, which carries with it the connotations of a contact zone in comparison to the binary language underpinning the English "frontier," the rigid, defining, and singular extreme limit between civilization and everything else. In turn, some interpretations of this broad concept of the borderlands have encouraged a number of critics and writers, both within and outside of the study of Chicana/o literature, to transplant such borderlands to any number of places, and to use it to describe any number of situations in which "two or more cultures edge each other" (Anzaldúa, *Borderlands* 19). Such readings incorporate both physical traits of geography and literal barriers, as well as less tangible characteristics that simultaneously separate and draw together nations, cultures, ethnicities, religions, genders, and even families.

As a result, others worry that "border literature" has come to mean any literature that places an emphasis on the border as a liminal space and in which characters confront an internal or external divide, attempting to work out identity in that space between. The centrality of the specific U.S.-Mexico border often and easily gives way to analyses of the borders between the United States and any number of countries or between any two countries (or cultures, or families, or even individuals) anywhere. Scholarly calls for site specificity proceed in direct response to the borrowing or even cooption of the concept of the border by postmodern and postcolonial theorists working with a wide variety of geographic locations. Claire Fox, for example, cautions against "the de facto emergence of the metropolis as site of 'border crossings' in the work of the postmodern theorists, in the wake of allegedly collapsed national boundaries" (130). Furthermore, many critics continue to express concern over those whose voices are silenced in the move toward "liberating the border from its spatial referent," as Claudia Sadowski-Smith argues (*Border Fictions* 35). The celebration of a hybrid or borderlands identity can overshadow the realities in which being "between" nations offers not a liberating, antiessentialist, fluid site of agency but rather a confining, dangerous, and exploitative reality, a reality migrant and other bodies aim to pass through as quickly as possible rather than revel in. In the interest of avoiding the remarginalization—or the continued marginalization, perhaps, of the voices of those whose lives depend on literally negotiating a very real border—these critics ask that we examine our reasons for expanding the spaces and places of the border to include these metaphorical imaginings.[4]

If employing metaphors potentially dislocates the border from the lived experiences of the systemic racism it enacts and supports, the same might be said of scholarship that has recently turned toward postnational, transnational, and hemispheric "remappings" of Latina/o and Chicana/o narrative and history.[5] Such criticisms demand that we attend to what is described by Neil Larsen as the "persistent haunting of a would-be transnationalized . . . by the specters of the national" (xii). But by joining those critics interested in pursuing the way Chicana/o literature invokes the mobility and metaphors of the border, including José David Saldívar, Ramón Saldívar, and Alicia Schmidt Camacho, or by describing the U.S.-Mexico border as constantly under construction, I do not mean to suggest that it exerts no specific, directed, or local control.[6] The border is, most certainly, "a site of juridical control where people are policed, detained, and turned away—often violently—where people's legitimacy, their very humanity is determined by their citizenship status" (Mendoza 250). Its perpetual geographic un-fixedness, its resistance to firm location, rather, only amplifies and serves those with the power to authorize or legislate its locations to suit their changing needs. It is also that characteristic, however, that opens up spaces for subversion, for a reconceptualization of that authorizing power. It is what allows undocumented immigrants to locate the literal gaps in the fences as well as what invites us to recognize the border as both a lived reality and a narrative, a story we tell about where one part of the world ends and another begins. The description of the U.S.-Mexico border as an ever-changing narrative does not diminish but rather emphasizes its power in the physical world: that narrative has material consequences, legislating and altering the lived experience of those on or near it.

Describing the experience of the geographic U.S.-Mexico border in ways that include its more metaphoric uses, then, seems both an inevitable and fundamental part of the defining process. This is perhaps especially so in the context of Chicana/o imaginings of that border, both political and literary. This material/metaphoric slippage of the border most clearly manifests itself via one of the foundations of Chicana/o literary and political history: the concept of Aztlán. As the purported home of the Nahua people as well as an identifier taken up by Chicano activists and poets in the 1960s and 1970s in an effort to reclaim their homeland, Aztlán worked as a metaphorical gathering space around which a new identity might coalesce. It also, in many maps, layers neatly over much of the territory lost by Mexico to the United States in 1848. Referring to a real, or perhaps only legendary, geographic place for which we have lost the maps, an unknown geography that is nevertheless home, Aztlán slides between material and metaphor. In the Chicano Movement, the varying aims of different activists with regard to the question of whether Aztlán was meant to be an actual, lived, geographic space to be reclaimed by Chicanos or more of an imagined community further suggests the slippage between material and metaphor.

When we turn from the language of Aztlán to the language of the borderlands, that blurring of the material and metaphor continues. Describing the links between those terms, for example, Monika Kaup suggests, "Chicano authors insisted that the space of their culture, the *mexicano* borderlands of the Southwest, was not the peripheral fringe of the American historical process, but a place in its own right, home, Aztlán, the native homeland of different peoples than Anglo Americans" (*Rewriting* 1). Mixing the geographical border zone with the metaphoric "fringe of the American historical process," Kaup's language demonstrates the appeal of talking about the lived realities, geographies, and histories of the U.S.-Mexico border via the metaphoric borderlands of nation and history. The metaphorical language of the "periphery," that term from postcolonial theory akin to the metaphorical language of the border, likewise appears in the work of Ramón Saldívar as he describes the subversive ways Chicana/o narratives "intentionally exploit their peripheral status to and exclusion from the body of works that we might call majority literature" ("Narrative" 11). In privileging border spaces unifying a genre of literature, we frequently if not always walk the tightrope between material and metaphor.

Renegotiating the Third Space between Material and Metaphor

Rather than avoiding such a tightrope, foundational border literary criticism suggests and even celebrates the inevitability of that collapsing of material and metaphor: Brady acknowledges the insights Chicana/o literature offers into the fungibility of borders, applauding texts that "refus[e] a too-rigid binary between the material and the discursive" (*Extinct Lands* 6), while Anzaldúa almost lovingly describes the U.S.-Mexico border as "home / this thin edge of / barbwire" (13). Anzaldúa's language carves out a third space precariously balanced upon the interdependent material and metaphorical boundary lines that separate and draw together nations. These coexistent conceptions of the border are supported by postmodern geographers like Edward Soja, who argues for an understanding of space as "a simultaneously real-and-imagined, actual-and-virtual locus of structured individuality and collective experience and agency" (11). By extension, border scholars and postmodern geographers alike also ask readers to conceptualize both space and place as text, reading each as interdependent: as Yi-Fu Tuan argues, "From the security and stability of place we are aware of the openness, freedom, and threat of space, and vice versa" (6). In the case of the U.S.-Mexico border, the space of the borderlands, in both allowing and directing movement, is connected to and dependent on what Tuan calls the "pause" that constitutes the border as place (6). In his study of the effects of the Treaty of Waitangi on the Maori, textual scholar McKenzie makes a similar argument: "When the case for Aboriginal land rights is being most successfully made, against the literally entrenched opposition of those with mining rights, it is by virtue of the stories which the land holds, the codification in landscape of a whole tribal culture. It is the narrative power of the land, its textual status, which now supports a political structure dedicated to the belated preservation of the texts which make up a culture" (41). The language of the textual scholar echoes that of the border literary scholars and writers: each insists that places must be read, that they contain and constitute narratives. Joining this call for attentiveness to space and place in Chicana/o literary narrative, Patrick Hamilton argues for the use of "cognitive mapping," analyzing the "mental representation or understanding of the physical environment" (14) afforded by literary texts.

If we recognize place as textual and discursive, the call for critical attentiveness to space and place in border literature can extend beyond its narrative contents to include the material elements that make up border books, the spaces they travel across, their multiple temporalities, the agents of their production and circulation, and the places they come to be in our lives. If we relegate the material construction and social life of texts to the "background, a setting, rich and interesting, but not in any sense interactive or formative" (Brady, *Extinct Lands* 8), we miss how those histories and lives interact with and shape border literatures. As a consequence, Neil Freistat has argued for "a better understanding [of] the book as place" (14): put another way, if place is a text to be read, can we not also read the material text, the physical object of the book, as place? Expanding the scope of the definition of borders beyond, or perhaps between, the conflicts of physical and metaphorical / identity-based emphases, the textual scrutiny of the material borders of any work of border literature calls attention to the social lives of texts.

Of course, such a move might be met with suspicion. Introducing the language of material, textual borders into a discussion of U.S.-Mexico border literature may on its surface seem too neat, too close to a conflation of material and metaphor for comfort. While Jacques Derrida's essay "Living On: Borderlines," which in part discusses the ways the material text itself frustrates its own boundaries, undoing our understanding of "the supposed end and beginning of a work, the unity of a corpus, the title, the margins, the signatures, the referential realm outside the frame, and so forth" (69), might offer general insights into border literature, perhaps it is also "too unspecific," as Kaup suggests, particularly because "a major lesson of Chicano literature is that geopolitical position matters" (*Rewriting* 16). But if we extend or reorient our definition of geopolitical position to include the text as place, we might fruitfully expand the horizons of Chicana/o border discourse in ways that ground the processes of book production, publication, and reception in a material history that only further emphasizes the politics of location. Such a focus exposes various moments in the social life of a text, demonstrating how political, social, and cultural forces shape the visible aspects as well as the interpretive possibilities of Chicana/o border literature. Widening the scope of the study of the formative nature of border literature to include the evidence of its physical pages and print, its covers and prefaces, as well as the literal white spaces of the margins, then, extends the requirement to be attentive to space and place. In this case, the spaces the books themselves occupy, the places they become for readers, the shapes they take, and the uses to which they are put can offer as much insight into the changing landscapes of the border as any other site of study.

In short, the materiality of any given text is a place worth reading. As a mediator between narrative and reader, the components of that material text constitute another borderland that contributes to the meaning-making potential of any Chicana/o border text. To use the language of borderlands to describe this emphasis on the textual materiality of Chicana/o border literature is not to collapse or conflate the lived geographical borderlands with the metaphorical or the textual. Instead it is meant to highlight the way the lived always intersects with the imagined. It recognizes that our discussions of border literature depend on the extension of the material, lived borderlands into the world of metaphor, and it, in turn, extends the metaphors of borderlands back toward the material, lived place of the physical text. Place, and in this case the material text, registers the lived experience of the struggle to publish and circulate narratives of the border.

The Borders of Border Texts: Textual Scholarship in/of the Margins

Like the U.S.-Mexico border, the material text is a place in the process of becoming, a place under negotiation not by cartographers and historians but by authors, publishers, editors, printers, and readers, though those negotiations are equally political. Textual theorists and book historians in particular have for the past three decades argued for a broadening of our understanding of the social life of a text, from production to distribution to reception, recognizing the author as but one (significant) player in the shaping of texts. Sonia Saldívar-Hull acknowledges that theorizing the border comes with its difficulties: she writes, "Because our work has been ignored by the men and women in charge of the modes of cultural production, we must be innovative in our search. Hegemony has so constructed the ideas of method and theory that often we cannot recognize anything that is different from what the dominant discourse constructs. As a consequence, we have to look in nontraditional places for our theories" (46). One of the most important "nontraditional" places to look for theories of the border might be the material texts themselves.

Recent textual scholarship has argued that in focusing our attention on the material borders of literary texts, we can locate or expose literary-political negotiations as they unfold.[7] Roger Chartier argues that "there is no text apart from the physical support that offers it for reading . . . hence there is no comprehension of any written piece that does not at least in part depend upon the forms in which it reaches its reader" (9). Those forms, or the material elements like cover pages and introductory materials, typefaces and titles, act as liminal spaces between narratives and the sociopolitical worlds in which they circulate. They are also often sites in which authors, publishers, and editors contest for authority over the meaning of a text. Cover pages, attractive fonts, and reviewer blurbs attempt to entice and accommodate readers, often shading expectations and even interpretations of the texts they advertise. Introductions from well-known authors or the inclusion of a critical apparatus—notes from the editor, historical background, bibliography, and so on—all guide readers in their understanding of a work and its place in academic and popular culture. Michele Moylan and Lane Stiles write, "Clearly, when we read books, we really read books—that is, we read the physicality or materiality of the book as well as and in relation to the text itself" (2). Such emphasis on the material borders of the text draws on Gerárd Genette's notion of the paratext, or that which "enables a text to become a book and to be offered as such to its readers and, more generally, to the public. More than a boundary or a sealed border, the paratext is, rather, a threshold, or—a word Borges used apropos of a preface—a 'vestibule' that offers the world at large the possibility of either steeping inside or turning back" (2). Genette's language of the threshold or vestibule, like Anzaldúa's borderlands, insists on the simultaneity of the object and the experience of it. Genette begins the exploration of these material textual elements in his work, translated as *Paratexts: Thresholds of Interpretation*, in which he further subdivides the paratext into "peritext," or textual elements ranging from the title page, epigraphs, prefaces, and introductions to intertitles, notes, and "epitext," or those textual documents that circulate around a text, including diaries, interviews, and letters. These elements, also expanded by McGann to include ink, typefaces, paper, images, illustrations, and other visual elements and relabeled "bibliographic codes" (*Textual Condition* 57), offer insight into how the various actors involved in the production of a text aim to present that text: their desires, interpretations, and assumptions shape the narrative from the edges of the text.

But while Genette's work clearly lays out the distinctions between paratexts that are autographic (generated by the author) and allographic (generated by some other entity, such as a publisher, editor, or literary executor), emphasizing the role and responsibility of the publisher in generating paratext, his discussion also—perhaps inadvertently—produces the illusion of complete authorial autonomy and control over the meaning and message of a book. While Genette acknowledges that paratexts are "authorial or more or less legitimated by the author" (7), the scope of his work does not allow him to begin to explore the question of what "more or less" looks like. Instead, he concludes, "Whatever aesthetic intention may come into play as well, the main issue for the paratext is not to 'look nice' around the text but rather to ensure for the text a destiny consistent with the author's purpose" (407). Such a vision of the paratext as transmitter of authorial purpose neglects the situations in which the author's purpose does not neatly overlap the purposes of those designing, implementing, and adding the paratext. In contrast, Florian Sedlmeier argues that paratexts also function as "a contested site where institutionalized strategies of marking and marketing ethnic literatures collide with the textual effects, which express diverging constructions of the literary" (221).

More specifically, paratexts and bibliographic codes function as the border space between the text and the social and political world it inhabits, but they also record and render visible the politics of publishing border literature in the contexts of American racism and linguistic ethnocentrism. For instance, in reading the spaces between the intentions of authors, publishers, critics, and readers, we can locate sites from which to critique the notion of stable narratives, texts, and histories. In one sense, that instability is leveled on Chicana/o border writers from the outside: publishers, editors, and readers with different understandings and expectations of what a Chicana/o text should be can potentially undermine narratives via competing insertions of cover pages, glossaries, review blurbs, introductory remarks, and even marginalia.[8] Attending more carefully to what it means for a paratext to be "more or less legitimated by the author" means exposing the obstacles to authorial autonomy experienced by Chicana/o border writers, studying how, if at all, authors overcome those obstacles. It also requires adjusting our sense of Chicana/o border literature away from the notion of a seamlessly transmitted, uninterrupted message from author to reader and toward a notion of the collaboratively produced and social text, the product of intentions both supportive of and in competition with the author's. Reading the margins of border texts reveals the ways authorial control is subverted by dominant culture interests, generating unstable material texts wherein the paratext and narrative compete in the meaning-making process.

Likewise, border writers and artists sometimes embrace instability by countering, revising, or ignoring dominant narratives and histories in their own work.[9] Their narratives offer competing versions of historical events, they open up to multiple narrative voices, and they redraw the boundaries between genres by producing literatures that take on less "stable" forms: from the periodical to the story cycle, the telenovela to the comic book series, notions of the incomplete, the in-progress, the unstable abound. Because of their particularly fraught relationship to the industries of book production and reception, Chicana/o border writers are perhaps even more keenly aware of "the symbolic and signifying dimensions of the physical medium" of the material text (McGann, *Textual Condition* 56). These writers create narratives that invite readers to reflect on the instability common to literary texts and border identity, and their books make that instability material. The result is what I term "border textuality," or the condition under which the material text renders visible the link between narratives of struggle over border identity and the very struggle to produce and publish those narratives. Literature that invokes border textuality not only narrates instability but materially instantiates it.

This is not to say that writers of border literature are always (or in some cases, ever) aware of and in control of the material transmission of instability. Just as we must necessarily mind the way the celebratory metaphors of borderlands identity can undermine the material realities of lived border crossings, the fact that books are many things to different people can be both oppressive and liberating: oppressive to those seeking to be heard yet subverted by the voices and intentions of others and liberating to those who find ways to celebrate the communal nature of literary production. As Paul Gutjahr and Megan Benton write, "Strategies of production usually attempt to influence tactics of consumption, and sometimes they succeed, but they certainly do not control them" (4). In other words, Chicana/o border writers and their narratives are variously constrained and liberated by the paratextual borderlands. In some instances, writers' texts participate in border textuality despite their best efforts to control and stabilize them in the face of perceived threats from publishers and readers. Likewise, readers interpret the material text and the narrative it produces in a variety of ways, contributing in turn to the cycle of a work's social life. Instead of seeing "instability" as something to be celebrated or maligned, *From the Edge* highlights the ways the interdependent relationships between writers, publishers, critics, archivists, reviewers, and readers lead to the production of border textuality in their struggles for and against stability, and it shows how those relationships are exposed in the material margins of the text. The politics of border literary production and reception are always already being played out on the page; furthermore, as those politics intersect with border literary narratives of the struggle to construct an identity, they materially shape the interpretive possibilities of the text. Border textuality demands that readers more fully attend to narrative instability—unstable languages, geographies, histories, and identities—by navigating the instability of the material text.

This combination of material and narrative instability is hardly unique to Chicana/o literature, or even Chicana/o literature of the U.S.-Mexico border. Sedlmeier, as well as Beth McCoy and John Young, for example, have each argued convincingly for attention to the way racial politics—and particularly African American racial politics—are mapped onto textual production with particular emphasis on paratext. Further, a great deal of scholarship of the social text insists that every material text registers a kind of productive instability. To that end, this book aims to broaden the reach of these arguments, drawing them toward this comparatively understudied field within Chicana/o border literature. But it also recognizes—and asks practitioners of textual scholarship to recognize—that such instability is experienced and communicated in vastly different ways by different groups of writers and texts. Whereas in other texts the language of borders and margins is frequently either metaphorical or material, the language of Chicana/o border literature, rooted in the complex intersections of those terms, demands to be read as both/and. Because the narratives of border texts are so frequently concerned with the literal, the material, and geographic experiences of the border even as they pursue narrative negotiations of the spaces between languages, geographies, temporalities, and identities, the material spaces between text and reader take on even greater significance.

The materiality of Chicana/o border literature is also marked by specific kinds of instability expressed differently in or even entirely absent from other literatures, even racially or ethnically marked ones: namely, in the paratextual evidence of Spanish-English negotiations; of the simultaneous embrace and rejection of readers both familiar and unfamiliar with Chicana/o border identity, history, politics, and voices; and of an editorial politics of recovery that aims to establish and preserve Chicana/o border literary traditions. These border paratexts offer us glossaries, translations, explanations, and justifications; they offer us lists, wide margins, and maps. Though certainly all kinds of texts employ similar paratexts, it is in the act of reading them that their stories—and politics—unfold differently. The particular iterations of instability seen in Chicana/o border texts draw us to consider the competing mappings, necessarily both literal and metaphorical, of border spaces performed by authors, editors, publishers, scholars, and readers.

Attending to the specificity of the U.S.-Mexico border as variously depicted in each of these Chicana/o narratives, each of the book's five chapters attempts to view examples of border textuality from a different phase of what Robert Darnton has termed the "communications circuit," or the network of interested parties in any given publication, including but not limited to authors, editors, publishers, printers, distributors, booksellers, reviewers, and readers. The communications circuit "transmits messages, transforming them en route, as they pass from thought to writing to printed characters and back to thought again" (Darnton 11). Such a system proposes not only to study texts as historical artifacts, explicating the processes of publication and reception at various points in time, but also to trace the effects of a text's material existence on interpretation. Beginning with a focus on the author (chapter 1), then on the publisher (chapters 2 and 3), followed by the scholarly editors and archivists (chapter 4) and finally the teacher and reader (chapter 5), each phase offers a new entry point into reading the evidence of the production and reception of border texts found in the material text. Yet as each chapter develops, invariably even these phases blend and blur, and taken as a whole, it becomes difficult to separate these various phases of the communications circuit as they interact with one another, revealing the complex web of intentions and expectations that interact with one another and shape the social life of every border text.

The first chapter focuses on the relationship between border authors and authority over their own work, studying writers Rolando Hinojosa and Ana Castillo and their revisions of previously published novels, *Estampas del valle y otras obras* (1973) and *Sapogonia: (An Anti-Romance in 3/8 Meter)* (1990). The published revisions of their work serve as subversive commentaries on the notion of textual and narrative stability. The second and third chapters are a paired exploration of the role of writers and publishers in transmitting political discourses about the role of Spanish in English texts. They study the material impact of attempts to visually distinguish between languages with the use of glossaries in *Caballero: A Historical Novel* (1996) by Jovita González and Eve Raleigh and in Ernesto Galarza's *Barrio Boy* (1971) and italicization in *Memories of the Alhambra* (1977) by Nash Candelaria and in Richard Yañez's "Desert Vista" (2003), respectively. These chapters expand the well-established conversations surrounding code-switching border texts by specifically analyzing the visual impact of the representation of language, tracing the competing interests of publishers, authors, editors, and audiences for linguistic accommodation or resistance. The fourth chapter turns to critics, reviewers, and archivists and their role in materially shaping the interpretive possibilities of recovery project texts, especially the work of María Amparo Ruiz de Burton, whose reentry into Chicana/o letters is supported by the Recovering the U.S.-Hispanic Literary Heritage project. Emphasizing the significance of "recovery" and "preservation" to the Chicana/o and border literary canons, the chapter explores the material texts of recovery projects for evidence of how recoverers, editors, and publishers shape interpretation from the margins in both Ruiz de Burton's *The Squatter and the Don* (1885) and Margarita Cota Cárdenas's *Puppet: A Chicano Novella* (1985). The fifth chapter focuses on readers and their manipulations of the literal borders of the text, identifying and examining the marginalia in copies of Sandra Cisneros's *The House on Mango Street*. Studying such marginalia demonstrates how the materiality of the text acts in the service of developing for readers a material relationship to the history, politics, and identities of the border, creating opportunities for readers to wrest authority from the author.

In attempting to trace these literary social lives, the scope of this book is limited to those writers who might identify as or have their texts identified as Chicana/o and who are also (in some cases, arguably) border writers, making the U.S.-Mexico border a central figure in their work. This narrows the focus to the specific challenges to and opportunities for publication facing this already quite diverse group of writers, particularly as they are complicated by matters of race, class, gender, politics, and language. In so doing, however, it only begins to attest to the diversity of literary voices and narratives whose experiences of the border are likely or even necessarily shaped in very different ways, including but not limited to those from Mexican, Central American, indigenous, Native American, Asian, African American, and Anglo-European American backgrounds.[10] Even within the category of Chicana/o border literature, any number of texts might have been chosen that would highlight the politics of publishing unfolding in the paratext. That this book cannot begin to cover all of the Chicana/o border texts with interesting paratextual and publishing histories—from Daniel Venegas's *Las aventuras de don Chipote o cuando los pericos mamen* (1928), translated and republished in 2000 as *The Adventures of Don Chipote; or, When Parrots Breastfeed*, to Roberta Fernández's *Intaglio: A Novel in Six Stories* (1990) and from Norma Elia Cantú's *Canícula: Snapshots of a Girlhood en la Frontera* (1995) to Javier O. Huerta's *American Copia* (2012)—suggests what is, I hope, only the opening of a discussion, a significant but by no means comprehensive contribution to a continuing conversation about the politics of border literary production.

Given the wealth of possible texts, some of those selected for discussion might seem unlikely, perhaps even marginal to the canon of Chicana/o literature, particularly from a mainstream perspective. But this book aims to model the way scholarship itself can participate in the social lives of texts, promoting their preservation and continued reception. Drawing together a wide range of familiar and less familiar texts, it demonstrates the way each materially registers complicated publishing histories—a reality experienced by countless other Chicana/o border texts. Furthermore, it shows the variety of ways these materialities have silently contributed to discourses surrounding the merits of their accompanying narratives. It considers to what extent the material instability that marks each of these texts has shaped both critical and popular reception. Occasionally, we read that instability as a positive attribute, a sign of purposeful authorial intentions and proof of the narrative's success, as may be the case with works by Hinojosa and Cisneros, the first and last texts under scrutiny here. In other cases, readers treat that instability as a problem: it is evidence of the author's comparative lack of control and, by extension, of the narrative's flaws or even its unsuitability for study, as is conceivably true with Castillo's "most neglected" ("Interview" 26) novel and a number of the other texts under discussion, perhaps especially including those texts whose instability is bound up in the practices and politics of literary recovery.

Examining these competing narratives about the merits or demerits of instability encourages more reflection on the way we celebrate the fiction of complete authorial control, even as we recognize the political forces undermining such control, particularly for Chicana/o border writers. By emphasizing textual instability as an essential feature rather than a flaw, one that every author encounters and negotiates and one with the potential for great insight into the successes and failures that accompany any border literary production, this book reintroduces some of these occasionally neglected texts into critical conversations with more familiar texts both within and beyond the borders of Chicana/o literary studies. Even studying Cisneros's *The House on Mango Street*—arguably the most famous work of Chicana literature—not only surfaces a narrative of its complicated publishing history but also draws on the book's comparative popularity in order to devote scholarly attention to anonymous readerly marginalia, another set of neglected texts that compete with the author's and reader's sense of stability. It suggests that the material margins of Chicana/o border texts—even those whose authors have met with mainstream success—both conceal and reveal narratives of the struggle to assert a border identity.

Michael F. Suarez writes that "because books cross borders, book history must do so as well" (149); this book is a response to that challenge. Recognizing the material text as a space that reveals interpretation as continuously under construction by authors, publishers, critics, reviewers, editors, archivists, and readers, the stories told by the margins of the texts are compelling evidence of the complex history of Chicana/o border literary production. Examining the social life of border texts exposes the struggle to publish, to keep in print, and to recover border literature. It also recognizes the meanings of border literatures as embedded in the very material elements of narratives of border identity: through paratext and bibliographic codes, the material text(s) of border literatures shape our understandings of border identity. This study asks us to see authors in dialogue or even in competition with publishers and readers regarding the shape and meaning of their narratives, as only part of the circulation of the text's meanings. It also demands that we link our own experience of texts to the history of border literary production, seeing ourselves as actors in the continuing narrative of border literature and culture.

1

"A Touch-Up Here and There"

Authorial Revisions and Their Paratexts

> If I were able I'd say it.
> Say make me, remake me.
> —Toni Morrison, *Jazz*

Chapter 5 of Ana Castillo's novel *Sapogonia* (1990) begins with the line "It wasn't that he had fallen in love with her" (17). That is, of course, provided you are reading the 1990 Bilingual Press edition, which you may have checked out of a library or ordered (used) from Amazon.com. Just as likely, you are reading a newer copy of the 1994 Anchor Books edition put out by Doubleday, in which case chapter 5 begins "Máximo lived in Barcelona for three months before he decided to look for his father" (16). Chapter 5 from 1994 reads nothing like its earlier counterpart, because in 1990 its contents would have been found in chapter 7. The contents of the 1990 chapter 5 can now be found in chapter 15 of the 1994 edition, nearly a hundred pages away from their earlier home. Although the paperback of the 1994 edition does not hide the fact that it is a revision, most casual readers are likely unaware of the content and context of the substantial changes made to Castillo's novel between its two publication dates. In fact, roughly half of the small number of literary critics who tackle this novel are unaware of those changes or do not mention them at all.

Recent textual scholarship increasingly advocates attention to competing versions of texts. As John Bryant argues, most of what we read comes to us in multiple versions:

> Consider the Bible, Qur'an, or any foundation text in its variously constructed and continuously translated forms; consider the matter of scribal invention in the variant *Piers Plowmans* or *Canterbury Tales*, or the record of performance versions in the quarto *Hamlets*, or the existence of two *Lears*. . . . There are ideological revisions in Paine's *Common Sense* and the Declaration of Independence, three versions of Frederick Douglass's life, two of *Moby-Dick*, and the manuscript and print revisions in Coleridge, Wordsworth, Whitman, Dickinson, James, Eliot, and Woolf. There is *Ulysses* in typescript, first edition, and a genetic edition. ("Witness and Access" 19)

Scholars like Bryant emphasize that the practical problems encountered while writing about "fluid" texts, or "written work that exists in multiple material versions due to revisions (authorial, editorial, cultural) upon which we may construct an interpretation" ("Witness and Access" 17), present opportunities to discuss the evidence of a text's social life and of the impact of publishers, editors, and readers as well as authorial second-guesses on any text's stability. Furthermore, theorizers of the social text including D. F. McKenzie and Jerome McGann have shifted their attention away from the notion of a stable, coherent, singular, definitive text, instead focusing on "the human motives and interactions which texts involve at every stage of their production, transmission, and consumption" (McKenzie 15). Such a "sociology of texts," McKenzie argues, "alerts us to the roles of institutions, and their own complex structures, in affecting the forms of social discourse, past and present" (15). Approaches that categorize all texts as social texts, as products of a variety of collaborative and competing forces, ground our scholarship in the material and political history of border writers and their work. They also highlight the discourses of political power and authority as they are literally worked out on the page, and those discourses are all the more complicated in nontraditional literatures like those of the border.

Chicana/o border literature often advocates sustained attention to the instability of identity and history, asserting borderlands or *mestiza/o* identity as a valorization of the spaces between traditionally conceived binaries implied by nation, race, ethnicity, gender, and sexuality. By expanding the field of inquiry to include the material borders of and between texts, we can begin the work of contextualizing the histories and politics of production, publication, and reception particular to border writers. The dual versions of a novel like *Sapogonia (An Anti-Romance in 3/8 Meter)*, as well as Rolando Hinojosa's *Estampas del valle y otras obras* (1973) / *The Valley* (1983), contain evidence of the particular nature and circumstances of border publishing and offer insights into the relationship between a text's material embodiment—its social life—and our interpretation of its subject matter. Each posits the spaces between them as a site from which to critique the notion of stable narratives, texts, and histories.

On a narrative level, these works by Hinojosa and Castillo have quite a lot in common. Both writers create imagined geographic border spaces: Hinojosa renders his fictive version of the Río Grande Valley as Belken County, often favorably compared to Faulkner's Yoknapatawpha, while Castillo's Sapogonia, "a distinct place in the Americas where all mestizos reside, regardless of nationality, individual racial composition, or legal residential status—or, perhaps, because of all these" (5, 1) renders place in slightly more vague terms.[1] Both novels are made up of often short, episodic chapters or vignettes, and both offer multiple narrators and shifting points of view while at the same time privileging two characters as the primary and secondary protagonists: Hinojosa gives readers Jehú Malacara and Rafe Buenrostro, while Castillo alternates between Máximo Madrigal and Pastora Velásquez Aké. Both authors also demonstrate a self-conscious concern with versioning, revision, bibliography, and multiple interpretations within their narratives.

But perhaps more important, the instability of storytelling as a topic in each of these texts is mirrored by the instability of the texts' material social lives, inviting readers to make choices about which version matters most. This is because both of these novels have been subject to substantial revisions after their initial publication. Hinojosa took up the task of translating and revising his 1973 novel in 1983. Castillo revised her novel when the smaller Bilingual Press sold the rights to Doubleday. With many works of Chicana/o border literature, multiple versions of a text register or render visible the author's struggle to be heard. For Hinojosa, this struggle is bound up at least in part in the political dimensions of linguistic accommodation, while for Castillo, the struggle is connected more visibly to gendered discourses of narrative and authorial control. In examining the ways the authors' narrative concern with versions is amplified by the proliferation of materially distinct versions of their texts, this chapter links a postmodern understanding of what McGann calls the "textual condition" to the particularities of border consciousness, participating in a form of border textuality. In border textuality, writers like Hinojosa and Castillo create narratives that invite readers to reflect on the instability common to literary texts and border identity, and their revisions make that instability material.

Rolando Hinojosa's *Sketches* and *Estampas*

Defining the scope of Rolando Hinojosa's Klail City Death Trip Series is an extraordinarily difficult task. The books that comprise the series range across a multitude of genres, settings, and languages, weaving a complicated web of characters whose lives intersect in the fictional Mexican American community of Belken County along the U.S.-Mexico border.

Even organizing the order of the series is next to impossible, as is evident when one asks which book is the first in the series. In 1973, Quinto Sol, an independent Chicano publishing house in Berkeley, California, published Rolando Hinojosa's *Estampas del valle y otras obras*, a collection of sketches divided into four parts that includes a translation from Spanish into English by Gustavo Valdéz and José Reyna as *Sketches of the Valley and Other Works*. After Quinto Sol split into Editorial Justa and Tonatiuh International in 1975, a second edition, which attempted to correct some editorial mistakes, was brought out under Editorial Justa in 1977, and a third edition appeared in 1980. At this point, Hinojosa's longer project of linked novels was already well under way—five other books had been written—and the shape of this first text was undoubtedly altered by its new position as the first installment of a much larger series.[2] When a fourth 1983 Bilingual Press edition—entitled *The Valley*—was published, the book was almost an entirely new animal: not only was *The Valley* published entirely in English but Hinojosa had also reorganized, revised, and restructured a substantial portion of the text. Could this book accurately be called a replacement for the edition that appeared ten years before? A supplement? Or something else? Given the linguistic, narrative, and other editorial changes introduced into the 1983 edition, it is certainly possible to argue these are two entirely different texts. If that is the case, where do we place this 1983 version in the series? Is it telling the same story as the one that came before?

The multiple material versions of *Estampas del valle* and *The Valley* participate in a proliferation of histories, generating additions and erasures that would frustrate any bibliographer. Actively pursuing textual and linguistic borderlands by publishing "rendition" (Zilles 4)—Hinojosa's word for these transcultural versions—after rendition of this text as Hinojosa does results in the material multiplicity of versions, none of which can claim ultimate authority: there is no single version of his story. Likewise, on a narrative level, there is no single version of many of the stories his characters tell. Instead, the characters themselves, along with their narratives, are actively engaged in a process of storytelling that challenges any singular notion of history, ethnicity, or even geography. Repeatedly, characters participate in or are subjected to counternarratives, counterhistories, and competing authorities, and version after version of events clamber over one another in a game of collaborative storytelling.

The combined narrative and material elaborations on border identity—where stories of self and community are told, retold, bent, altered, and distorted—exemplify border textuality. Taken together, these multiple editions demonstrate the unique relationship between narratives of border literature and the material, political circumstances under which those narratives are produced and published.

Specifically, Hinojosa's reworking of his 1973 work registers the instability of border identity through paratextual instability. The paratextual changes Hinojosa introduces to the 1983 edition of his text combine to create a coherent, more streamlined novel that is accessible to an Anglo, English-reading audience, as many critics have noted, but also those changes almost paradoxically demand to be read and studied within the context of its multiple versions.[3] The novel renders itself legible to one readership at the same time that it insists that legibility is only partial. These complex efforts at (il)legibility present themselves in peritexts we might deem autographic, such as Hinojosa's title(s) for his work, or allographic, such as the letter from the editor, or even in some cases first autographic and later allographic, as in the case of the map that precedes the text. Further complicating Hinojosa's narrative are the internal and "fictionalized" peritexts—the intentional print mistakes, notes, and footnotes introduced by fictional characters that demonstrate a metafictional awareness of their status in print—an exploration of which demonstrates the way Hinojosa's texts highlight the fallibility of both oral and print culture. These gaps and errors narratively and materially involve the reader in the multiplication of versions and insist on the incomplete nature of any single version of a text. The notes and footnotes reveal that when even the characters themselves get into the act of creating, compiling, and revising versions of stories, they replicate Hinojosa's own celebration of versioning from within the narrative of the text, insisting that one cannot read *The Valley* without reading *Estampas* or, at the very least, acknowledging that another version exists. The question of whether *Estampas* and *The Valley* are telling the same story can be answered in this way: neither story is quite the same, but neither story is quite complete without the other.[4]

Autographic/Allographic Peritexts: Letters, Titles, and Maps

Whether or not we view them as different texts, the 1973 *Estampas* and the 1983 *The Valley* share at least one feature: the visible attempt to accommodate dual linguistic audiences. In the case of the 1973 edition, this accommodation was attempted largely by the editors. When Hinojosa first wrote and published *Estampas del valle y otras obras* (1973), he wrote in Spanish because, as Joyce Glover Lee notes, "there was some stigma attached to writing in English during the early days of the Chicano movement" (51); in *Estampas*, Hinojosa wrote for a Spanish-reading audience. But his editors attempted to accommodate a dual audience with English translations, and these competing intentions—somewhat at odds with Hinojosa's—are transmitted through paratext. The letter from the editor, written by Herminio Rios, which precedes the first edition of *Estampas*, is written in both Spanish and English, demonstrating an allographic attempt to accommodate both the Spanish- and English-reading audiences. While the letter itself explicitly claims to have two "públicos lectores" (4) or "reading publics" (7)—those presently involved in the Chicano Movement and those who will want to learn about it in the future—the fact that such a letter is rendered in both English and Spanish implies a recognition of the further subdivision of those "reading publics" along linguistic lines: there are now at least four potential audiences, not two. For the editors, this tacit commitment to linguistic accessibility necessitated a nontraditional format for the publication and translation of the text, which meant including English-language translations of each section immediately following Hinojosa's Spanish. But which, if any, of these "reading publics" laid out by the editors did Hinojosa have in mind? From the literal beginning of his book, even the word "we" suggests that Hinojosa's narratives are addressed to multiple readerships, multiplying narrative experiences.

Some evidence suggests that Hinojosa's opinions at one time differed slightly from those of his editors: in 1974, a year after the publication of *Estampas*, Hinojosa himself claimed that "the Chicano writer has been forced to write in English" (quoted in Lee 50). But by the time Hinojosa returned to this text in 1983, his Klail City Death Trip Series had expanded alongside his willingness to employ English in his work. A number of critics have noted the shift throughout the series toward a greater accommodation and use of English. John Akers points out that the later novels *Rites and Witnesses, Partners in Crime*, and *Becky and Her Friends* do not have Spanish-language antecedents, while the earlier *The Valley, Dear Rafe*, and *Klail City* each did. In "The Sense of Place," Hinojosa reframes his earlier reliance on Spanish by highlighting his attempts at linguistic realism:

> When the characters stayed in the Spanish-speaking milieu or society, the Spanish language worked well, and then it was in the natural order of things that English made its entrance when the characters strayed or found themselves in Anglo institutions. . . . Later on I discovered that generational and class differences also dictated not only usage but which language as well. From this came the how they said what they said. (23)

While Hinojosa creates characters throughout the series that navigate increased interaction with Anglo Americans and the English language, the texts themselves increasingly incorporate the English language. As a result, *The Valley* (1983) aims to acknowledge his English-reading audience but does so in a way that the translation of his 1973 version did not: Hinojosa takes a more active role in engaging that English-reading audience.

While others have traced linguistic alterations, revisions, and differences in many parts of Hinojosa's work, a brief examination of his paratextual changes to the titles will draw out both the narrative and the material impulses toward textual instability. As is perhaps indicated by the dual-language letter from the editor, the title of Hinojosa's 1973 *Estampas del valle y otras obras* presents a number of challenges that hint at both narrative and material instability all on its own. Specifically, how does the title suggest that we categorize the genre of this text? Is it a novel? A short story collection, in which "the order of the constituent parts is most often arbitrary" (Genette 312)? Akers argues that the title, with its use of the phrase "y otras obras," "indicate[s] that originally Hinojosa did not envision *Estampas* as one novel but rather as a collection of four independent works" (92). In that case, the phrase *Estampas del Valle* applies only to the first part of the collection, while the "other works" are those of the three distinct sections that follow. With its use of intertitles, the 1973 edition further indicates to readers that the text is a collection of sketches, its four parts entitled "Estampas del valle," "Por esas cosas que pasan," "Vidas y milagros," and "Una vida de Rafe Buenrostro." Each of the first three parts is followed immediately by its English translation, "Sketches of the Valley" (translated by Gustavo Valdéz), "One of Those Things" (translated by José Reyna), and "Lives and Miracles" (Valdéz). The final section, "Una vida de Rafe Buenrostro," also translated by Valdéz, is a series of paragraphs and extremely short vignettes, each small segment presented in Spanish at the top of the page and English at the bottom.

While Akers is correct that readers confronting the title, not to mention these intertitles, are encouraged to see the sections as discrete, one can't help but note the significant presence of characters, settings, and stories that cross the boundaries of those sections. As with many story cycles, it is certainly true that the four sections that constitute this text might be read independently, particularly the section "Por esas cosas que pasan," which is occasionally separately anthologized. However, the reading experience is clearly also rewarded by taking these individual sections to be part of a larger whole, especially as stories are retold and characters recontextualized by each ensuing sketch, story, or fragment. Thus these 1973 paratextual elements—the title and the intertitles—present sketches that overlap, while at the same time the formal boundaries of sketch, story, collection, and novel are blurred.

By 1983, Hinojosa had changed the title of his collection to *The Valley: A Recreation in Narrative Prose of a Portfolio of Etchings, Engravings, Sketches, and Silhouettes by Various Artists in Various Styles, Plus a Set of Photographs from a Family Album*. Though not every critic sees a strong distinction between these two versions of the novel—Lee, for instance, argues that "the variety of titles for essentially the same material all confound the newcomer" (23)—many others do. Calling it a "recast" rather than a translation, Klaus Zilles (9) points to the changing of the title and the addition of a new subtitle as the first clues that Hinojosa moves beyond linguistic translation and into the territory of what Manuel Martín-Rodríguez calls a "transcultural version" (*Life* 123). For instance, Hinojosa's change of the title reveals his attempts to make his work more appealing to an English-reading (and specifically Anglo American) audience and culture by distancing itself from more traditional Spanish-language genres and forms: Zilles claims that Hinojosa "must have been aware of relinquishing to some degree the novel's relationship with Spanish literary history" (9) by removing the word "estampas" and its associations with the literary form of character sketches from the title.[5] By shifting the focus from a character sketch to re-creations of visual, material objects, Zilles argues, "[Hinojosa] achieves . . . the same objectivity and impartiality that one would associate with today's powerful documents in photojournalism or with literary portraits in the Spanish medieval tradition" (10). He also escapes the likely unfamiliar genre by replacing it with a far more familiar one: the portfolio.

The new title, especially when shortened to *The Valley*, as it almost always is, would seem to be a clear indication of a change in audience and an attempt to accommodate that new audience via a new autographic paratext. But, more important, the changed title also draws the reader's attention to the book as a set of material objects that are "*re-creations* in narrative prose": this writing is already a revision, already a version of some other preexisting text. The new subtitle also gestures toward the complicated layering of versions that must take place in order to "convert" an image into prose. Whereas a word like "sketches" could refer to either images or prose and simultaneously gesture toward an unfinished quality in both, the revised subtitle, which refers to the books as a set of material objects that are re-creations in narrative prose, turns readers' attention to the idea that images and prose act as separate layers in this text. The subtitle asks readers to consider that these material objects exist but also that they have been materially altered through their "re-creation" in prose. Therefore readers must confront the question of whether it's possible to re-create objects without fundamentally changing them. This is precisely the question that readers might ask of these two versions of Hinojosa's text. In a moment of border textuality, the altered subtitle layers version upon version: the fictional etchings and sketches are layered beneath the fictional re-creations, which are themselves offered to readers in a 1983 version that is substantially different from the one published a decade before. The long subtitle gestures not necessarily toward Hinojosa's attempt to introduce "novelistic cohesion" (Akers 94) into this new version but perhaps instead toward a sense of purposeful compilation: there are "etchings, engravings, silhouettes" competing with photographs, and the subtitle works to emphasize that these

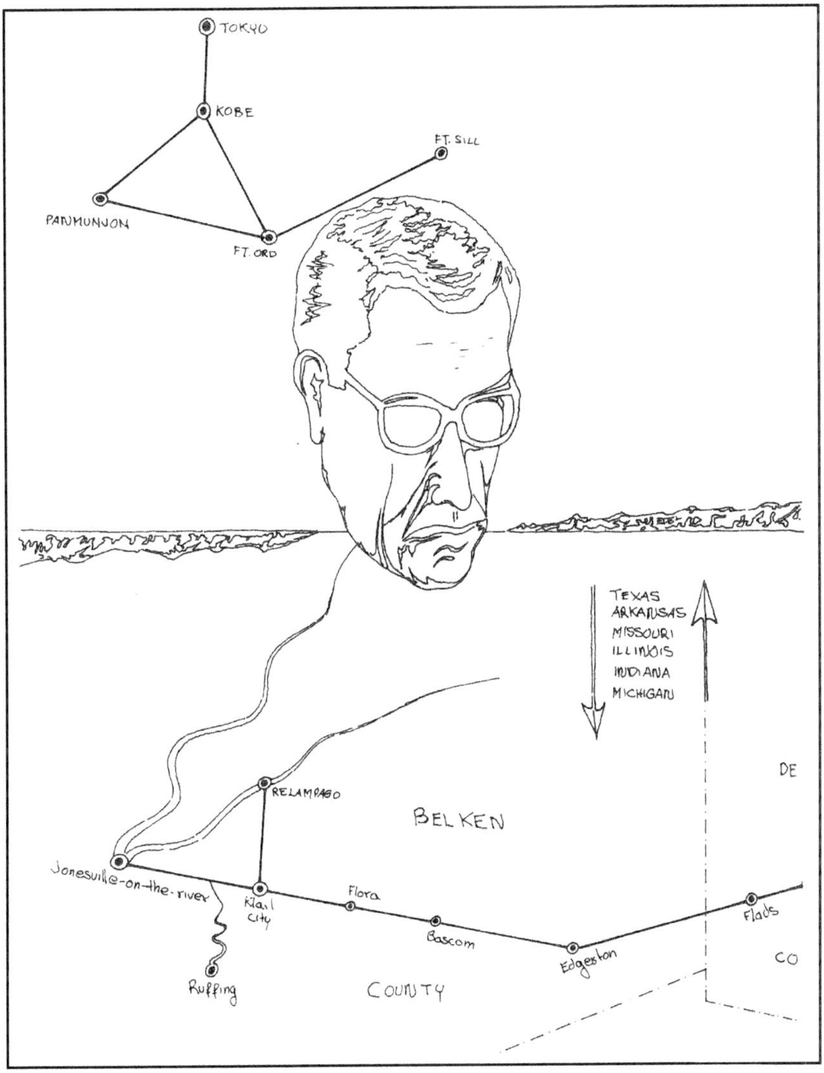

FIGURE 1 The map accompanying the 1973 Quinto Sol text of *Estampas del valle y otras obras* by Rolando Hinojosa. (Reprinted with the permission of the author.)

works are created by multiple hands, then reinvented in prose. Both *Estampas* and *The Valley* insist on themselves as collections where the links between the parts are potentially tenuous, but also where the arrangement of the materials matters as much as the materials themselves.

Hinojosa's changing texts for changing audiences have altered the possibilities for how we read and even categorize his work: Zilles, for example, argues: "Hinojosa's recasts must be . . . considered essentially new texts in their own right and are therefore counted among the fourteen installments of the KCDTS [Klail City Death Trip Series]" (4). At a time when "foreignizing" translations have gained currency, translation theorists and border critics alike might fault Hinojosa for appearing too accommodating of English-speaking audiences: he supplies not only an English version but also completely changes and rearranges it to suit that readership. But, as Martín-Rodríguez argues, "authors of transcultural texts . . . seem to be much more aware of their texts being different things to different people, as well as of their need to transcend barriers and borders that could impede the reader's interaction and thus the need to come up with novel strategies" (123). But the dual linguistic impulse is only a small part of the larger dual impulse toward narrative singularity and multiplicity, toward border stability and instability that involves readers on a material level. The titles all gesture in different ways toward that sense of narrative multiplicity.

A larger portrait of overlapping textual and border stability is painted in the maps that accompany the 1973 and 1983 versions of the novel (see figures 1 and 2).

Héctor Calderón describes the autographic peritextual map that precedes *Estampas del valle y otras obras* (see figure 1) this way:

> At the top portion of the map toward the left, hanging in space, Hinojosa situates Kobe, Tokyo, Panmunjon, Fort Sill, and Fort Ord with lines of relation to each other. These are the cities that throughout the Korean War will affect the Mexican families of Belken County. In the center there is also a list of states in inverted geographic order, with Texas in the north, followed by Arkansas, Missouri, Illinois, Indiana, and Michigan to the south. On either side of the list are arrows pointing down and up. These states are well known to the migrant worker stream that flows back and forth on a seasonal basis from the Valley. These two schematic versions of the real world are juxtaposed against the expanding fictional world of Belken County. At the bottom of the map, near the international border with the Rio Grande flowing north (Hinojosa's conceit), is the fictional Belken County. (148–149)

Further complicating the illustration is the presence of a man's face hovering between the maps of Belken County, the migrant stream, and the Korean War locations. The man, with glasses but no eyes, looks down over a lightly sketched horizon onto the map. He is not identified, and it is unclear whom the image might represent, though one or more of the series' narrators—Jehú Malacara, Rafa/Rafe Buenrostro, Esteban Echevarría, or P. Galindo—might be considered as a possibility. Whether or not we label the face of the man in the map, we must acknowledge his presence at the center of the horizon. We might think of the face as that of neither the author nor one of the narrators but instead the cartographer: the image insists to readers that they recognize the map as well as the maker of the map, that we must experience the desire to locate ourselves in a text simultaneously with the recognition that even the tools we use to locate ourselves are fabrications of someone else's imagination. Readers must confront the intersection of the literal and the narrative constructions of place and space in this map.

Much of recent Chicana/o scholarship has sought to emphasize and insist upon the centrality of space and place to an understanding of notions of nations and borders. In particular, scholars are beginning to look for ways to revise traditional understandings of Chicana/o borderlands space and place, as evidenced, for example, by Patrick Hamilton's uses of "cognitive mapping" in Chicana/o texts and Marissa López's turn to a hemispheric, transnational understanding of the Chicana/o nation. Almost as a complement to this new turn in scholarship, Hinojosa's 1973 map seems to use the centrality of space and place to insist on complicating our notions of the physical border. The borderlands as mapped by Hinojosa in this 1973 text are meant to "create and contain Chicana/o spaces," as López might argue, as "part of a larger story about the partitioning of hemispheric space" (*Chicano Nations* 5). Thus the borderlands region is contained by Belken County, but it also extends throughout the Midwest, and it is also extended throughout the places of international conflict. José David Saldívar writes that the narrative of *Estampas del valle y otras obras* "engages the reader in an alternative reconstruction of Texas border history" (178) that counters the narratives of early historians like Walter Prescott Webb, and the map participates in that "alternative reconstruction" by alerting readers to the wide range of geography into which the borderlands extends its reach. Its layering of multiple geographies insists that readers recognize mobility as essential to characters whose lives depend on migration streams for employment and are then forever changed by their entry into war in service of the United States of America. In turn, its inclusion of the horizon and the hovering face—whether we read that face as a sort of benevolent, godlike overseer, a frame narrator, or the author—directs readers to recognize the very construction of maps as occurring at the intersection of the material, physical shape of reality with the narrative, literary construction of reality. The map addresses readers' desire to locate themselves in the geographical spaces constructed in the narrative by asking them to consider the relative "reality" of those spaces.

However, this map and the accompanying image of the man's face disappear from the 1977 and 1980 editions of *Estampas del valle*, and in 1983 the map is replaced with a different, more straightforward map of Belken County (see figure 2).

Calderón notes that although Hinojosa drew the 1973 map, the map included in *The Valley* "was drawn by someone at Bilingual Press / Editorial Bilingüe" (241n14). This more recent allographic map plots only the towns of Belken County and the national border, leaving out the north-south

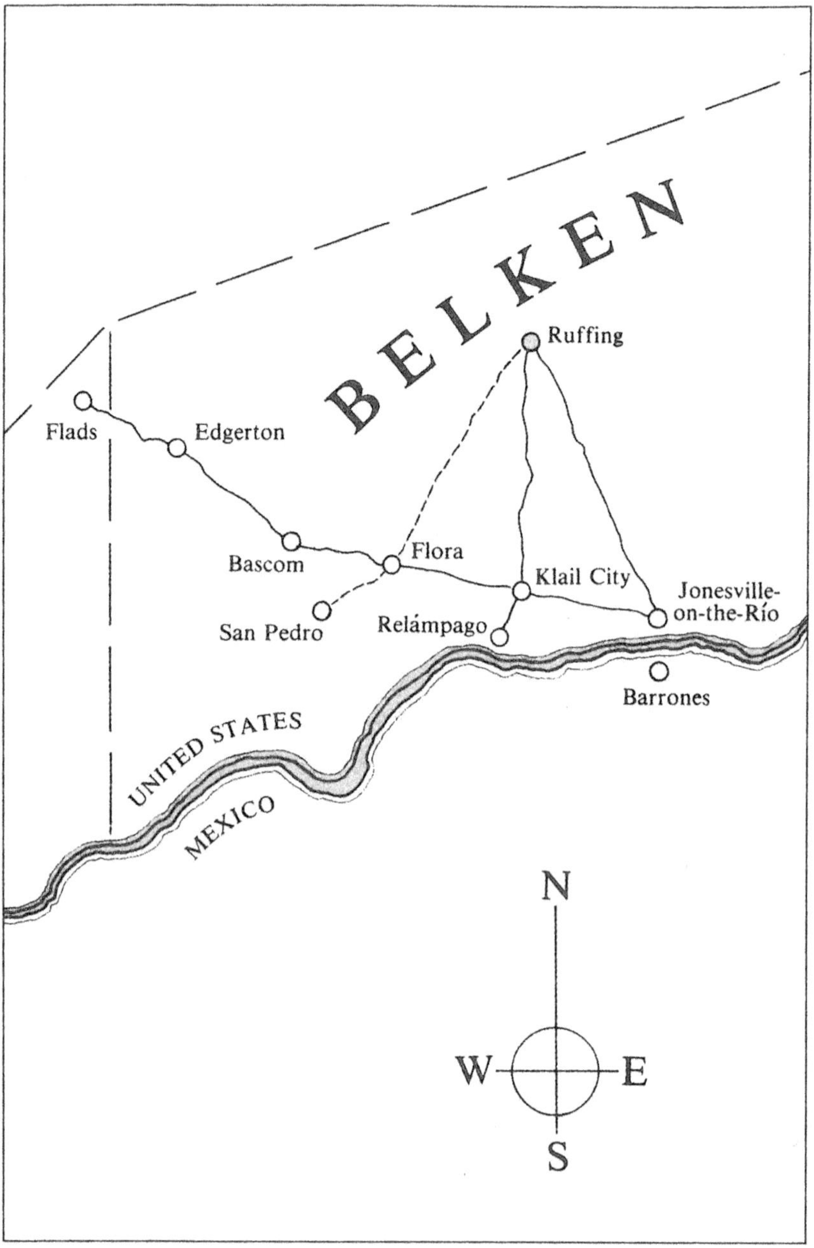

FIGURE 2 The map accompanying the 1983 text of *The Valley*. (Reprinted with permission from the publisher of *The Valley / Estampas del Valle* by Rolando Hinojosa [©2014 Arte Público Press–University of Houston].)

migratory pattern and the references to international cities. The mysterious face has disappeared. All in all, this map appears to aim at a more commonly understood realistic representation of a map of a fictional county, one slightly more recognizable than the multiple plot points and disparate geographic locations of the first map. And for many critics, it accurately represents Hinojosa's blend of history and fiction: both Hinojosa and the map "present factual incidents yet within a fictional structure . . . which creates the illusion that history arises from the story and not vice-versa" (Neate 92). But it also communicates a different story about the relationships between the county and the rest of the country, as well as the world at large. Although this version was written and published after the series had already begun to expand in multiple geographic directions, and after Hinojosa had grown more accommodating of the English-speaking and -reading parts of the United States, the map insulates itself from the rest of the world. The paratextual map sets a different stage for readers of the 1983 English version, one in which only Belken County matters. Although the narrative still references migration as well as the Korean War, those plot points are no longer geographically located on the map, and readers are encouraged to focus more closely on the community as rooted in a stable yet also isolated geographic location. While the 1973 autographic map plays with readers' expectations for maps and legends, complicating the outlines of borders and boundaries with overlapping geographies, the 1983 allographic map aims at a more conventional form of realism, asking readers to believe from the very first page that Belken County is a place one can travel to, with definitely drawn borders.

In many ways, this multiplication of maps reflects the historical and longstanding debates surrounding the drawing and redrawing of the actual U.S.-Mexico border dating from before the Mexican-American War. Those historical maps, particularly when laid side by side, bear the traces of nationalist, racist, and classist interactions between Mexico and the United States. In turn, the fictional world of Belken County, represented in multiple maps, works to call attention to the constructed nature not just of the fictional border described in Hinojosa's work but also the "real" border on which the fiction is built. McKenzie, arguing that we must read maps as texts, claims, "The visual adjacency of territories, the border-line definition of linguistic, ethnographic, religious, or political boundaries, may be an accurate record of the current facts, but the four forms seldom correspond exactly. A visual definition in terms of any one may be a subversive political act in terms of another" (47). When two different maps, each of which draws different boundaries around what constitutes Belken County, introduce the "same" text, we confront at least two different political acts.

Furthermore, that one of these maps was drawn not by Hinojosa but on behalf of the publisher only multiplies the intentions and potential interpretations of these maps when laid side by side. It also neatly parallels the power struggle over defining authority: who is authorized to draw the boundaries between the United States and Mexico? Between Belken County and the rest of the world? We could therefore argue that Hinojosa's map, as the product of his own intentions, is the "correct" or "real" map of Belken County, that the publisher-included map is a kind of interference with the text. But in many ways "interference" is at least partially the point: there is no map, real or fictional, that does not construct a different world for readers, nor is there one that is not politically motivated. These maps instead interfere with each other, multiplying the possibilities for charting this fictional world, competing with one another and registering for readers the impossibility of singularity, or even stability, when trying to chart a territory. Alone, each map conveys a sense of borderlands geography: perhaps one defines a space, the other a place. Together, the maps insist on an understanding that the border is unstable, always in the incomplete process of being fixed, always bound up in a political, hierarchical, quasi-Edenic struggle over who gets to name the world.

Metafictional Paratexts: A Celebration of Versions, Oral and Print

The letter, titles, and maps bear the marks of the changes Hinojosa and his editors introduced between *Estampas* and *The Valley*, changes that were arguably meant to streamline the English-language reading experience but also most certainly destabilize any sense of textual singularity. These kinds of changes, or repetitions with a difference, highlight Hinojosa's preoccupation with versioning—the introduction of competing, complementary, or conflicting versions of narratives as another attempt at the realistic depiction of how stories are shaped by their tellers and hearers—on both a material and a narrative level. Emphasizing fluidity, resisting linearity, and pushing at the edges of fact and fiction, the narrative itself resembles its 1973 paratextual map, "realistic" in terms of its attempt to most accurately portray the complexity of border life.

For instance, the opening sketch in both versions of the book, entitled "Braulio Tapia," enacts this narrative emphasis on repetition while also hinting at the instability and revisionist possibilities of oral history. In this sketch, Jehú Malacara's grandfather, Jehú Vilches, describes watching Roque Malacara (the younger Jehú's father) walk up the steps of his home to ask Vilches for his daughter's hand in marriage. Vilches narrates, "Turning my head slightly to the right, I catch a glimpse, or think I do, of my late father-in-law, don Braulio Tapia . . . don Braulio raises his hand to shake mine as he did years ago when I first came here to this house to ask for Matilde's hand. . . . Who did don Braulio see when he walked up these steps to ask for his wife's hand?" (*The Valley* 12). Juan Bruce-Novoa argues that in this scene "continued observance of a traditional ritual proves the health of communal customs. However, when the old man wonders whom his father-in-law dealt with when he played the suitor's role, we glimpse a potential breakdown in the oral tradition, a ritual as central to communal health as betrothal" (155). The silence or gap in community memory that leads to don Braulio's uncertainty also leads to misremembering, as evidenced by Klaus Zilles's examination of referenced birth dates: although Braulio Tapia is supposedly Jehú Malacara's great-grandfather, he is only about fifty years older than he (109). Luis Leal argues for the importance of the characters' oral histories in spite of their lapses and gaps, claiming, "Their stories become creative narratives that feed their imagination and that of the inhabitants of the barrio, however unreliable they may be to the professional historian" (105). But it is also precisely these confusions, multiple versions, and even what appear to be mistakes of memory that are at the heart of the narrative and its construction of border identity. In these moments of confusion, the places where the numbers don't add up or the restitched seams of the story show through, readers experience that instability. In turn, they are invited to participate materially in the construction and reconstruction of narratives that challenge traditional notions of history and progress.

The narrative example of the "Braulio Tapia" sketch challenges the notion of a coherent or consistent oral history. But the narrative, like its material versions, is equally committed to highlighting the instability of print culture as well. Hinojosa's texts go even further in blurring the boundary between the material text and the fictional world it presents to readers: not only does he materially alter the paratexts of his editions of the work but he also introduces stories and characters whose stories are shaped by changing fictional paratexts within the narrative. Martín-Rodríguez begins to hint at this link between the narrative and its material manifestations when he argues that Hinojosa "exploits in his text many of the strategies associated with print culture and reading" (*Life* 30). One of the more subtle ways Hinojosa "exploits" those strategies can be seen in the occasional footnotes and references to bibliography that appear in both versions of the novel.

For example, in the collection of recollections entitled "Por esos cosas que pasan" and translated as "One of Those Things" (1973) or "Sometimes It Just Happens That Way, That's All" (1983), eyewitness statements and newspaper accounts are used to create a constellation of versions of the events surrounding a murder, drawing the reader's attention in particular to the stark differences between four versions of what happened: the lengthy, complicated descriptions offered by Balde, his sister Marta, and his best friend, Beto, and the tersely worded English-language newspaper stories that merely (and incorrectly) record the names of those involved in a fatal stabbing and the outcome of the trial. Zilles describes this section as emphasizing "the indifference of Anglo jurisprudence towards Texas Mexicans" (186), but the multiple tellings, each with its own additions and erasures, complicate readerly access to the facts surrounding the incident. These versions also draw a distinct line between the motivations, emotions, and details of the event and the institutional, bureaucratic enforcement of the law. Hamilton convincingly argues that the significance of the kinds of narratives employed to explain the murder of Ernesto Tamez—newspaper accounts that represent the Anglo justice system versus the first-person narrative accounts that represent the Chicana/o experience—rests not so much in their ability to provide an answer as to "why" the murder occurred as in their demonstration of the "distance and conflict between the cultural positions from which these epistemological perspectives emanate" (41). In combination, these testimonials, print and oral, emphasize both historical and textual instability.

Hinojosa introduces metafictional paratexts in this chapter through his use of references to newspapers and footnotes in order to further emphasize narrative instability through the materiality of print. The newspaper articles that flank the narrative are always—regardless of edition—printed in English, emphasizing the oppressive authority of language in the United States. Further, in the 1983 version, the penultimate line of the newspaper article detailing the sentencing Balde receives for his murder conviction contains the phrase "ETAOIN SHRUDLU PICK UP." ETAOIN SHRUDLU is a nonsense phrase used by typecasting machine operators to highlight composing errors: this phrase was meant to indicate a mistake, to call out to composers the need to recast the line, but occasionally the phrase was overlooked and the mistaken line was printed as is, with ETAOIN SHRUDLU appearing erroneously alongside the original mistake in print. Including this phrase in the 1983 version of the text certainly reemphasizes print culture for readers, because it functions as a sort of ghosted paratext: an item that was never supposed to appear in print but whose presence nevertheless confirms the status of that printed object as such. In other words, readers are led to "know" they are looking at a newspaper article by the presence of this (fictional) error. But, more important, including the phrase emphasizes the instability of that print culture, its failures, errors, and mistakes (that the phrase is introduced only in the 1983 version, and does not appear in the 1973 version, only multiplies the confusion). Hamilton argues that the inclusion of the phrase symbolizes Anglo inattention to Chicana/o issues as a whole, seeing them as "the equivalent of randomly striking the keys" (41), but the presence of that phrase also causes readers to question which part of the line is meant to be erased, which part contains the error, the mistake. If the "Braulio Tapia" story transmits messages about the instability of oral history and memory, "Sometimes It Just Happens That Way, That's All" does the same for print communication.

Additionally, between the newspaper articles are a variety of testimonials from involved parties that emphasize print and narrative instability at the same time. Included are two footnotes that communicate to readers that part of what they see is the transcription of cassette recordings from March 16 and 17, 1970, when Baldemar and Marta spoke their versions of the story into a recorder. In *Estampas*, these notes describe "tape recordings," while in *The Valley* they describe "cassette recordings," but otherwise, they are substantially the same, and they both indicate the way oral testimonies have been mediated by written transcripts. The inclusion of the footnotes aims at verisimilitude, asking readers to believe that they are reading a collection of authentic, nonfictional documents, while the presentation of multiple stories gives readers access to the complexities of narrating any event. But, more important, readers are given a written transcript of an oral recording and asked to consider the potential interferences, mistakes, gaps, and relative values of the oral depositions versus the written and other testimonials offered in this story. How does one weigh the truth claims of a taped testimony versus those of a signed deposition? Against a newspaper article? The multiple versions of this text underscore the numerous competing perspectives and stories found within the novel itself, while the use of fictional paratexts blends fiction and reality, in the process demonstrating the unreliability of both. The narrative and its paratexts, both fictional and non-, insist that readers attend to the differences introduced by material texts, whether they are meant to mediate oral or print communication.

Even the characters themselves appear concerned with multiple representations of texts, as when Jehú introduces entries from Victor Paláez's diary in "Otra vez la muerte" / "Death Once Again" (1973), later changed to "But Since He Died" (1983). In that introductory paratext, Jehú describes the man who took him under his wing after the death of his parents and offers the set of excerpts to the reader, claiming, "I assume full responsibility for its order (or lack of it) and for a touch-up here and there (commas and the like) although no changes were made in the content, which, after all, is as it should be" (*The Valley* 27). Jehú's attempts to interfere as little as possible in the transmission of Paláez's diary, when paired with Hinojosa's willingness to radically alter a text in pursuit of accommodating different audiences, may not seem at all similar. But by offering readers a character and narrator who is aware of his own and others' influences on texts, even in editing them in the slightest ways, Hinojosa also offers readers an opportunity to reflect on the relationships between the texts Jehú handles and the texts of *Estampas del valle* and *The Valley*.

When critics investigate the significance of these narrative repetitions and emphases on storytelling, they often also cite the complicated, multiple, and varying forms Hinojosa employs in his sketches as representative of a larger theme or argument about the status of Chicana/o identity. For example, Héctor Torres claims, "The sense that there is no ending in *The Valley* is itself equivalent to the notion that that the Valley is becoming itself, and those Chicanos from that community are in the very process of living out the potentials of that region" (92). Such arguments could be extended beyond the pages of one version of the novel: elements are, as Zilles describes them, "drawn in and drifting apart" (xiii) not only within any particular version of the novel but also between those versions as well. Hinojosa complicates any readerly progression through a chronology of texts in his series, frustrates editorial endeavors by creating "recasts" (Zilles 4) rather than faithful translations and emphasizes the relationship between borderlands identity and the borders of textuality. His paratextual emendations are echoed or even amplified by narrative concerns with the multiplication of versions and paratexts, and readers must work through a narrative that aims to both simplify access to the world of Belken County and frustrate any sense of the singularity of that place or its stories.

The narratives of *Estampas del valle y otras obras* and *The Valley* show readers how versions of a story multiply and complicate one another as they compete for a handle on reality, history, or even truth: versions of community history that ignore its oral and ritual components, as well as racist or indifferent histories offered by mainstream media and the court system, share space with the tellings and retellings of the history of Belken County by its own citizens. José David Saldívar has argued that the narrative of Hinojosa's Klail City Death Trip Series "counters historical amnesia by restoring to the materiality of its signifiers that buried reality of south Texas history" (175); Hinojosa's texts unearth that "buried reality" by presenting not one but many histories that run counter to the progressive Western traditional narratives of the border. But he also goes one step further by presenting those multiple histories in materially different versions, highlighting the failures of not only oral but also print culture to adequately capture a historical moment on their own. Readers and critics who confront the changes to the text—paratextual, linguistic, and lexical—are invited to participate materially in these repetitions with a difference, and therefore to participate in the construction and experience of counterhistories. Combined, these paratexts act as enmeshed commentaries on the instability of border narratives, calling attention to one another and demanding to be read in the context of the presence of their alternate versions. Confronting these paratexts, readers are repeatedly asked to choose their version of the story, and to recognize that choice as political.

Many scholars have noted with approval Hinojosa's control over the ever-expanding universe of texts in the Klail City Death Trip Series, celebrating the genius of multiplying versions, of offering recasts or renditions alongside more traditional translations, as a subversive commentary on the politics of publishing Chicana/o literature. For instance, with the publication of *The Valley*, Akers argues, Hinojosa has "consciously stepped over the boundary demarcating translation and initiated a postmodernist literary pursuit into a virtually unexplored but growing area" (94). Describing Hinojosa as "consciously" pursuing the multiplication of material versions of his own text, Akers gives full credit to Hinojosa for an intentional and authoritative foray into the destabilization of a singular text. This celebration of Hinojosa's efforts is countered, however, by the political realities experienced by other Chicana/o authors as they publish and revise their texts. More specifically, the occasional scholarly tendency to attribute power and control over versions to male-authored texts like Hinojosa's is reversed in responses to the publishing history of a female-authored text like Ana Castillo's, which by contrast occasionally emphasizes impotence and lack of control.

Ana Castillo's Two *Sapogonias*

Ana Castillo and her two versions of *Sapogonia* offer readers an opportunity to link the materiality of the text, as well as the attempt to accommodate multiple audiences, to narrative concerns with border identity, just as Hinojosa's work does. The first of the following two sections explores that accommodation of multiple audiences in a similar fashion, tracing the path that led to the distinct material textual differences between the 1990 Bilingual Press version and the 1994 Anchor-Doubleday version. The second section records the interpretive effects of Castillo's revisions, suggesting that reading the narratives of the two *Sapogonias* alongside one another is to participate in Castillo's own definition of *Xicanisma*, a definition she says demands that we "reinsert the forsaken feminine into our consciousness" (*Massacre* 12). For while Hinojosa is labeled as having gained and maintained a certain level of control over the publication of versions of his work, and in turn is lauded by scholars for such seeming control, the critical and even authorial language surrounding Castillo's novel is frequently tinged with a sense of failure. Marissa López notes that *Sapogonia* is "rarely taught and even more rarely mentioned in discussions of Castillo's oeuvre" ("Chicana/o Literature" 147); even the praise of otherwise enthusiastic readers of Castillo's work ranges from "succeeds in its own quirky way" (Spurgeon 26) to "not so successful as a novel per se" (Castillo, "An Interview" 26). Though there is a range of reasons that *Sapogonia* and its status as a revision are less likely to be celebrated than her other work, this difference in treatment is shaped at least in part by the fact that Castillo's revisions, not to mention her discussions of those revisions, are more visibly bound up in narrative negotiations—and renegotiations—of femininity.

"The Most Neglected": Tracing the Publication and Reception of Sapogonia

Just as in the case of Hinojosa's work, the material textual history of *Sapogonia* can be summarized as "difficult," though that may be putting it lightly. At each turn in what Robert Darnton calls the "communications circuit" (11), the cycle of participants in book production from author to publisher to bookseller to audience, the novel faced a set of complicating factors that had major effects on the shape of Castillo's second novel. How do the interests, assumed audiences, marketing abilities, and even the popularity of two vastly different publishers shape the documentary, material, and interpretive possibilities of *Sapogonia*? Is the structural complexity of the 1990 edition related in any way to a press that might be more comfortable publishing experimental and/or nontraditional texts? Likewise, does the 1994 edition, whose back cover boasts was "restructured and refocused" for Doubleday, suggest a link between linearity and marketability? How should the fact that Castillo seems dissatisfied by both editions shape critical interpretation? Castillo's dealings with her publishers, the audiences implied by multiple markets, and the critical reception of the multiple versions of *Sapogonia* reveal the complex historical situation that shaped and continues to shape our understanding of this novel.

Perhaps the most complicated aspect of *Sapogonia* is its publication by two different presses. Although Castillo initially published *The Mixquiahuala Letters* (1986) and *Sapogonia (An Anti-Romance in 3/8 Meter)* (1990) with Bilingual Press, Anchor Books, a division of Doubleday, would later release them in 1992 and 1994, respectively. After another of Bilingual Press's publications, Aristeo Brito's *The Devil in Texas / El diablo en Texas*, won the Western States Book Award, Doubleday sought out the Press for recommendations of Latina/o authors, and as a result acquired subsidiary rights to *The Mixquiahuala Letters* (Van Hooft, "Re: Castillo"). When that first book proved successful, Doubleday purchased subsidiary rights to *Sapogonia* (Van Hooft); Doubleday would later publish *Peel My Love Like an Onion* (1999). This sale, according to Samuel Baker, "annoyed Castillo, who would have liked to have had more involvement in the publication" (59). As the editors at Bilingual Press have noted, negotiating subsidiary rights without notifying the author "is standard publishing practice, especially in the case of first-time authors publishing with small, independent, or university presses" (Van Hooft). Thus Castillo's frustration and "annoyance" are at least partially self-directed: as Baker notes, "Her chief comment on the matter now is to urge young writers to have their contracts vetted, no matter how small and friendly the press" (59).

This was not the first difficulty Castillo claims to have encountered in her relationship with Bilingual Press: she also alleges that the 1990 edition of *Sapogonia* that was published by the smaller press came out before Castillo had any chance to make revisions. The version of the novel that did appear, Castillo claims in an interview with Bryce Milligan, "did not get edited. When I saw that they were just going to publish it as it was, I tried to pull it out, but that was not possible. So it was published unedited. I felt very uncomfortable about that edition" ("An Interview" 26). Bilingual Press disputes these claims: executive editor Karen Van Hooft explains, "It has always been our practice to copy edit the material we publish and also to send the author both the copy edited manuscript and the galleys for approval. If Ana had any concerns about the editing, they were addressed at the time" (Van Hooft).

These conflicting narratives of the production process only multiply the confusion: the press's description presents Castillo as a willing actor with full knowledge of the editing and publishing process, while in Castillo's own version of events she had considerably less control: she describes herself as "annoyed" and "uncomfortable" but ultimately at a loss to do much to correct the novel, of which Castillo says, "had I had the opportunity, I would not have published as it was" ("An Interview" 26). Even in her discussion of her work with Doubleday, which she says "agreed to allow some minimal changes, so I gave it some liposuction and a facelift" ("An Interview" 26), Castillo expresses her sense of limited control over the shape of the novel, though the presses themselves might disagree with such a characterization. In these competing versions of the story of *Sapogonia*'s publication we catch the first glimpse of the overlapping though not always parallel interests of the various actors on the communications circuit: publishers, editors, writers. We also witness the way that the story of a book's publication is always already a story, a narrative written and rewritten with constantly changing interpretive results.

According to Castillo's narrative, control over her work was precluded by the fine print of her contract. Given the role of both the small and large presses in publishing *Sapogonia*, it is worth considering the impact of each publishing company on the interpretive possibilities of the novel. Each press caters to different audiences, publishing texts that Martín-Rodríguez argues can be distinguished in terms of "the market" and "*la marketa*." He defines the market as "those works that are now directed to the literary establishment" and *la marketa* as texts "that are addressed to the (always elusive when it comes to definition) Chicano/a community" (*Life* 110), citing Bilingual Press / Editorial Bilingüe as a top producer of books for *la marketa*. While *la marketa* also indicates a class distinction, Martín-Rodríguez's argument primarily centers on language use: the market is categorized as monolingual and unaccepting of the presence of Spanish or *Caló*, while *la marketa* and the presses associated with it allow and encourage linguistic diversity. Therefore, while Castillo's poetry often features *marketa*-directed bilingualism, her novels are far more accessible, particularly *So Far from God*, where, as Peter Carr argues, Spanish is "restricted largely to occasions where context facilitates comprehension" (28).

Alternatively, Frederick Luis Aldama argues that although Castillo often functions as "grist for a publishing mill that, in order to maximize profits and satisfy stock market goals, carefully determines which group of readers is willing to spend the most money on what book" (93), she nevertheless addresses *marketa* readers even in market-directed texts. He claims: "Castillo uses a double voice—writing to and against the mainstream—in ways that make her fiction more appealing as crossover material. This does not mean to suggest that she 'sells out'; her skill at crafting fictions that complicate and challenge at every turn is undeniable" (113). Aldama sees Castillo's writing as appealing to the market and *la marketa*, layered one on top of the other.

But while Martín-Rodríguez addresses the market appeal of Castillo's *So Far from God*, in contrast to her work for *la marketa*, as a sign of her shift from "well-known in Chicana/o literary circles" to "well-known writer" and Aldama sees Castillo challenging two audiences in a single text, a book like *Sapogonia*, which has been produced in two different versions for the market and *la marketa*, offers a third avenue for exploring the impact of competing audiences on Castillo's work.[6] Aldama argues that "perhaps Ana Castillo is an example of an author who is constantly discovering new ways to negotiate the articulation of a Xicanista identity within the mainstream" (113). But *Sapogonia* has yet to join that mainstream fully, even on the coattails of its successful younger and older sisters, and even with its revisions. Instead, its multiple material versions jointly occupy a border zone between the market and *la marketa*, defying categorization.

Castillo notes this complicated negotiation of the market and *la marketa*, saying, "The kind of literature I write is not directed for the mainstream, although *So Far from God* did very well, and I'm hoping that we're entering a new era now where it will be more and more the case that writers from the fringes occupy the mainstream" (quoted in Baker 59). The audience Castillo has in mind for her work may not be quite the same as the audience sought and procured by her publishers; the response from that unanticipated audience feeds back to Castillo, who interprets her popularity somewhat optimistically in terms of changing reader tastes. Yet it is important to recognize that readers are responding not simply to Castillo's narrative but, more specifically, to the narrative as it is shaped by publishers, booksellers, and reviewers. For instance, the success of *So Far from God* likely had much to do with its promotion. Carr notes: "Upon its release, *So Far From God* was heavily promoted—advertised on the cover of the *Los Angeles Times* Book Review of May 16, 1993, for example—and received widespread media attention. The *Los Angeles Times* called it the novel to read if Gabriel García Márquez seems too complex, being a cross between *One Hundred Years of Solitude* and the television soap 'General Hospital'" (quoted in Carr 24). By contrast, *Sapogonia* received no such promotion, because its link to magical realism is tenuous at best and reviewers would be at pains to describe it as a literary telenovela. Somehow, *Sapogonia* resists the kind of paternalistic comparison to *One Hundred Years of Solitude* often launched by reviewers of *So Far from God*, wherein "Castillo's reputation is here transferred from her position as a leading voice in the innovative contemporary Chicana/o literary arena to that of an undemanding late offspring of the highly patriarchal Latin American magical realist trend" (Martín-Rodríguez 127). In going too far afield of that trend, *Sapogonia* misses out on the García Márquez bump.

The relationship between *Sapogonia* and *So Far from God* is important not only because it demonstrates a difference in the way mainstream publishers like Doubleday and Norton were able to promote those two novels but also because the historical hiccup in the double publication by Bilingual Press and Doubleday caused *Sapogonia* to be published both before and after this more successful novel. A close examination of the way both presses attempted to advertise *Sapogonia* through book covers shows a few glimpses of the impact of these conflicting chronologies. The back of the Bilingual Press paperback advertises Castillo by first referencing her two bilingual poetry collections (*My Father Was a Toltec* [1988] and *Women Are Not Roses* [1984]), also mentioning the titles of two chapbooks and finally *The Mixquiahuala Letters* as evidence of Castillo's craft. By contrast, Doubleday is able to advertise Castillo on both the front and the back of the paperback as the author of *So Far from God*. The presence of this more famous title on the cover, a clear and often-used attempt to establish a positive comparison between the two, encourages readers to see *Sapogonia* as another potentially palatable magical realist, southwestern—and, in the end, mainstream—success. The complicated publication history makes *Sapogonia* either the descendent of Castillo's bilingual poetry, as Bilingual's *marketa*-oriented cover indicates, or the heir to Castillo's market success, *So Far from God*. Ultimately, the chronology of publication shapes the way publishers market Castillo's work, and that, in turn, potentially shapes the way her work is received.

Further evidence of the competing potential audiences served by Bilingual and Doubleday can be seen in their use of celebratory blurbs to sell Castillo's novel. For example, the Bilingual edition quotes the San Francisco Women's Foundation, which named Castillo a Women of Words honoree for "pioneering excellence in literature." In contrast, the Doubleday edition quotes author Clarissa Pinkola Estés regarding Castillo: "A writer with enormous integrity, she is blessed with common sense and lyric sense, the very rarest of gifts." On their own, each of those quotes is wonderfully celebratory; in comparison, they seem to be celebrating two different versions of Castillo. A pioneer and a woman possessed of common sense are not nearly antonymous, but they do suggest a distinction between experimentation and approachability. These respective *marketa*- and market-oriented blurbs, offered on the one hand by a small feminist organization and on the other by an author of a bestseller, aim in different ways to entice readers with their portraits of Castillo.

Additionally, both publications use the same quote from Rudolfo Anaya, a respected canonical Chicano writer, to sell copies. On the back of the Bilingual edition, Anaya elaborates, "*Sapogonia* is a complex, engaging novel. It explores the depth of passion, which makes for great literature. Here is Ana Castillo at her best, a literary triumph. *Sapogonia* will establish Castillo as one of our finest Chicana novelists; its qualities make it a novel to be read by all." Doubleday imports this quotation onto the front cover of the 1994 version, cutting it to read, "A complex, engaging novel. . . . *Sapogonia* will establish Castillo as one of our finest Chicana novelists," interestingly erasing the reference to "literature" and "literary" and thereby emphasizing the more mainstream "novel" and "novelists." Is *Sapogonia* an example of experimental, pioneering, poetic literature or a complex yet common-sense novel, another *So Far from God*? Given the coexistence of the Bilingual Press and Doubleday editions, which aim to serve *la marketa* and the market in different ways, it is possible to see how the interpretive possibilities of this novel can be shaped before a reader even opens the book.

Those possibilities only multiply when the narratives themselves prove to be different from one another. While Castillo uses labels that emphasize her discomfort with the novel in singular terms, calling it "her middle child . . . the most neglected" ("An Interview" 26), Doubleday makes visible the two versions before singularizing them once again. The back of the 1994 edition's paperback proclaims, "Anchor Books is proud to present a revised edition of prize-winning poet and novelist Ana Castillo's second novel, *Sapogonia*. Originally published in 1990, this newly edited version brilliantly demonstrates why she is one of America's leading Chicana writers." Rather than ignoring its status as a revision, Doubleday embraces it as an improvement over the implicitly inferior original, conforming to or creating readers' expectations of one definitive version of a text. Supplanting one text with another attempts to assign stability to *Sapogonia*.

When faced with a text that celebrates rather than conceals its instability while also making public the messy writing and revising process, perhaps we assume too quickly that the text is fatally flawed, in this case making Castillo's dissatisfaction with *Sapogonia* our own. Köhler, for example, argues that because of the lack of revision, "The narrative partially seems to sound uneven" before dismissing such unevenness as a "technical issue" (103). But I would suggest that the uneven narratives of each edition represent more than a technical issue: they are a reflection of a novel in progress, an identity in progress, and a sign of competing narratives worth examining side by side. Castillo and her publishers, audiences, and critics all shape the production and continuing reception of *Sapogonia* in ways that assume a progressive improvement of the text in its revision. But what might happen if readers engaged the instability of its versions instead? Instead of taking Castillo at her word, we might confront the fluidity of the text, attending to the borders between versions as carefully as we attend to the borders between nations, ethnicities, races, and genders.

"Someone Who Dominates": The Effects of the Revision of *Sapogonia* on Interpretation

Once readers move beyond the cover pages and dive into the novel, they meet challenges regardless of which edition they read. The designation of the narrative of *Sapogonia* as border literature is certainly debatable, because the novel does not feature the U.S.-Mexico border in any way, instead taking place in various U.S. cities (Chicago, Los Angeles, and New York), Spain, and the invented Latin American nation of Sapogonia. Even Sapogonia is difficult to describe: Joy Lynch claims, "In *Sapogonia*, Castillo creates a mythological landscape which she endows with the qualities of a psychological imprint from a past denied integration into the present . . . [reminding] us of the 'presence' of the past in our present lives" (134–135). Such an invented space suggests that it echoes and resonates with a geographic borderlands; in turn, a sizeable number of critics have variously invoked it as an example of border literature in a more metaphorical sense, involving "border subjects" (Walter 82) and "[merging] the mythical Aztlán with the contemporary and argumentative borderlands" (Socolovsky 76).

The novel tells the story of the relationship between Máximo Madrigal (Max), a Sapogón who leaves his home for Europe, finds his father, and eventually ends up in the United States, and Pastora, a woman of indigenous heritage and a musician committed to social uplift, who ends up spending time in jail for transporting unauthorized immigrants into the country. The two characters move in and out of each other's lives, and their purely sexual relationship is frustrating to Max, who is more accustomed to women developing attachments to him. Not only does Castillo weave together the stories of two characters as they drift in and out of each other's lives but she also constantly shifts points of view, from first, second, and third person to multiple focalizations of the main and secondary characters. Yvonne Yarbro-Bejarano describes this technique as Castillo's "negotiation with and translation of male narrative form and male point of view" (68); Castillo's play with point of view alternately draws readers toward and pushes them away from Max.

In addition, readers confronting both Max's narration and Pastora's, among others, must make decisions about the situatedness of the claims each makes about the other. For example, from Max's perspective, Pastora is a witch, while Pastora argues, "Latino men always thought that a woman who allowed herself to be thought of sexually and denied any reason to feel shameful of it and had none of the inhibitions or insecurities with relation to commitments as it was considered women should—had to be a witch" (1990, 125). The narrative, by alternating perspectives, neither encourages nor discourages either interpretation. To further confuse matters, in 1994 the sentence conveying Pastora's response was edited to read, "She said that Latino men always thought that a sexually open woman who had none of the insecurities with relation to commitment—as it was considered women should—had to be a witch" (161). Both lines appear to convey the same sentiment, but the first contains a passive construction, "a woman who allowed herself to be thought of sexually," and the second makes the woman active by referring to her as "a sexually open woman." Because of the subject of the discussion, this revision serves as more than a grammatical preference. The difference centers on the woman's—in this case, Pastora's—relationship to her own sexuality. Though the use of the word "allowing" suggests a degree of agency, the first version places the focus on the gaze, on the one who thinks of her sexually. Meanwhile, "a sexually open woman" more clearly focuses on female pleasure by comparison. Is Pastora's sexuality passive or active? And finally, the language of "allowing" also reminds us of Castillo's own language to describe the work she did to revise the novel for Doubleday, who "allowed" the changes to her book to be made: as a result, the narrative change suggests a subordination that Castillo erases in the act of revising, even as the need for revision itself may have made her felt subordinate to her publisher.

Faced with these competing sentences, chapters, and versions, critical arguments about the narrative might be expanded to acknowledge their effects on interpretation. López's argument for "critical strategies that take account of a text's literariness by granting full consideration to literary and textual elements, viewing them as vehicles for meaning" ("Chicana/o Literature" 147), which she makes in the context of exploring the formal qualities of *Sapogonia*'s narration, can be expanded to include the material existence of dual versions of *Sapogonia*. Likewise, Elsa Saeta's description of the internal difficulty of following the complex narration of *Sapogonia*—"It is difficult to judge what is real or accurate when the whole structure of the game is constantly changing" (69)—might easily be broadened to encompass the experience of discovering the differences between the two published versions. If readers are confused, destabilized, or frustrated by the competing narrations of Pastora and Max, not to mention all of the other characters through whom the third-person narration is focalized, it is likely that those confusions will be multiplied exponentially when readers are faced with two versions of the same text. Köhler argues of *Sapogonia*, "If we need to tell and re-tell stories in order to make sense of what is going on around us, in order to understand life, then the distinctions between reality and fiction must be blurred" (111); this is also true of the two materially different versions of *Sapogonia* from which readers have to choose. The different versions tell the same story in two different ways, in the same way that we get two different versions of events within the narrative: Pastora's and Max's.

Although Castillo describes revisions such as the one just discussed as a sort of elective surgery, implying that surface problems may have improved without addressing root problems, the changes she made significantly alter the reading experience. This might not be apparent at first glance, since every chapter in the 1990 version finds its way into the 1994 version, albeit in a different order. Sentences are chopped or expanded, chapters are divided into sections, and descriptions become clearer, but the plot of each chapter essentially makes the transition from one version to the next. However, the changes Castillo makes shape new interpretive possibilities, particularly for Pastora's character. This is especially interesting given Castillo's description of her revision as "liposuction and a facelift," which implies a feminized notion of the text, a docile body shaped by cultural norms ("An Interview" 26). This revision "procedure" paradoxically involves intensifying the focus on the masculine characteristics of the novel by more clearly centering on Max's character. Most of the revisions Castillo makes present a more coherent portrait of Max, ultimately altering readers' access to Pastora; as Castillo writes, "woman in the flesh, thereafter, was subordinated" (*Massacre* 12).

In fact, many of these revisions reflect the culmination of a series of changes to the character sketches that began in the mid- to late 1970s and resulted in the more fully fleshed Máximo and Pastora, including "Death of a Chicken" and "Antihero," housed in the archives at the University of California, Santa Barbara. For example, in two of the sketches and the published version(s) of the novel Max imagines killing Pastora. Readers of the sketches will note the shift from Max's use of a pistol ("A gun to his head would cure him of his misery. But first, first he would manage the strength to walk all the way back if need be and put the first bullet into hers" ["Death" 2]) to his use of his own bare hands ("I wanted to put my hands tightly around her bird-like neck and crush the delicate bones within. I swore that night it would be well worth it if I had to spend the rest of my days in prison. But of course, I didn't do it" ["Antihero" 2]), and finally to the published version, in which scissors from Pastora's sewing basket become the murder weapon. As Castillo revises, the phallic gun changes to the brutal yet intimate image of his bare hands and changes again to the scissors—both feminine and phallic.

As the sketches preceding the publication of the novel indicate, Pastora and Max were at the forefront of Castillo's narrative creation, but in those sketches Pastora is almost always seen through the lens of Max's narration. This hierarchy of Max over Pastora continues in the 1990 edition of *Sapogonia*, which begins with Máximo's story but quickly shifts to Pastora's concurrent story in chapter 5. Though readers again more frequently see Max's perspective on events and characterizations, the novel also more frequently moves between the stories of Max's and Pastora's lives until their meeting. The revisions Castillo made to the 1994 edition do more than simply reorganize chapters: they emphasize even more directly the importance of Max's narration to the whole of the novel. This move centralizes the point of view of the displaced Sapogón, relegating Pastora to the background. Furthermore, it functions to make the narrative of each character more distinct and linear. For example, rather than switching back and forth between characters as they must in the 1990 version, readers do not meet Pastora until chapter 15; the first hundred pages of the novel are dedicated to Max's story. Again, the back cover of the 1994 edition claims that Castillo's revision "has captured even more vividly the struggle of Máximo Madrigal, an expatriate of Sapogonia, with his obsession for Pastora Aké, a woman of his native blood whom he can never control." The 1994 revised edition delivers a primary and secondary narrative rather than a set of competing narratives.

Castillo might argue that Max was always meant to be the primary character: she acknowledges, "Coming from the early Chicano Latino Movement, which was dominated by men, I was compelled to understand the individual. I found him seductive and at the same time repulsive, but someone who dominates. It was very important for me, as a woman and as a feminist, to try to get into the workings of this kind of person's mind and try to understand him" ("Ana Castillo" 183–184). However, early commentaries on *Sapogonia*, relying on the 1990 edition of the novel, approach both characters and their stories as equally important. For instance, Yarbro-Bejarano argues, "*Sapogonia* is a fascinating text that explores male fantasy, its potential for violence against women and the female subject's struggle to interpret herself both within and outside of this discourse on femininity" (69). Perhaps in the version where both characters are introduced early, critics can more easily identify and argue for the presence of a yin/yang of femininity and masculinity. Furthermore, despite Castillo's intentions, the reorganization of chapters orients a reader to each character in a different way: the duality or call-and-response qualities of the chapters' moving between Max and Pastora give way to a more sustained attention to Max before introducing Pastora, reinforcing a market-driven concern for linear progress. For example, when Pastora's character is developed in chapter 6 of the 1990 edition, she is participating in a performance, and Máximo is observing her. Chapter 7 abruptly shifts back in time to the period before Máximo comes to the United States, working backward from Barcelona to France and Sapogonia. In the 1994 revision, that chronology is straightened out. First readers learn Máximo's backstory, and then they are introduced to Pastora, in chronological order. Thus readers can prioritize the narrators and story lines, perhaps at the expense of a more balanced exploration of how each character's narration enhances or conflicts with the other's.

Rather than seeing Castillo's revisions as improvements, we might see them as opportunities to recognize the advantages and disadvantages of presenting the narrative in structures of different order. While Pastora and Max compete for a reader's attention, twisting her version of events around his, the 1990 and 1994 editions of *Sapogonia* weave a double narrative, telling their stories from different vantage points. In the spaces between these versions, we find a valorization of the unstable, a call to reconsider the notion of the solitary, unified text from which we typically launch our literary analyses. A close examination of one deletion from the 1994 version reveals not only a further centralization of Máximo's character in all of its complexity but also the elimination of some of the complexity of Pastora's character.

A little more than halfway through each of the editions of *Sapogonia*, the chapters begin to align with one another and, for the most part, match each other in plot. This realignment begins at chapter 34 as Máximo considers the possibility of "surrendering" to Pastora. As he reflects on her power over him, he thinks of his own birth: "[S]he had managed to take something so vital and potent from his being, like the umbilical cord his grandmother had severed with her teeth the dawn he was born; the remains, shriveled ten days later, wrapped and hidden away to protect his soul" (172/192). Max's simultaneous attraction to and repulsion from Pastora often figures itself in terms of the combination of her sexuality and maternity. Pastora undermines the whore/mother, Malinche/Guadalupe dichotomy throughout the novel because, as Roland Walter argues, "The implicit deconstruction of the patriarchal order . . . is based on female agency, a (mythical) revaluation of woman's life-giving powers, a rendering visible of the female body and mind as text, as discourse that reclaims the indigenous matriarchal social structure and way of thinking" (88–89). In this chapter, Max recognizes his own inability to surrender to Pastora, to a "matriarchal social structure," and from here she drifts further away from him, first to prison and then to Eduardo. That the chapters from this point onward proceed in the same order perhaps indicates that this moment is the novel's climax, a turning point with a predetermined resolution that occurs no matter which edition one reads.

But one significant change is made to that final half of the novel: the sixteen paragraphs that begin chapter 48 disappear. Although the plot of each chapter continues to match the other from that point forward, this large portion of chapter 48 from the 1990 edition is deleted from the 1994 edition. The deleted paragraphs describe Pastora's realization that she is pregnant and the events that lead to Eduardo's return to her life. For example, missing from the 1994 edition are the following opening paragraphs:

> She was going to have a baby. She had known for only a few days that she was seven weeks along. Pregnancy had not occurred to her before. She had been careful to use a contraceptive and the intrauterine device was checked regularly to make certain it was in place. Worried that she was suffering from an illness, she went to a doctor and was given the unexpected news.

> She rejoiced over the child that was sprouting from her very soul, whom she would offer all that she had to give. She whispered the secret to friends, although she had yet to tell her family. Motherhood without marriage would mean only hardship in her mother's point of view and endless criticism from her stepfather. (1990, 242)

These original opening paragraphs of chapter 48 demonstrate Pastora's initial joy and the effect of the pregnancy on her, asserting that "Pastora's telepathy was sharper than usual recently, possibly because she now was accompanied by the spirit guides of the new soul she carried within" (242). However, the 1994 edition begins more abruptly with the seventeenth paragraph of the 1990 edition: "Pastora didn't look pregnant when Eduardo appeared at her door" (243/274). Without those opening descriptions of the 1990 edition, the 1994 edition is more guarded and pessimistic about Pastora's relationship to her pregnancy: "[S]he didn't know what happened to the joy with which she had planned to share her news" (243). The 1994 edition contains only the shadow of a former joy. This deletion demands our attention because it is the only significant change made in the last twenty-five chapters of the book and it eliminates not just a phrase or a paragraph but sixteen paragraphs.

Why remove these paragraphs that add a positive dimension to Pastora's pregnancy and advance the plot, indicating how and why Eduardo reappears in Pastora's life? One answer is that the line "Pregnancy had not occurred to her before" rings false; readers know from their first introduction to Pastora that she has had an abortion. Moreover, readers are aware throughout the novel of the agony and sadness with which Pastora regards her reproductive abilities. When readers first meet Pastora, she is described by Diego, the would-be father, as "mourning" (18/106) and "punctured through to her soul" (17/106) by her recent abortion. Like Máximo, for whom thoughts of Pastora lead to thoughts of the loss of his umbilical cord and loss of his power, Diego experiences a peculiar sense of reproductive loss: "He felt a tug at an absent womb in his lower abdomen and he cried" (18/106). The 1994 edition appends the words "with her" (106) to the end of that sentence, shifting the focus from emasculation (in the sense of deprived strength) to shared grief.

In what male characters describe in Pastora as an uncharacteristic behavior, she "hardly restrain[s] herself" (17/106) from thinking about the child she would have had, her emotions a complex portrait of the impact of abortion on her life. Throughout the ensuing chapters, readers are periodically reminded of the abortion just as Pastora's body continues to remind her. In chapter 6/17, the narrative describes Pastora in the bathroom: "Although it was barely a trickle, she continued to bleed the final vestiges of the fetus she had eliminated" (23/121).[7] When she sits down to pray in chapter 30/31, Pastora continues to ask for "solace and consolation" nearly three years after the abortion.

Kelli Lyon Johnson notes that the description of Pastora's reaction to her abortion is a measure of her grief not simply over her lost child but also over violence: "The decision to abort for . . . Pastora is the result of fear of men and their institutionalized cultural and physical power over women" (47). As she prays, Pastora thinks, "To women, abortion was self-defense and preservation of the species. . . . Abortion was instinct beyond ideas. Abortion was fear (the cat that devours its litter when a predator nears)" (164/185–186). As an act of self-defense, Pastora's abortion leads to a prolonged and terrible grief, which is continually impressed upon readers throughout the narrative.

The language of depression and sadness with which Pastora responds to her abortion also extends to her reproductive abilities in general. For example, in chapter 18/24, the narrative describes the experience of Pastora's menstruation as "a fruitless labor" (109/156). When she menstruates, Pastora feels "that everything in life was defeated, as if the failure to be fertilized each month meant failure in life" (1994, 156).[8] Pastora's relationship to her potential maternity is characterized by loss; when she does successfully conceive a child, she experiences great difficulty with her pregnancy, and this leaves her demoralized to the point where she merely "allowed herself to sound irritable rather than depressed" (245/276).[9] Although she feels "exhilarated" (246/277) by the experience of giving birth, when she meets Máximo and describes being a parent, she claims, "One's wings are heavy" (267/302). The language of "wings" is reminiscent of Diego's description of her in the midst of postabortion grief: he describes her as "a great bird whose wings had been injured" (17/105–106). She sacrifices much for her son, including nine years of her own life, and although Máximo bristles at the space the child occupies that would otherwise belong to him, Pastora's relationship to her son—like her relationship to Máximo—is paradoxically all-consuming and distant. What was once a monthly failure has produced a son, and though she "would teach it to fly" (244/275), as Pastora explains to Máximo, he "is not a continuation of you or me . . . but a continuity of the species, a simple and humble fact" (269/304). Her emphasis on biological facts mutes the emotional intensity Máximo brings to the discussion, but it also mutes Pastora's entire experience of motherhood.

Thus, in a novel that frames Pastora and her reproductive abilities in terms of depression, sadness, failure, heaviness, distance, and even death, these deleted opening paragraphs of chapter 48 present an opportunity to consider a new perspective on both Pastora's relationship to reproduction and her relationships with other people. The opening sentences, "She was going to have a baby. She had known for only a few days that she was seven weeks along" (1990, 242), startling and crisp in their simplicity, offer a momentary reprieve from the deep gloom that pervades many of the depictions of reproduction in this novel. Not only does this original opening sequence describe her as "rejoic[ing]" over her pregnancy but it also quickly introduces her vulnerabilities and concerns for the opinions of others. She repeatedly worries about how her mother and father will feel, and she spends the bulk of these sixteen paragraphs in telephone conversations with Eduardo, trying to determine how to share her secret as well as whether to accept him back into her life. Her questions—"Who wanted the divorce?" (242)—and her accusations—"It's taken quite a while for you to admit that I am important to you and it comes when you are unequivocally alone" (243)—betray her uncertainty and her wounded, passive aggression, which can be quite startling given her otherwise strong and sometimes cold demeanor. When she does accept Eduardo at her doorstep (as the chapter in the 1994 edition begins), it is after an intense phone call concluding in Pastora hanging up on Eduardo in addition to a letter from Eduardo begging to see her. Just as Máximo thinks Pastora's life has begun taking cues from a "propagandist women's magazine" or a "Spanish soap opera" (267/302) in the aftermath of motherhood, this earlier instance of romantic drama casts Pastora in a new and vulnerable light.

The deletion of those sixteen paragraphs limits access to a more complex understanding of Pastora's relationship to her own body and to other people in her life. In effect, this deletion provides a more coherent portrait of Pastora's pregnancy and tightens the focus on Máximo, which is one of the major effects of Castillo's reorganization of the novel as a whole. However, the 1990 edition carries a trace of this narrative construction of Pastora, and its disappearance alone creates an instability in the text(s) we call *Sapogonia*. The novel, in each of its versions, narratively emphasizes that there are two versions of Pastora: the version Max sees (Coatlicue, or a witch) and the version Pastora presents (a sexual, maternal, complex woman). On a material level, readers are offered two more versions of Pastora: the one who initially feels joyful and vulnerable at the discovery of her pregnancy and the one whose joy is withheld, distanced from readers, who can experience it only in the past tense. She is a woman whose emotions surrounding pregnancy occasionally spark into happiness and extreme closeness to others as her telepathy heightens and also a woman whose "wings" are constantly weighted, distancing her from Máximo, Eduardo, and even her son.

The *marketa* text—advertised in light of Castillo's status as a literary pioneer and winner of the Women of Words Award—offers a novel more balanced in its representation of protagonists but also a complex representation of Pastora's connection to her own body. The text produced for the market—complete with liposuction and facelift—streamlines the narrative into a more approachable, linear novel, subordinating Pastora and elevating Max along the way. Though we might take such a reading to mean that the more balanced gender representation in the first version renders it the better or more valuable one, the question need not be whether one of these versions is more apt, more consistent, or more coherent. Instead, the 1990 and 1994 versions of *Sapogonia* multiply the versions of Pastora described in the narrative, placing an accurate description of her identity out of reach. Neither Max nor readers can pin her down.

In chapter 47 of both versions, in the aftermath of Max's grandparents' horrific death, Max relates how he used wood from his grandfather's land to create his most recent sculptures: "the works I produced were indisputably my finest work thus far" (234/265). When the sculptures arrive from Sapogonia, they have been completely destroyed: "What resulted was not from stupid handling from tossing about on a plane or down conveyor belts. They were hatefully smashed so that what was left could not be salvaged as the original piece" (234/265). After a bout of anger, Max decides to re-create the art "from what remained of [his] damaged pieces" (234/266). The narration of this moment is subtly different in the 1990 and 1994 versions. Before the discovery of the pieces' damaged state, the 1990 version includes an additional narration to the effect that they "were the beginning of a series that surpassed all my past work and I could never duplicate them." Furthermore, the 1990 version contains Máximo's specific assertion that "the work would be salvaged despite the vandals' desire to destroy art. I would work on a series of small pieces" (234). These additional details heighten the tension of this moment. Máximo first feels the project can never be duplicated, then finds a way to "salvage[]" his work through smaller pieces, partially as a targeted response to the vandals who nearly stood in the way of his art. The more concise narrative of the 1994 version merely implies this motivation.

Socolovsky argues for the significance of this moment in the narrative, claiming, "Max thus rewrites the myth of an attachment to land by quite literally transplanting the land, and settling down elsewhere. His use of the ranch's wood for his artwork demonstrates the way in which the place follows the migrant, rather than the migrant returning to the place and calling it home" (82). But beyond the significance of the origins of his sculptures, one is also reminded of the possibilities for imagining and reimagining art as it is reshaped by circumstances beyond our control. Max not only conceives of his work in terms of a series—not a solitary, stable object—but, when faced with disaster, he also refashions his sculptures into something new, related to and yet distinct from their earlier forms. Yet while Max embraces fluidity in his artwork, extending that embrace to the fluid identities (sexual, gender, religious, and maternal) of a woman like Pastora comes with an edge. When the novel concludes, it is possible to see Pastora as just another work of art: "it was Máximo alone who concocted Pastora" (311/354). But unlike in the case of his other works of art, he finds himself on the side of destruction when her identity slips out of his control. In the 1990 version, as he attempts to confess his deepest feelings to her, Max finds himself holding back: "I would aim to destroy her in order to recreate her as mine" (288). In a similar way, Castillo narrates the story of her book's publication—a story, it should be noted, with multiple versions—as one in which she had less control over the shape of her text in its first and second publications, but yet, rather than destroy it, she worked within the text, rewriting even these very moments, to create a new version that bears a resemblance to but can never be mistaken for the old.

Castillo may not have meant to create a novel with multiple versions, but her interactions with textual versions in the borderlands between Chicana/o and mass-market publishing houses need not be seen simply as corruptions or barriers in the way of her producing her intended text. Instead, they highlight the problems unique to an author navigating between the margins and the mainstream and act as shaping forces in the possibilities for interpreting the text(s), making material the narrative concern with multiple sides to the same story. Perhaps the story of Pastora's narrative subordination to Máximo in the development of these revised versions reflects Castillo's own sense of subordination to the impulses of her *marketa* and market publishers. But by reading them side by side, we have an opportunity not only to "reinsert the forsaken feminine" (Castillo, *Massacre* 12), to reflect on the impact of revision on Pastora's character, but also to begin a discussion of how our own interpretations might differently depend on these "damaged pieces." Literature and criticism of the border have long championed the value of contesting dominant narratives of history, the politics of location, and the instability that undermines any attempt at defining a solitary truth. They have taught us to value identities in process: the contingent, the contradictory, the "act of kneading" (Anzaldúa, *Borderlands* 103). For those of us who find *Sapogonia* to be a moving reflection on the way stories are told and heard differently from every location and point of view, exploring how the competing versions and the circumstances of their production replicate that narrative can help deepen an understanding of this process.

Conclusion

By revising and reintroducing new versions of their novels, both Rolando Hinojosa and Ana Castillo offer readers texts that call attention to themselves as material objects and demand to be studied in the context of their publication histories. Hinojosa voluntarily revised his novel, creating a "transcultural version" that tests the notions of textual stability, the constraints of translation, and the efforts of editors and critics of his Klail City Death Trip series looking to pin down a chronology. Castillo, in pursuing publication with both Bilingual Press and Doubleday, had less room to revise. While she likely envisioned her revision as a replacement and not a "duo-text" (Zilles 3), or a text composed of an original and a newer rendition, she nonetheless created competing versions whose paratexts and organization tell two slightly different stories, with different emphases on gendered narration. Many critics of Hinojosa are attentive to these multiple versions as such, though some confuse or conflate the versions in the way that many critics of *Sapogonia* do, generating arguments based on and responding to critics who operate from completely different versions of the texts. But, perhaps most important, the availability of both Hinojosa's and Castillo's texts in multiple versions links textuality to Chicana/o borderlands identity: both novels emphasize the instability of Chicana/o history and storytelling via unstable material texts, highlighting the experience of borderlands identity via characters concerned with versioning, revising, and remaking art (or texts) from elements of previously existing art.

This concern with alternative histories and counterhistories is a political one: Hinojosa and Castillo both underscore the importance of narrative as well as editorial and even authorial power in the face of the version of Western history that attempts to speak for the borderlands rather than from them. Thus revision is a powerful tool that aims not simply to correct the mistakes of past narratives but to place new narratives beside them. As readers, we are meant to see not only the end product of those revisions and contestations of the dominant narratives of history but also the subversive act of revision as it happens or, as Bryant argues, "actual struggle, not allegories of struggle" (*Melville Unfolding* 54). In these stories of revision, border writers, characters, and texts negotiate language choices, multiple audiences, the mainstream and the margins from within the narrative of the text. But those negotiations are also extended to the material text, where readers find themselves asking the same questions as the characters they read: which version of the story matters, and why?

2

Translating in the Margins

Transcultural Glossaries

Words fail me in both languages.
—Gustavo Pérez Firmat

In narrative and in interview, in fiction and in fact, Chicana/o border writers frequently pursue—or are hounded by—the question of language. Whether they speak some Spanish or none at all, the question of whether and how to include Spanish in their literary texts is both personal and political. For bilingual Chicana/o border writers, inhabiting both English and Spanish can be a dangerous and yet incredibly powerful position: they and their characters often describe being cast out or mistrusted by speakers on either side of the divide, even feared by those who recognize in them the power to destabilize language, knowledge, and reality. As is the case with many Latina/o writers, they can belong fully to both and/or neither language, but they must at some point negotiate the boundaries between them as they aim to communicate with readers. Such boundaries are the product of and a gesture toward the lived experience of the U.S.-Mexico border: "it is this border context," argues Alfred Arteaga, "that differentiates the styles of linguistic interplay of Chicano poetry from other styles of polyglot poetics" (10). As Chicana/o border writers and in turn their characters negotiate their own linguistic identities, the question of whether, when, and how much to translate occupies a central part of Chicana/o border narratives. Martha Cutter is right that "translation evokes a crossing of borders" (7); the crossing of those borders happens not only within the narrative but also in the physical, material borderlands of the text as decisions are made about how best to represent the presence of Spanish in an English-language text. Authors frequently must contend with editors, publishers, and readers over how much to accommodate monolingual English readers, and the evidence of that negotiation is sometimes written into the material text in the form of a Spanish-English glossary.

Reading the bilingual glossary as paratext, we recognize the glossary as "more than a boundary or a sealed border" between languages and audiences; it is, "rather, a *threshold*, or—a word Borges used apropos of a preface—a 'vestibule' that offers the world at large the possibility of either stepping inside or turning back" (Genette 2). This particular threshold between text and not-text, much like the borderlands between the United States and Mexico, is more a contact zone than a dividing line, a space filled with activity and yet often elided in discussions of national and ethnic as well as linguistic difference. Even its blurred status as autographic (chosen by the author) or allographic (chosen by the publisher) suggests that this concept of the paratext can be very helpful in illuminating the ways border narratives are variously supported or undermined by their own materiality. However, as Beth McCoy notes,

> Arguing for a practical and theoretical link between the bookish realm of paratextuality and the larger political realm of racialized power is not easy. Doing so, after all, requires attention to that which the culture at large determines is marginal, minor, and beyond the reach of interpretation, as suggested by the moral adage "Don't judge a book by its cover." It also demands more intense exploration of how white power might be transacted through such inconsequential spaces, a possibility that for many remains counterintuitive: how could something so minor perform such a major function? (158)

The "inconsequential spaces" of the bilingual glossary in a Chicana/o border text can seem like a minor addition, a neutral tool that guides understanding. And yet that glossary performs the major function of addressing readers' expectations of the relationships between Spanish and English. That it does so from the margins not only potentially conceals its work but also reveals the impact of competing narratives of language. In this case, the margins register "the visible, graphic aspects of language contact, and in particular the concrete manifestations of bilingualism in various national settings" (Hodgson and Sarkonak 21).

On the surface, the insertion of a Spanish-English glossary into a border literary text would seem to be an example of near-complete English-language accommodation, perhaps to editors, publishers, or readers; as Lourdes Torres explains, "A glossary . . . provides further assurances that the monolingual reader does not have to languish in unfamiliar territory" (82). The glossary, which sometimes precedes but more typically follows a narrative, alerts readers to the employment of multiple languages but also, and perhaps more important, defines a visible boundary line of white space between those languages where one might not otherwise exist. Opposing one language to the other suggests a clear-cut equivalency that potentially distracts readers from the complexities of existing between or among languages.

But the glossary, when examined closely, can also work to subversively highlight those linguistic complexities. As McCoy argues, paratextual elements, which include bilingual glossaries, "have functioned centrally as a zone transacting ever-changing modes of white domination and of resistance to that domination" (158): in the case of many works of Chicana/o border literature, glossaries are themselves a kind of border zone, providing insight into the working relationships between author, editor, publisher, and reader, as well as a sense of competing interests in the representation of Spanish in predominantly English texts. Glossaries shape interpretive possibilities by manipulating the role of Spanish in English (and vice versa) in a visible way. As a site where linguistic domination and resistance rely on the instability of language, these marginal spaces often reflect a fundamental mistrust of the translating ability and accuracy of the writer as well as the reader, as well as a desire to make the reading experience (and thus, the identification experience) easier. Like the historical Malinche, the Chicana/o border writer operates between languages in a volatile political context, caught between the desires and the demands of the publisher and the reading audience, who sometimes insist that she erase her own linguistic identity in favor of transparency.[1] Border identity is enacted not only in linguistic choice but also in the material elements that support or supplant that identity, over which the author sometimes has less control.

The fight for control over meaning takes place both within the narrative subject matter of border literature and on the material fringes of the text, pointing out its own production and reception, generating border textuality. Works such as the recovered *Caballero: A Historical Novel* (1996) by Jovita González and Margaret Eimer (pseudonym Eve Raleigh) and *Barrio Boy* (1971) by Ernesto Galarza demonstrate different usages of and potential interpretive repercussions for the employment of a Spanish-English glossary in border literary texts. In both cases, the bilingual glossary appears to offer useful information to a monolingual audience unfamiliar with the terms, and yet what the glossary includes and omits signals a resistance, a withholding, and a necessary silence in the face of a demand for translation. As a result, the glossary subtly shapes narratives of assimilation in *Caballero* and of acculturation in *Barrio Boy*.[2] More specifically, the glossary in *Caballero* perhaps reflects the competing intentions and compromises reached by its two authors, as well as its later editors, with different interests and audiences in mind. In contrast, the glossary in Galarza's autobiography seems to gesture toward the competing intentions and allegiances Galarza and his narrator each experiences within himself. The texts under investigation here both contain narratives of border identity, placing characters and situations on the physical border between the United States and Mexico but also navigating the borders between cultures and languages, developing plots and themes that push readers to pursue various constructions of border identity. But a textual-materialist focus on the physical margins of the texts further reveals competing tensions between the narrative treatment of border identity and the way those terms and identities are worked out by authors, editors, and publishers on the margins of the page. The narrative—the subject matter, the linguistic code—is inevitably affected by the work happening in the margins surrounding it. Thus, these texts are representative of border textuality, or a working out of border identity on two levels: the linguistic and the bibliographic, or the narrative and the paratextual. At times, these levels are antagonistic, driving readers to different conclusions about the relationship between languages; at other times, they work in concert to produce a coherent picture. But they are always influencing one another, always providing opportunities for readers to reflect not only on a character's quest for identity but also on the competing discourses of identity at work in shaping the book they are reading. Chicana/o border literature almost demands an attention to its material margins, constantly exposing itself as a product of the discourses on identity it takes as its subject.

The result of close analysis of these glossaries is evidence of what Mary Louise Pratt calls a "phenomenon of the contact zone" (7): transculturation. Pratt's use of the term is connected to Angel Rama's coinage of "transculturación narrativa," which he defines in place of acculturation to gesture toward the combined process of acquiring, losing, and creating a new culture. In Rama's estimation, the transcultural author "ocupa el papel de mediador" 'occupies the role of mediator' (99, my translation). Explaining that transculturation is the process by which "marginal groups select and invent materials transmitted to them by a dominant or metropolitan culture" (8), Pratt's concept grants agency to marginalized writers working in response to white hegemony. Pratt focuses primarily on that agency in pursuit of understanding the way those writers adapt the genres, forms, and texts of the colonizers to new conditions, thereby enacting a specific resistance; in particular, she argues, "While subjugated peoples cannot readily control what the dominant culture visits upon them, they do determine to varying extents what they absorb into their own, how they use it, and what they make it mean" (7). While acknowledging the resistant role of the writer in employing and revising such textual appendages as a bilingual glossary (arguably an artifact of the dominant culture), it is also important to emphasize the space of the material text as a visible tug-of-war of domination and resistance that goes beyond the control of any single party: author, editor, publisher, reader, or otherwise. Instead, this analysis emphasizes the material result of "the relations among colonizers and colonized, or travelers and 'travelees' not in terms of separateness, but in terms of co-presence, interaction, interlocking understandings and practices, and often within radically asymmetrical relations of power" (Pratt 8): the experience of border textuality in these transcultural texts is influenced by those interested forces wrestling with the need for and meaning of linguistic assimilation/accommodation.

Registering and Resisting Assimilation in *Caballero: A Historical Novel*

Caballero: A Historical Novel was co-written by Mexican American Jovita González and Anglo American Margaret Eimer, writing under the pseudonym of Eve Raleigh, in the mid-1930s, though it was not published until it was recovered in 1996. María Cotera argues that the historical novel, which includes romances that cross ethnic boundaries at the risk of familial and patriarchal integrity, "provides a literary counterpoint to the emergent myth of the Chicano 'warrior hero' who battles the forces of outside oppression 'with his pistol in his hand,' while maintaining a patriarchal code of oppression within the home" ("Hombres Necios" 340). Cotera's overt reference to the title of Américo Paredes's foundational critical work, *With His Pistol in His Hand* (1958), calls attention to the dominant mode of critical discourse that privileged Chicano over Chicana interests and understandings of the relationships between Mexican-ness and patriarchy, between tradition and the suppression of the female voice. As the subtitle of the novel suggests, the narrative follows a historical and a romantic track, indicating a revision of the historically laudatory image of the Hispanic caballero. The story takes place in southern Texas, between the Rio Grande and the Nueces River, a site of contention for its proximity to the changing borders between the United States and Mexico. The patriarch, Don Santiago de Mendoza y Soría, retains a possessive hold over the land he was given and has cultivated; of his four children, only Alvaro pleases his father by imitating his rashness, his violent nature, and his desire to prevent Anglo domination. His son Luis runs away with an artist, while his daughters Susanita and Maria de los Angeles alienate him by marrying Americans (Susanita for love and Maria out of a sense of pragmatism).

These marriages, then, serve as the sites of productive assimilation into American society, while Santiago's death at the end of the narrative indicates his fading patriarchal as well as nationalist grasp on his Mexican family.

Since its publication in 1996, thanks largely to the work of Nicolás Kanellos and editors José E. Limón and Cotera, critics have begun to engage the text on a number of levels, interrogating its revisionist history, its implications for Chicana feminism, and its depictions of the U.S.-Mexico border zone as a site of cultural contact. Limón and Cotera write on the acknowledgments page that "our border heritage is inescapably bound up in this book" (xi); given that the narrative itself centers on the historical moment of redrawing the U.S.-Mexico border, such a description seems clear. By extension the paratext, particularly the glossary and the extension of the glossary format, makes the narrative concerns of the borderlands material for readers by establishing and undermining a series of visual boundaries between languages, characters, and authors.

Most recently, scholarship has zeroed in on the working relationship between the two authors, attempting to account for the racial and political as well as authorial hierarchies that may have developed during the writing of the novel. In his introduction, Limón carefully outlines the limited knowledge we have of that relationship, arguing, "I strongly believe Eimer had a strong authorial hand in shaping the romantic plot development of *Caballero* but always with the active participation of González in the crafting process" (xxi). The emphasis on strength in Limón's depiction of this collaborative relationship, to describe both his opinion and Eimer's role, runs slightly counter to the narrative of restorative justice implied by the recovery project's installation of González in the role of first author of this text. While the recovered edition seeks to right a potential historical wrong, Louis Gerard Mendoza argues that the problem of dual authorship requires critics to ask difficult questions "that are not easily answered but nevertheless force us to confront purist and racialist notions about Chicana/o literature" (42). Most compellingly, Cotera herself argues in "Feminism on the Border: *Caballero* and the Poetics of Collaboration" that "what makes *Caballero* interesting as both a work of borderlands feminism and a historical artifact is that it is a cross-cultural collaborative novel about the politics of cross-cultural collaboration" (201). Essentially describing what I have been calling border textuality, Cotera calls attention to the way the politics of publishing *Caballero* intersect with the politics at the heart of the narrative itself.

These conversations about collaborative authorship and *Caballero* can be productively connected to another area of critical focus—the politics of space—by focusing on the inclusion and placement of the glossary and, by extension, the placement of the character list and list of authors. The rhetoric of space in *Caballero* has been covered largely in terms of the space of the hacienda: Monika Kaup, who argues, "The *hacienda*, an ancestral Mexican house form, is the central focus, and perhaps the real protagonist-hero, of González and Raleigh's novel" ("Unsustainable" 570), is echoed by Rosemary King, who claims, "[Patriarch Don] Santiago internalizes the significance of the hacienda as a Mexican place; his internal embrace of external spatial dynamics shapes the loyalties and allegiances in the novel in such a way that Santiago believes an acceptance of anything or any one Anglo is a rejection of himself and his authority" (25). The fact that the 1996 edition includes González's drawing of a floor plan of the hacienda extends the significance of space for this novel. Kaup argues, for example, that the drawing serves as a feminist critique of the form of the hacienda: paradoxically, although the drawing assumes the status of a key or legend for the narrative, "according to [the narrative of] *Caballero*, the *hacienda* cannot be modernized and make the transition to a more democratic era, where women, servants, and peons attain equal citizenship rights" ("Unsustainable" 584). This paratextual element, inserted by the editors responsible for recovering the book, both supports and undermines the narrative itself. It also offers us an opportunity to extend the discussion of space in *Caballero* as it relates to the material spaces afforded to the glossary and other elements that reflect the collaboration between Mexican and Anglo, between Spanish and English. In particular, the function of the glossary, which traditionally works to support the notion that languages exist in one-to-one correlation with one another, is both established and subtly undermined even as its formal constraints are applied to the character list and the list of authors. The visual presence of these elements take their formal, visual cues from the format of the glossary at the same time that they work to undermine the simplicity of those same cues. The act of destabilizing the simple translation of Spanish to English is thereby also extended to the undermining of the relationship between characters and their descriptions as well as between author and co-author.

In *Caballero* the glossary functions as the readers' perhaps most obvious clue that the novel will concern linguistic and cultural assimilation.[3] The narrative concerns the varying degrees to which members of the Mendoza y Soría family assimilate themselves to the encroaching Anglo American way of life, from Don Santiago, who lives and literally dies clutching the earth that he feels rightfully belongs to him as an *hidalgo*, to Susanita, whose initial belief that "there were no frontiers in God's love" (11) persists throughout the novel and results in her marriage to—and productive cultural mixing with—the Anglo officer Robert Davis Warrener. As a precursor to a narrative that presents literal marriage, of both Susanita and María de los Angeles, as a fruitful solution to the problem of cultural clashes between Mexicans and Americans, the glossary itself appears to function as an assimilative tool. If "to assimilate" is "to make or be like" or "to be or become like," but also "to render accordant, or less discordant" and "to conform to," the job of a bilingual glossary is to render the Spanish words more accordant, or less discordant, with the English words, to make the languages conform to one another. That the glossary is always in the process of making or rendering words to be like each other, as opposed to reflecting or showing their innate likeness, is key. The glossary represents the fiction of a one-to-one linguistic correlation between Spanish and English at the same time that it performs the work of rendering those words similar. Thus monolingual English readers, like the characters, are given an opportunity to gauge their own willingness to assimilate—to render less discordant—the Spanish used in the text by replacing it with English equivalents.

It is important that, unlike in many narratives, including Ernesto Galarza's, which include a glossary at the conclusion of the text, the glossary here appears at the front of the book, after the original title page, a reproduction of a note accompanying González and Raleigh's manuscript entitled "Authors' Notes," and a character list. Like a signpost erected to highlight an otherwise invisible national boundary, the glossary creates an expectation of a boundary line: one that leads to linguistic confusion or one that assumes the need to translate on the part of the reader. But a quick glance reveals a first, very subtle, undermining of what we might assume is the privileged and assimilative position that English holds in this novel. The narrative's wedding plots, seemingly straightforward advancements of the ease of assimilation, actually offer complicated reflections on the process itself: Susanita's marriage to Robert allows her the equally romantic and assimilative freedom to "keep her face toward the future, without lingering glances for what was past and gone" (293), but that of María de los Angeles approaches assimilation from an angle of practicality: as the kind of "person who needs a life—filled" (312), María de los Angeles views her marriage to Red McLane as a means to an end. For her, it is an opportunity to devote herself to charity. In his pursuit of María de los Angeles, McLane thinks to himself, "Love? He did not need it" (214); neither does she. This double marriage plot complicates any straightforward sense of a singular path toward assimilation, of what the picture of mixing Anglo and Mexican families might be. Likewise, the glossary doubles its own narratives of linguistic assimilation, challenging our expectations of linguistic hierarchy.

For instance, the traditional format of italicizing the Spanish word, as is done throughout the text of the novel, has been reversed, so that the translations, not the words themselves, appear in italics. For example, an entry reads, "palomita. *Little dove.*" The glossary reflects not only a bicultural attempt to negotiate between English and Spanish but also a visual upending of the traditional hierarchy implied by the novel's presentation in English. This visual reversal of the hierarchy of standard to nonstandard typography puts into question the relative rankings of the two languages. The glossary also provides multiple as well as slightly misleading translations, undermining the sense of ease of translation implied by the layout. It offers the multiple meanings of a word in a straightforward manner: "posadas: *Literally, an inn. As used: Services which are held from the sixteenth of December through the twenty-fourth in commemoration of the birth of Christ*" (xxxiv). Significantly, the authors attempt to explain specific usages that confound one-to-one translation: even though the format of the glossary encourages a single word on one side and a single translation on the other, the translations themselves multiply meanings, undermining the singular correlation between a word and its translation. The assimilative process, whether linguistic or matrimonial, is neither singular nor simple.

In addition, the translations themselves can be incomplete or even misleading: the description of Luis Gonzaga as a "marica" is slightly fogged when readers turn to the glossary and see "marica" defined as "*Milksop. An effeminate man.*" As Mendoza notes, "In common parlance, and in Spanish-language dictionaries, a *marica* or *maricón* is a gay man, a homosexual. Its contemporary English approximate as a derogatory term would be 'fag' or 'queer'" (305). Though there may be many reasons for providing a more "genteel" translation of the term, the interpretive effect is undeniably significant. The distance between someone who is "feeble, timid, or ineffectual" as the *OED* defines "milksop," and one who is homosexual is not automatically crossed given the definition of the word "marica" that González and Raleigh have provided. And though the narrative is not entirely coy, with its subplot involving Luis running away with another man, this careful exclusion of reference to homosexuality reflects some inability to fully translate: whether or not that inability is imposed from without (perhaps in an attempt to avoid censorship), less careful or knowledgeable readers will be fooled into a sense of transparency via a glossary that partially acts to obscure meaning. The glossary both encourages readers to think of Spanish as easily translated and leaves them unsettled with translations that are even borderline incorrect. Both pretending at and undermining the sense of fluid movement between linguistic boundaries, the glossary works to demonstrate the complexity of language as well as the multiple allegiances one might hold while acting as a cultural "informant."

The visual, spatial reinforcement of a singular correlation between one side (Mexican, Spanish, foreign) and the other (Anglo, English, familiar)—locations on either side of a borderland with white space in between—is repeated in the character list that also precedes the narrative. In expansive novels that incorporate large casts of characters, such a paratextual inclusion is not unheard of: the 1970 English translation of Gabriel García Márquez's *Cien años de soledad*, for example, includes a helpful family tree of the Buendía family to assist readers in navigating who's who. However, that family tree does not appear in the paratext of the original Spanish edition, suggesting that the addition was made not only in service of a complicated cast list but also to offer even more support to English-language readers than that offered to those who read in Spanish. Likewise, some overlap in purpose is suggested by the character list in *Caballero*. Like the glossary, this list is meant to render the foreign familiar. Characters' names run down the left-hand column in romanized print, and the descriptions and translations of said characters in the right-hand column are printed in italics. These visual parallels link language and characterization as aids to the reader, constructing border zones by highlighting areas of assumed readerly confusion. If we follow Limón's argument that González was drawing on "composites and fictive renditions of actual Mexican personages from her familial ancestral background" (xx) and therefore was responsible for contributing the "specific narrative delineation of at least the Mexican characters—by far the great majority—in the novel and likely the Anglos as well" (xx), we might read in the character list a visual representation of the communication between González and Eimer in the construction of the narrative. An explanation of the mostly Mexican cast aids the reader in keeping the multiple names straight, and it visually mimics the glossary's word-and-its-English-counterpart strategy of defining and redefining each individual. Both the glossary and the character list assume that a reader who comes across a Spanish term or a name can use these paratextual elements to find and replace, with either a translation or a description, the difficult word. They alert readers, before they have even reached the narrative, that such work may be necessary.

However, the character list is incomplete: a section in the middle of the list names seven men with no description of their title or relationship of any to the rest of the characters. Unlike "Don Santiago de Mendoza y Soría / *patriarch, owner of Rancho la Palma*" and "Doña María Petronill / *his wife*" (xxxi), characters from José Antonio Carbajal to Juan de Cisneros have no descriptive characteristics to aid readers in locating their place in the narrative. Most of these characters turn out to be some of Santiago's fellow hacendados, who meet under the cover of night to debate their options with regard to the encroaching Texas Rangers. And yet, in the absence of descriptors, they blend one into the other, given less attention than the five women simply listed as "*house servant at Rancho la Palma*" (xxxii). Perhaps there are no words to adequately describe them, just as there exist in Spanish words with no satisfactory English equivalent. Or, more important, perhaps the character list is meant to both encourage and discourage a sense of completion, of balance: it encourages readers to seek out, to label, to know each of the characters, but it also prevents complete knowledge by leaving some descriptions blank.

The character list is not only visually but also narratively incomplete: names or descriptions included in the text are missing, misleading, and, in at least one case, irretrievable. For example, once readers reach the narrative itself, they quickly encounter characters whose names do not appear on the list at all, including "Fulgencio . . . aloof in the importance of his position" and "Juan

Bautista; personal servant and coachman, carrying his double duty with the dignity becoming to his gray hair; Nicolasa the baker, witch-like with her stoop and peering eyes" (5). Nicolasa, the baker, is in fact included in the list but is described only as one of the five female "house servant[s]" mentioned above. The choice to remove her distinctive attributes in the character list casts her as part of an indistinguishable group of servants, the list in turn competing with the narrative regarding her significance as an individual. Juan Bautista is not mentioned in the character list at all, in spite of the fact that we have a clear sense of his occupation and relationship to Don Santiago. And Fulgencio is a special case: after the mention of his name in the narrative, the editors have inserted a tabbed blank space and a footnote. Visually, then, the narrative gestures toward an absence that the footnote explains is the result of the editors' having to meld together two manuscript versions of the text. Explaining that MS-2, their base text, is missing three pages, for which they have substituted similar pages from MS-1, the note states, "The social identification of Fulgencio is left unclear" (347n2). Readers will never know what position Fulgencio holds that leads him to feel so "aloof" but for two different reasons: the character list omits him, while the narrative gap turns him into a sort of palimpsest, there and not there.

Taken together with the narrative, the characters list is both complete and incomplete. It is also, like the glossary, not to mention the map of the hacienda, both reliable and unreliable in terms of the story it tells, which is slightly different from the story of the narrative. As Erin Murrah-Mandril points out, the organization of the character list emphasizes the hierarchical relationships between characters as they are described and ordered by their relationship to the patriarch Don Santiago at the same time that the narrative works to undermine that centrality: "this list of characters invokes the structure of historical romance that ostensibly revolves around the decline of the Mexican patriarch . . . but only by negating Luis Gonzaga's and the Mendoza y Soría women's acquisition of power" (137). The novel itself is admittedly unfinished; so, too, the character list. But the effect of reading the unfinished character list is one that teaches readers to seek out complete understanding at the same time that it withholds or even confounds such understanding.

If both of these paratextual elements—the glossary and the character list—work as spatialized markers of linguistic instability, of untranslatability, of incompletion, or of the always imbalanced hierarchy of languages and cultures, the position of the authors' names can be read in a similarly spatialized manner. The glossary uses the space of a word, a borderlands area, and its translation to both encourage and discourage a sense of the equality between the two. The characters list similarly uses the space of a name, a borderlands area, and an extended description or translation to encourage and discourage a sense of complete knowledge of all of the characters. And, despite the general appearance of balance on the character list and glossary pages, each actually develops a hierarchy that either leaves significant gaps for readers (as in the characters list) or trains their eyes to accept Spanish as the normalized language (as in the glossary). Readers who must rely on the character descriptions or the potentially inaccurate translations are therefore at a disadvantage: the translations in either case are flawed or incomplete. This kind of spatial hierarchy is repeated, then, in the ordering of the authors' names on the title page. In some ways, the order of the names takes on the format of the glossary: the name of the Mexican American writer and the name of the Anglo American cultural translator—the path to assimilation—function as two halves of a whole. As Cotera writes, "The dual voices of the *Caballero* manuscript . . . constitute a material reminder that the text itself was forged in the borderlands between at least two historical perspectives" ("Feminism" 201). But just as the glossary and character list resolve into problematic hierarchies, so does the author order.

This repeated materially spatialized hierarchy is especially significant given the fact that the original title page lists Raleigh as first author and González as second, while the published 1996 edition reverses the order. Limón cites letters in which González describes the production of the book using "we" rather than "I," along with a letter from Eimer to González in which she describes being advised by a publisher to list her own name first on the title page, changing the order that was used on the original manuscript. Kaup argues that González's efforts to involve a nonnative co-author reflect a sensibility that recognized the success of writers like Fabiola Cabeza de Baca, whose role as an informant to Anglo audiences and cultivation of Spanish—as opposed to Mexican—roots appealed to a popular reading audience. Limón appears to concur, arguing,

> I . . . believe that [Eimer's] claim and role in the construction of the work are outweighed by González's far larger role in the genesis and overall execution of the project. Thus, and in keeping with the early recognition of the authors themselves, in this finally published edition of *Caballero*, my co-editor and I wish to restore Jovita González's name to the first-author status affirming what we see as her primary role in the production of *Caballero*. (xxi)

Though they include a facsimile of the original title page from the manuscript in their edition, listing Eve Raleigh as first author, as Genette notes, "Recording the name on the title page and recording it on the cover fulfill two different functions" (38). The presence of the facsimile indicates a fidelity to history, to fact, and to the very specific (and only—all other copies have been destroyed or lost) title page found among González's papers. Had the work been published in the 1930s, as desired by the two writers, Raleigh would have been named as first author. Again, Limón carefully notes that the manuscript he and Cotera used for their edition "does show Eve Raleigh as first author, but we have no record that González necessarily accepted this new arrangement" (xxi). They also share no evidence that she necessarily rejected the new arrangement, either, leaving us only the evidence of that manuscript title page as a testament to the ethnic hierarchy established between these two writers.

However, the editorial decision to alter the cover page of their edition, to restore or return to an ideal manuscript of which we have no evidence aside from the letter, attempts to right a perceived wrong in the hierarchy of authors' names. Even in a collaborative effort, the editors argue, one woman must have done more (or at least more important) work than the other, and that woman was González. Following D. F. McKenzie's dictum "Editors make, as well as mend" (30), Limón and Cotera attempt to "generate the meanings that most matter to [them]" (30). As a perhaps unintended result, some scholars have turned to representing this novel as singly authored. Just as the title of the novel shifts from a Spanish term to an English-language descriptor that fails to translate (*Caballero: A Historical Novel*), the editors repeat the hierarchy of language and character with the restored primacy of González's Hispanic name.

While the hierarchies generated by the glossary and character list suggest narrative attempts to both serve and undermine the interests of readers who expect a one-to-one linguistic and cultural translation, the shifting hierarchies of author order suggest a continuing conversation about the stakes of publishing border literature in general and the hierarchies of authorial identity that develop as a result. Calling the novel "a layered memory-site that spans and connects the setting of the narrative with the contexts in which the novel was written and eventually recovered and published" (138), Murrah-Mandril emphasizes the way that this novel speaks to and about our contemporary concerns for accurately representing the history of this book at the same time that we unavoidably alter that history. Most specifically, the politics of the recovery project that allowed *Caballero* to be restored depended heavily on restoring, first and foremost, a Mexican American writer. As Mendoza points out, "If we accept that *Caballero* is undoubtedly a work of Chicana/o literature, this assessment must be based on two criteria: its subject matter and the known identity and reputation of Jovita González" (42); listing González's name first further ensures that claims of dual authorship don't cloud claims of Chicana/o or Mexican American literary heritage. And while her editorial decisions convey an interest in restoring González to top billing, Cotera's later explorations of the novel's history turn increasingly toward the notion of collaborative authorship: she even notes that this kind of attention to the novel "may lead to its exile from the world of Chicana/o letters" ("Feminism" 202). The parameters of what counts as Chicana/o literature exclude or at least complicate the possibility of including a co-authored work like this.

But given that this is a novel whose narrative often seems to vacillate between assimilation and a valorization of Texas-Mexican culture—as Jaime Javier Rodriguez writes, "The historical novel *Caballero* wants to follow the rules. It desires to be known, recognized, deemed worthy, and assimilated.... But in its efforts at typicality *Caballero* never persuades" (117)—this emphatic reversal only further participates in the establishment and the continued undermining of any linguistic, ethnic, or authorial hierarchy. The process of establishing and altering the author order works in a similar way to the glossary: the glossary demonstrates linguistic assimilation in process rather than as a result, while the continued editorial decisions about author order demonstrate the establishment of a politically defined authorship in process. Both emphasize a dialogue between perceived opposites attempting to be drawn together, to be made alike and coherent, even as Cotera asks, "Can we see in *Caballero* not one ambivalent and politically contradictory voice, but two voices that may or may not always agree and may even contradict one another?" ("Feminism" 203).

In each element of the margins—the glossary, the character list, the order of authors, and even the title—a visual representation of assimilation is suggested but also undermined, mimicking the narrative's own push and pull between ethnic assimilation, especially as seen in the double marriage plot. Whether or not the narrative "relishes the possibility of true cultural integration" (Miner and Sager 193) is at least partly dependent on the way we read the paratext. And that paratext reveals a transcultural text in which elements of language are organized into a hierarchy that appears to aid monolingual readers but in one way or another unsettles our faith in those hierarchies. The glossary appears to aim at comprehensiveness but ultimately shifts italicization—otherization—onto the English translations. The character list, with its gaps and refusals to fully define all of the Spanish-surnamed characters, and the novel's title, which does not translate but visibly preserves the Spanish word over and above the English subtitle (perhaps as often as Raleigh's name is left out from authorship attribution, critics and reviewers elect to drop the subtitle), both point to attempts to erase English, to supplant it with Spanish, or to at least refuse the erasure of Spanish. This repeated visual hierarchy of language works in a subtle way, and control over it is not restricted to its original authors: for example, recent editors have become complicit in the manipulations of these hierarchies by reversing the order of the authors, aiming to correct previous manipulations by other editorial forces. In *Caballero,* the presence of both the original title page and the rearranged author order work to establish and undermine a sense of the hierarchy between authors, showing how editorial intervention continues to shape our understanding of this novel as negotiating the hierarchies of linguistic, cultural, and authorial identity even from the spaces of the paratext. These actors—authors, editors, and the narrative itself—together generate a materially transcultural text.

Contesting Narratives of Acculturation in *Barrio Boy*

If the material text of *Caballero* registers and resists the process of assimilation through its use of the glossary, Galarza's work—including his semifictional memoir, *Barrio Boy*, as well as his activist works *Strangers in Our Fields* (1956) and *Merchants of Labor* (1964)—likewise performs a similarly complex negotiation of acculturation. An early cover of the 1971 memoir displays the original subtitle—"The Story of a Boy's Acculturation"—and paratextually insists from the opening that Galarza's story is not one of loss but rather of gain, of a relatively unproblematic adoption of American culture. Throughout his memoir, but most particularly in its final two parts, "Life in the Lower Part of Town" and "On the Edge of the Barrio," Galarza carefully narrates a perspective on adjusting to life in the United States that is inclusive of his Mexican identity as well as encouraging of his growing American identity, leading Ilan Stavans to describe Galarza as "not an American per se, but an *Americanized* person" (xxiii). For example, as Ernesto attends Lincoln elementary school, he pauses to note, "At Lincoln, making us into Americans did not mean scrubbing away what made us originally foreign" (236). Describing the school as "not so much a melting pot as a griddle where Miss Hopley and her helpers warmed knowledge into us and roasted racial hatreds out of us" (236), Galarza forcefully rejects any sentiment of cultural, linguistic, or ethnic loss as the result of his education in America. Maria Montes de Oca Ricks explains that Galarza was never interested in "the loss-of-identity-theme so harped on by psychologists and social scientists studying the Chicano community" (95); instead his narrative reads as a testament to the way his identity was supplemented by such experiences. Manuel Luis Martínez further claims that "as an activist, Galarza . . . practiced and advocated *Americanismo* in response to a very narrow and exclusionary view of the public sphere, democratic participation, and definition of citizenship held not only by mainstream Americans but also by advocates of separatist and nationalist agendas" ("Telling" 58). In other words, Galarza was interested not in advocating a Mexican or Chicana/o nationalist identity or even a borderlands identity but rather in expanding the definitions of an American identity to make it more inclusive of arriving immigrants and laborers.

While his investigations of the Bracero Program functioned as a kind of journalistic advocacy of those ideals, Galarza's representation of his own life in *Barrio Boy* more clearly expresses his interest in solidifying that more inclusive identity. Antonio Márquez describes the work as "autobiography in service to nostalgia and cultural integrity, and . . . also in service to the cultural myth called 'The American Dream'" (57). In contrast, Lauro Flores focuses more exclusively on the way the autobiography works to demonstrate Galarza's relationship to "the human group he belongs to and which he aptly calls *la raza*"

(87), arguing that the tension in this autobiography, as in many Chicana/o autobiographies, rests in the relationship between self and community. Ramón Saldívar argues that, unlike fellow memoirist Richard Rodriguez, whose narratives valorize a sense of individuality and singular experience, Galarza "establishes a continuing correspondence between personal identity and social identity" ("Ideologies" 32). Galarza writes a memoir of himself and his family, his community, and his fellow immigrants that seeks common ground in terms of not only ethnic heritage but also shared history in the United States.

Choosing the form of Chicana/o autobiography to navigate both individual and collective identities, as Juan Velasco notes, allows Galarza's narrative to participate in "the cultivation of agency" rather than "confession and sympathy" (321). One of the other ways that Galarza prioritizes a narrative of coherent identity and agency is through humor. His process of acculturation, imbalanced though it may be, is frequently narrated with a dry, deadpan sense of humor that undercuts any sense of shame or discomfort Galarza may have experienced during his adjustment period in the United States. At the very least, it would seem that Galarza does not want his readers to associate acculturation with shame and discomfort, and his narrative most frequently works to minimize those moments. Accordingly, a number have scholars have taken note of the way humor functions in Galarza's narrative.[4] Renato Rosaldo describes *Barrio Boy* as participating in a "politics of laughter, where chuckles and wit [become] subversive" (67); in contrast to a scholar like Martínez, who insists that we attend to the "palpable sense of loss and nostalgia" (*Countering* 295) in Galarza's work rather than valorize Ernesto's liminal border identity, Rosaldo argues the memoir is characterized by a "border discourse, marked by bilingual heteroglossia, understatement, and humor" (82). What permeates the narrative—and much of the scholarship—is a sense that humor functions as a method of self-deprecation at the same time that it functions as a method of resistance: Rosaldo concludes regarding *Barrio Boy*, "its understated humor can readily be missed, but it is barbed" (86). But resistance to what? The threat of assimilation? Americanization? National, cultural, and/or ethnic erasure? It may be any one of those things. According to Galarza himself, humor can also be a sign of resistance to the threat of homogenous narratives of Mexican American identity.

As Ilan Stavans as well as Galarza's own introduction indicate, the narrative of *Barrio Boy* uses humor in part as a counterweight to the proliferation of a certain kind of Mexican American narrative of identity that focuses on themes of suffering, erasure, and loss. Further, the author's manipulation of the paratext emphasizes his own understanding of the significance of the material text in supporting such counternarratives. Thus he uses his introduction to the book to respond to "the rumor that these Mexican immigrants and their offspring have lost their 'self-image,'" saying, "I can't remember a time I didn't know who I was; and I have heard much testimony from my friends and other more detached persons to the effect that I thought too highly of what I thought I was" (xxviii). His introductory insistence on self-deprecating humor seeks to set itself apart from the frequently lofty, more serious tones invoked by other Chicana/o nationalist writers working at the time, including Tomás Rivera, Rodolfo "Corky" Gonzales, and José Antonio Villareal. That the narrative is not always consistent in its execution of that humor—moments of loss and erasure creep in at the edges—suggests an internal struggle over the kind of narrative Galarza wants for the book.

Galarza's resistant humor and his attempts to change the course of the canonical Chicano novel are expressed most frequently and perhaps most clearly in his narrative depictions of language acquisition as well as in his inclusion of a glossary. Rather than cast himself as a lost child in a world where foreign language shuts him out, he narrates his own growing confidence with the English language through humorous moments of dawning linguistic understanding. On the train on the way to the United States, Ernesto notes that some words actually are the same in Spanish and English: "we agreed that a gringo conductor would not be wearing Mexican letters on his cap, and that *conductor* in Spanish was the same as conductor in English" (210). This begins a game between Ernesto and his mother to learn which other words are exactly the same; they find that when words are closely related but not spelled quite the same, "we thought English spelling idiotic" (210).

This is not to say that all of Galarza's depictions of language acquisition are without political edge: there is something bittersweet about his description of his one-on-one and notably one-sided English lessons with Miss Ryan, wherein he describes the way he "tried interrupting to tell Miss Ryan how we said it in Spanish. It didn't work. She only said 'oh' and went on with *pasture, bow-wow-wow*, and *pretty*. It was as if in that closet we were both discovering together the secrets of the English language" (235). Only Ernesto is experiencing the process of acculturation: he is the other, Miss Ryan the host. But even in that depiction, he embraces "the secrets of the English language," pressing on in his acculturation.

Although Ernesto seems to delight in linguistic equivalence on the train ride mentioned earlier, Galarza insists throughout the rest of the narrative that the singularity of any language is itself a fiction. "To begin with, we didn't hear one but many sorts of English" (262), he narrates, describing the way one neighbor "nibbled his words, like a rabbit working on a carrot" and another "spoke English in his own way, brittle and choppy, hard to understand unless you watched his lips" (262). Galarza also emphasizes the differences within language as frequently as he differentiates between chicanos (recent immigrants from Mexico) and pochos (longtime U.S. inhabitants of Mexican descent). For example, he notes that "*pocho* talk" (263)—"*yarda* for yard, *yonque* for junk, *donas* for doughnuts" (264)—was unacceptable to his mother. These loanwords suggest a mingling of English and Spanish that destroys the singular integrity of each language, destroys the blank space between a word and a translation, and Galarza's mother will not suffer it. Yet the process of linguistic acculturation can't be stopped. Even his own family "invented its own versions of American talk" (263): thus, even his mother can't help but say "Yo no pick een-glees" (263) when the situation calls for it.

Thus it might seem strange that a narrative that frequently argues that languages hardly exist in one-to-one correlation with one another, that they are frequently changing and borrowing from one another, and that they structure our experiences in different ways—such as when Ernesto tries to explain "that in Mexico roosters said 'qui-qui-ri-qui' and not 'cock-a-doodle-doo'" (236) and is subsequently told that "Mexican roosters were crazy" (236)—would conclude with a glossary.[5] While on the surface this glossary would seem to aim to give concrete access to translations of Spanish words, it does so with more than a subtle hint of humor. Just as the narrative goes to great lengths to inject humor into the process of translating Spanish to English and back again, so, too, does the glossary: many of the translations go beyond simple translation to uncover the humorous connotations of Spanish words used in Galarza's narrative. Because he alternates between direct and contextual translation within the narrative itself, not all of the Spanish words used in the work are found in the glossary. And many are translated in a straightforward manner. But many others aim to poke fun: "*comadre*: a lady's relationship to parents whose baby she has presented for baptism, of whom she is the *madrina*; *comadres* frequently become intimate to the point of not being on speaking terms" (301). For others, the humor works in pairs: "*palacio de gobierno*: the state capitol, where the important *autoridades* spent most of their time; *palacio municipal*: city hall, where the not-so-important *autoridades* did likewise" (305).

Occasionally, the glossary translation does not appear to be humorous unless read in the context of the narrative: "*lista de correo*: general delivery" (303) is a direct, simple translation unless we read it as an ironic commentary on the comic confusion experienced by Galarza and his family as they try to navigate the U.S. postal system. When receiving Uncle Gustavo's forwarding address, Galarza describes it as "puzzling. The best we could make out it was a General Delibri. It sounded as if generals were in charge of the mail in the United States, nothing like our *lista de correo*" (206). The misunderstanding becomes a source of self-directed humor, a way of gently mocking one's own linguistic incompetency. But it also demonstrates the way Galarza materially insists that language does not function in a one-to-one correlation in the ways we might expect. When readers reach the end of the narrative, or when they seek out a translation of a word, the included glossary seems at least on the surface to suggest that matching Spanish to English is quite simple: "*Lista de correo*: general delivery" (303). Ernie and his family are, on one level, the objects of humor for not being able to decipher this seemingly simple translation. But the very fact of its presence in the glossary turns the tables on readers in a subtle way: the reader who searches for the translation of *lista de correo* is perhaps as much confused as Galarza's family, and therefore by the transitive property the object of humor. Furthermore, mistaking general delivery for an actual general is all the more confusing given the U.S.-specific homonymic honorific of postmaster general, suggesting the convolutedness of the English language in the midst of gently mocking the English-language learners. The narrative tells us one story of the relationship between languages, while the glossary tells another, in each case making the (different) language learner the butt of a mild joke. Taken together, then, the book as a whole narrates the allure as well as the mistake of thinking of translation as a simple substitution of one language for another.

In this and many other instances, the glossary guides readers to experience linguistic and cultural translation as humorous and multifaceted rather than as treacherous or a sign of erasure. It turns our attention to the multiple translations of experiences buried within Galarza's own text, materially suggesting that the singular narrative of Chicano loss and erasure is itself a fiction. And the humor targets representatives of all cultures seemingly equally, both within the narrative and in the glossary. For example, Galarza spells his early attempts at English phonetically, emphasizing the mispronunciations—for example, "hua-tinees, plees" for "What time is it, please?" (211)—as a way of poking light fun at his own language acquisition. Likewise, he notes the strange American pronunciations of words, "Sackmenna" (262) for Sacramento, "Kellyphony" (263) for California, bringing the varieties of American accents under equally humorous scrutiny. Ernesto and his mother think English spellings are "idiotic," while American characters think some Spanish words are "crazy": there would seem to be a balance in the presentation of linguistic misunderstanding and the humorous repercussions. Even the glossary pays comic attention to Americans with its translation of *bolillo*: "a small French loaf, or an American; a name for both on account of the strong resemblance between them in complexion and crustiness" (300), and to Spaniards with *gachupín*: "a Spaniard; the only thing more disagreeable to a Mexican were two *gachupines*" (302).

Galarza is not beyond poking fun at himself or his family as they undergo the process of acculturation, but there are some lines he doesn't cross. In *Tender Accents of Sound: Spanish in the Chicano Novel in English*, Ernst Rudin studies Galarza's glossary and argues that the narrator "seems to identify rather with the culture for which the glossary is meant than with the culture that the glossary depicts," calling many of the entries "belittling" of Mexican culture (137). While Rudin's arguments fall in line with a general sense that Galarza wrote his work not to valorize a lost Mexican heritage undergoing erasure but rather to demonstrate the acculturative process as one that need not be so self-serious, such an argument misses some key moments in the glossary that stand out in their seriousness. Consider, for example, Galarza's glossary translation of "*chicano*," which is decidedly straightforward: "a Mexican recently arrived in the United States and definitely a working-class type; a term of sympathy and identity among persons of this class" (301). As the term that would most likely apply to Galarza and his family, chicano does not come up for even light ridicule: in fact, the translation stands out in its lack of whimsy, directly insisting on "sympathy" instead. Chicano, as a term, is not subjected to good-humored or even slightly more caustic translation because it doesn't connote the sense of power associated with Anglo Americans or Spaniards. Like *campesino*, which Galarza translates simply as "a peasant or country dweller, a man of the *campos* or fields" (300), chicano stands as a classed and ethnic marker that resists ridicule. Despite the appearance of balance in targeting identities as a source of humor, words like these belie the complex negotiation of identity that goes beyond a simple embrace of the acculturated Mexican American identity.

Likewise, the occasional somber moments in Galarza's narrative stand in sharper relief when placed against the backdrop of humorous acculturative encounters, especially when one reads the glossary closely. The description of Ernesto's mother's death from the Spanish flu is sudden and simple, and the jocular translation of *curandera* found in the glossary—"a woman who practices folk medicine with herbs, unguents, brews, compresses, poultices, a little prayer, and much faith on the part of the patient" (302)—contrasts sharply in tone with Galarza's lengthy narrative description of a curandera's complicated, somber attempt to heal a sick young neighborhood girl followed by the simple "In the morning the child died" (287).[6] Here the potential for narrative sympathy for the death of a child is undercut by a translation that calls into question the presumed naiveté of those who would put their trust in such healers. Just as the humorous narrative moment of translating "*lista de correo*" is altered by a reading of the straightforward glossary entry, the humorous glossary entry alters the reading of this more straightforward narrative depiction of a young girl's death. In this case, the narrative itself can't or won't call this seemingly problematic faith into question—Ernesto even joins the group of people praying over the body of the sick girl—but the glossary does, creating space for two narrative framings of this death. In this space where the narrative and its paratext give readers competing visions of the work of curanderas—somber and serious though ultimately unsuccessful on the one hand and lightly comic quackery on the other—readers experience a transcultural moment: the voice of the glossary condemns with humor what the narrative seems to observe with solemnity, unsettling our relationship to our narrator's point of view, driving uncertainty into this narrative of acculturation.

The narrative moments of linguistic failure and confusion that result in loss—rather than a humorous anecdote—also draw attention to themselves in the midst of a narrative that tends to describe pain and loss from the perspective of continued hope and perseverance. While Galarza spends most of his narrative making light of such linguistic and cultural confusion, demonstrating that, even as he struggled with the language, he and his family always got where they were going, one incident betrays the lightheartedness of his tone. When his aunt, uncle, and cousins are denied entry into the United States and instead permitted only a short visit with Ernesto's family on Angel Island before having to return to Mexico, Galarza emphasizes his own role as interpreter. In this case, it is not Ernesto's failure to understand English that stands in his way but his failure to understand America, "the rules and the laws and the orders" (240), his failure to acculturate. As Galarza narrates, "The man in uniform had merely shown us some papers but he had not told us why. He had not even said what would have to be done to bring our family back and take them home with us" (241). Meanwhile, his own family has an unending list of unanswered questions: "Were there any higher *Autoridades* who could change the orders? Where could we find a lawyer who spoke Spanish? How much would he charge? Did the *Autoridades* make a mistake, or did we? What was it?" (241). Galarza does not linger on this episode in his life; from here, he quickly moves on to describing his neighbors in the barrio in America. Nevertheless, the narrative records a moment when Ernesto's family is torn across national boundaries, where rules go unexplained, where questions go unanswered, where meaning remains untranslated in ways that have deleterious effects on Ernesto's familial and national identity, his acculturative process. The immigrant, the chicano, the young man waiting to welcome his relatives at Angel Island who is being denied that opportunity without explanation has neither acculturated (he doesn't understand, and therefore cannot adopt, the culture) nor assimilated (the society has yet to accept him). Here, as in other somber moments, the narrative resists the humorous treatment Galarza levels at most of his experiences as an immigrant American, and it intensifies the argument that linguistic and cultural translation frequently work to ensure American power differentials that put Chicanos like Galarza at a disadvantage.

Though the autobiography was originally subtitled "The Story of a Boy's Acculturation," perhaps the paratextual erasure of that subtitle in recent editions (it has been dropped in favor of a cover description calling the book "the best-selling story of a boy's journey through time and cultures") is the clearest sign that Galarza's narrative both is and is not about acculturation, linguistic or otherwise. The majority of the narrative works to inject light and even self-deprecating humor into the text, acting as a counterweight to the growing number of Chicana/o coming-of-age narratives that dealt with ethnic erasure, nostalgia, and loss. It works as a demonstration of the ways Galarza strives to achieve a balanced Mexican American identity: one that adopts the customs and culture of America without losing sight of the social institutions of his Mexican heritage. But just as a glossary pretends at balance through its fiction of one-to-one translations, Galarza's own work slyly undercuts that balance. Even the length of the narrative sections dedicated to life in Mexico (three sections, approximately 215 pages) compared to the length of the sections dedicated to life in the United States (two sections, approximately 85 pages) is an early indicator of the impossibilities of achieving such balance. Throughout, his examples of linguistic confusion both inject humor into the narrative and emphasize the multiplicity and untranslatability of language. Likewise, his glossary both confirms and contradicts the narrative, reinforcing the resistance to singular translations in both comic and tragic ways. Furthermore, the moments of frustration and loss that do appear are magnified by the contrast they present to the otherwise coherent and progressive narrative of acculturation. For some this inability to acculturate or assimilate may be a source of power, a sign of a refusal to fully capitulate to the demands of an oppressive American identity, and in many Chicano narratives this might be the case. But in this narrative, in these instances, it is a registering of the fact that the balance of identity—like a one-to-one glossary translation—sought by a writer like Galarza isn't always possible. A lighthearted rendering of the process of acculturation can't fully cover the moments of loss and erasure that attend it, and the glossary makes those gaps and inconsistencies all the more visible.

Conclusion

Control over the territory of language and, by extension, over the material text, is not and never has been limited to an author. Editors, publishers, and readers compete with authors over linguistic expectations in English-language literature, and they sometimes refuse or are unable to locate common ground. For example, Helena Maria Viramontes demonstrates an increasingly vocal, resistant approach to appeasing her readers when she argues,

> A few years ago a southwestern writer, Cormac McCarthy, wrote *All the Pretty Horses*. If I remember correctly, there were whole paragraphs in Spanish. Not one reviewer questioned it, not one reader said, 'I wish there was a glossary.' But if a Spanish-surnamed writer uses Spanish, it becomes an issue. Readers feel purposely excluded, like, why are you keeping this from me? Well, I'm sorry. How could I not give integrity to the characters? (quoted in Lourdes Torres 84)

For Viramontes, the narrative and its characters lose integrity when the languages they speak must be explained or co-opted by the paratextual presence of a glossary; furthermore, she contends that there is racial motivation behind a requirement that border Chicana/o writers do translation work that is not asked of Anglo writers. Viramontes recognizes the interpretive as well as the political power hidden in paratextual elements like glossaries, and she works to mitigate their effects by insisting that readers either work to understand Spanish on their own or learn to adjust to the sensation of being left out.

That isn't to say that writers and texts that employ glossaries are necessarily automatically accommodating their readers. In the case of both *Caballero* and *Barrio Boy*, the resistance to a simplified understanding of the correlations between Spanish and English is relatively subtle. The material texts, particularly the glossary, at times mimic and at others undermine the narrative depictions of the continuum of acculturation to assimilation, illuminating the fictions of linguistic balance, harmony, and equality experienced on that continuum. Just as "a tongue compensates for its deterritorialization through a reterritorialization of meaning" (Deleuze and Guattari 20), the paratexts of border literature can reterritorialize the meanings of the narratives they contain. These transcultural texts take readers' expectations of translation, of the kinds of knowledge the work of the glossary should foster, and refuse or are unable to meet them. The glossaries are incomplete and inaccurate, and they even occasionally compete with the narrative to assign meaning to characters, moments, and identities. They unsettle readerly expectations of smooth translation and, in so doing, call attention to the processes of problematic translation happening within the narrative as well as in the material production of the border literary text itself. As such, each is "a text that self-consciously enacts the politics of its production within its pages" (Cotera, "Feminism" 224). Whether subtly or more forthrightly, by calling attention to the shaping forces of the border elements of the material text, writers and their texts create yet another space in which they challenge readers to reflect on border identity itself, or the places where competing ideologies, identities, and languages come into contact with one another.

3

Making Language Visible

Transcultural Typography

> No matter how clear its glass, a window is perfectly visible when one simply alters one's gaze.
>
> —Paul Gutjahr and Megan Benton

The politics of linguistic choice are nearly inescapable for many if not all Chicana/o border writers. Choosing to translate, or not to translate, or to translate but only in certain ways or instances, or to insist that translation is impossible or even unnecessary, is not only an imperative faced by border writers but also the subject of many border narratives themselves. Literary critics of the border, in turn, find themselves practicing this art of negotiation as they strive to embody their own politics of language. For example, Héctor Calderón's *Narratives of Greater Mexico* includes this message: "Unless otherwise noted, translations are mine. Spanish is not a foreign language to me or to millions of citizens of the United States; for that reason, I have not italicized Spanish in my text" (xix). Likewise, in *Feminism on the Border*, Sonia Saldívar-Hull writes, "In a consciously political act, what Gloria Anzaldúa calls 'linguistic terrorism,' I will not italicize Spanish words or phrases unless they are italicized in direct quotations. I invite readers not fluent in Spanish to experience a sense of life on the border as we switch from English to Spanish" (173). Both critics, whose work forms part of the strong foundation of border literary scholarship, make political choices about the way Spanish will be represented on the page, and they also draw attention to those choices so that readers recognize their intentionality. They insist that readers notice the absence of distinctive markings in the text, and that they understand that absence as part of a larger attempt to equalize Spanish and English.

These explicit expressions of linguistic politics specifically emphasize the look and shape of italicized words as carriers of meaning. Italicization is a seemingly innocuous and common technique for representing foreign words: Lynn Truss, author of *Eats, Shoots & Leaves: The Zero Tolerance Approach to Punctuation*, explains, "Italics have developed to serve certain purposes for us that we never stop to question" and jokingly asks, "When was the last time you panicked in the face of italics, 'Hang on, this writing's gone all wobbly'?" (146). But for these critics, italicization is in need of questioning, is itself politicized; they reposition italicization as a participant in the creation of oppressive linguistic hierarchies.[1] Calderón explicitly connects italicization to foreignization, and therefore refuses to participate in the visual foreignization of Spanish words. Saldívar-Hull explains her reasoning for this choice as connected to readers' expectations for the reading experience: she anticipates that this visual choice might contribute to readerly frustration, and she argues for frustration as a meaningful part of the border reading experience.

These expressions of the critics' attempts to avoid the visual marginalization of Spanish appear in the material margins of the critical texts themselves: Calderón's explanation of his unitalicized Spanish turns up at the end of his introduction, for instance, while Sonia Saldívar-Hull places her explanation of her lack of italicization or translation in the first footnote, located at the back of her work. In these paratextual spaces, these material border elements that readers have learned to recognize as part of yet not quite the text itself, we find keys to understanding critics' own relationship to Spanish as well as how they feel about their readerships. Here the politics goes beyond a concern for how and whether to translate, further toward the question of how to represent the presence or absence of translation in a meaningful, visual way. As Saldívar-Hull herself notes, Chicana feminists "have to look in nontraditional places for our theories: in the prefaces to anthologies, in the interstices of autobiographies, in our cultural artifacts (the cuentos)" (46). When it comes to language, in the pages preceding and following a Chicana/o border narrative (or even a work of border literary criticism), but also in the visual and typographical vehicles that convey the text itself, we find a politics of language, a politics of engagement that asks readers to consider their role in the literal and figurative marginalization of Spanish. All of these spaces might be considered parts of the borderlands, for, as much as geography and language, they shape interpretation from the literal edges, from the material margins.

Textual and border literary critics alike have come to acknowledge the importance of the way the words look on the page as they guide readers to interpreting the narrative codes they embody. As Paul Gutjahr and Megan Benton explain, "In many ways, letterforms are the most immediate and visible link between the writer and reader" (15). What a story means, in other words, is inextricably bound up in the way the words that tell the story look. Such a concern with the visual politics of language is at the center of Damían Baca's *Mestiz@ Scripts: Digital Migrations and the Territories of Writing*, which explores the visual nature of mestiza/o writing in order to revise traditional notions of Mesoamerican literacy. He argues that "Mestiz@ scripts" work at the intersection of Western and Mesoamerican modes of communication, weaving together the alphabetic and the pictographic in ways that heavily rely on visual as well as linguistic interpretation. Claiming, "It is too often the case that efforts to clarify alphabetic literacy often overlook the pivotal role of illustration and image within language" (92), Baca's interests overlap with those of a textual scholar like Johanna Drucker, who defines "'writing' as the visible form of language from the level of the marks to the letters and [including] all the characteristic features of the visible medium" and contends that "these features contribute to structuring the linguistic significance of the text" (232). For example, throughout his text, Baca makes use of the "at" sign—@—in Mestiz@, "primarily for purposes of gender inclusivity" and also as "a marker of communal subjectivity among Mestiz@ cultures" (2), demonstrating the intersection between the linguistic and the graphic, the visual and the political significance of letters. Written texts are necessarily visual texts, and though we might often treat the shape of the words as mere conveyors of meaning, those shapes unavoidably contribute to the meaning as well.

The interpretive possibilities of italics in particular draw us into a paradox: italics are both an invisible, everyday occurrence that "we never stop to question" and an insistent visual marker of material textual difference. The use of italics to represent Spanish words in English texts, then, can be seen as a nearly invisible narrative of linguistic difference that privileges the normal or even logical English over the different or even seemingly handwritten (read: premodern) Spanish. A close examination of the use of italics in border narratives exposes efforts to control the presence of Spanish in English-language texts, as well as attempts to subvert that control. In performing this kind of examination of the materiality of language, this chapter is a partner to the previous one, and it continues the exploration of what it means to translate in the literal, material margins. It also similarly suggests that the work of italics as paratext can be autographic and/or allographic and that such designations have an impact on how we read the narratives themselves. While linguistic conflicts often occur in the pages surrounding the texts, the very words on the page register them as well. As Gutjahr and Benton argue, "Typography is an interpretive act, but one that must in turn be evaluated: Is it insightful, or obtuse? Consonant or dissonant with the linguistic text? 'Transparent' or obtrusive?" (6). Closely examining the role and effect of italicization in the work of Nash Candelaria and Richard Yañez, we can answer such questions and highlight the interpretive possibilities hidden in italics and accent marks.

This chapter investigates two examples of the typographic normalization—or nonitalicization—of Spanish in English-language texts, each with different goals and potential interpretive results. The first is Nash Candelaria's *Memories of the Alhambra* (1977), a work that crosses the U.S.-Mexico border and triangulates it with Spain, while the second extends the discussion to Richard Yañez's complex use of typography in his short story "Desert Vista" (2003). Both authors construct characters whose identities are bound up in language, whose status in between nations, cultures, and classes is related in their varying degrees of comfort in shifting from Spanish to English and back. Furthermore, these politics of identity are in turn extended to the reader, who must negotiate the normalized Spanish present in each work. In each case, the often overlooked process of italicization structures our expectations of the presence of Spanish in English texts, almost invisibly directing the creation or erasure of linguistic hierarchies.

Both authors also express a sense of concern for the materiality of the page and the politics of textual production: in the case of Candelaria, this material politics is expressed both through his reflections on his decision to self-publish his work and through the effects of such a decision. The typographic normalization necessitated by the material realities of self-publishing result in a multiple and varied discourse on language acquisition, retention, and preservation, highlighting simultaneously the subordination of Spanish to English and the persistence of Spanish in English, with a range of linguistic possibilities in between. In *Memories of the Alhambra*, the typography of the text is sometimes at odds with the narrative, threatening linguistic homogenization even as the narrative celebrates linguistic diversity. Yet the very existence of that typography perhaps unintentionally demonstrates the multiple narratives of loss, erasure, and recovery at the heart of Chicana/o border linguistic experience. In contrast, Yañez's work demonstrates a more conscious conversation about the materiality of language that extends even to the page, one that opens up a space to consider how typography communicates the process of acquiring knowledge and one that is supported and enabled by a university press with the means to produce it. "Desert Vista" manipulates the typographical use of italics to reflect critically on language acquisition and to advance a politics of knowing that goes beyond the skills of translation. Each text insists on attention to that which we might otherwise ignore: the visual construction of the borders between languages.

Erasing and Multiplying Linguistic Difference in Nash Candelaria's *Memories of the Alhambra*

Nash Candelaria's 1977 novel *Memories of the Alhambra* follows José Rafa, a New Mexican in search of his Spanish roots in the wake of his father's death. The narrative offers an extensive interrogation of the practice of rejecting indigenous Mexican roots in order to claim a European heritage, establishing itself as part of the larger Chicano Movement in its attempts to embrace the Indian, as well as the mestizo, over and above one's Hispanic or European roots. It questions the politics of identifying with Spanish heritage to the exclusion of all others, and ultimately advocates a multicultural fusion that allows the next generation to identify as Chicano. Though the novel is not frequently described as a border text, as the first installment of a trilogy that includes *Not by the Sword* (1982), which narrates the story of the Rafa family on the eve of the Mexican-American War in 1846, and *Inheritance of Strangers* (1985), which continues the story in the aftermath of the Mexican-American War, the narrative of *Memories* establishes itself as linked to U.S.-Mexico border history.[2] Furthermore, a major part of the narrative concerns José's travels from New Mexico to Mexico and then Spain in search of his identity, and the narrative choice to move José through these spaces magnifies the narrative expression of the connection between physical crossings of boundaries and realizations of ways that identities cross boundaries. Despite José's constant refrain, "I'm Spanish. Pure Spanish. Son of conquerors. Architects of the New World. We beat the Indians. Conquered them" (163), he must eventually come to terms with, even embrace, his indigenous Mexican heritage, and his border-crossing journey makes possible his recognition of himself as "Mestizo. Child of the Old World and the New" (173). The confrontation and ultimate realization of his ancestry leads to his death, though his son Joe eventually learns to respond to the question "Eres Mejicano?" (92) in the affirmative, demonstrating Candelaria's vision of the new Chicano generation's embrace of its mestizo heritage. Martha Cutter argues, "The father's problem of ethnic definition is played out through the son's struggle for linguistic identity" (192), noting that as Joe becomes more comfortable asserting his hybrid identity, his ability to translate Spanish into English and fit in with both his friends and his New Mexican family increases dramatically. Joe no longer questions which of these identifiers suits him, instead adapting to each specific situation, speaking Spanish in Spain and Spanglish in New Mexico, communicating with his children in English.

This increased level of comfort at shifting between languages invokes a further sense of comfort in occupying the spaces between the strict definitions of identity groups. Through much of the novel Joe and his father struggle with questions of definition that call into question the stability of language, particularly with what names and identifiers mean. For example, José and his brothers gather around the topic of name-calling, with Tomás asking, "What difference does it make what someone calls you. Mexican. Spanish. Indian for that matter. Does it put any more beans on your plate?" (78). Of course, the search for what one is called is at the heart of this novel, and the term "Mexican" means more than just "a person from Mexico" here: Theresa, José's wife, reacts to being called a Mexican by noting, "There was a cruel twist to the word so that it meant more than it said . . . [it] meant poor. Uneducated. Dark complexioned. Dirty. Don't enter here. Go back where you came from. I'm better than you" (123). Repeatedly, the narrative emphasizes the problem of definition, showing how each ethnic label or marker becomes a powerful tool depending on the connotations applied. Thus, in one telling scene Dandy insists, "One of their weapons is what [Anglos] call you. So they can steal from you and not feel guilty about it" (78). In turn, they argue over what to call themselves: Mexican? Spanish? American? New Mexican? As Joe watches in confusion, he notes that "this same conversation seemed to repeat and repeat. Endlessly. Never resolved" (80); the question of what to label oneself, as well as the problems of being labeled by others, has no end. Here Candelaria narrates the problems of choosing a national, ethnic, or political label: specifically, the problem that these definitions of self are always only temporary, impermanent assertions of existence and meaning.

For a young Joe, this permanently temporary identity is discomforting at first. He struggles to define terms like Mexican and Anglo: for example, he "wasn't sure what an Anglo was. It didn't seem right that Catholics were Anglos. . . . And a Jew? . . . As for calling a Negro an Anglo? Come on. The same for orientals. . . . So who did that leave to be an Anglo? Those others. The 'enemy.' Who were Protestants. Non-minority" (83). Here he works to make sense of who counts as an Anglo, the taxonomy of identity. As he grows up, he rebels against such labels, dating a young woman named Isabel and responding to his parents' questions about her Mexican heritage with "I don't go around broadcasting the ancestry of every girl I date. What does it matter?" (106). And finally, when asked that question, "Eres Mejicano?" he can verbally answer yes, but also in his head he can continue, "American. Mexican. Human. Ape descendent son of God. Yes. Yes. Yes" (92). By the end of the novel, both externally and internally, Joe embraces a borderlands sense of identity that refuses to limit itself to a single term. What previously made him uncomfortable—the never-ending conversation about labels and names and what to call oneself—becomes a source of relief as he answers to all in the affirmative. Just as he feels comfortable speaking both Spanish and English, he feels most comfortable inhabiting more than one identity, living at the intersections of these labels.

If Joe's new comfort with the spaces between identities and languages offers a singular example of Chicana/o border linguistic experience, one that is very different from that of his father, other material aspects of the text also work to diversify narratives of linguistic experience, giving readers further insight into the multiple and varied relationships to language possible in border spaces. It demonstrates in a tangible way the realities of not only linguistic acquisition but also erasure and loss, both voluntary and involuntary, as part of border identities-in-process. For example, while the progression of the narrative seems to lead toward increasingly celebrating linguistic diversity, it could be argued that the sparing use of Spanish, coupled with the nonitalicization and lack of diacritical marks throughout the text, develops out of a politics of conservative multiculturalism, or what Peter McLaren describes as the process by which "ethnic groups are reduced to 'add-ons' to the dominant culture. Before you can be 'added on' to the dominant United States culture you must first adopt a consensual view of culture and learn to accept the essentially Euro-American patriarchal norms of the 'host' country" (quoted in Poey 203). This add-on status is made perhaps most clear when we register the fact that Candelaria's novel is about the process of becoming fluent in two languages but that it is itself written in English. Manuel Villar Rasso and María Herrera-Sobek note that, on the whole, California Chicano writers, including Candelaria, have published mainly in English due "in part to the lack of publishing venues for works in Spanish in the United States and in part to the lack of interest in Chicano literature in Mexico and other Latin American countries" (25). The conditions for publishing this novel, shaped as they were by market considerations that presumed a lack of interest in Spanish-language texts as well as racial and national hierarchies that cast Chicana/o narratives as undesirable in all manner of locations, in turn shaped a narrative about linguistic fluency from the outside: the material novel itself is not as fluent as Joe is.

But the conditions for publishing this novel were also shaped by Candelaria's own abilities: given his own limitations in Spanish due to having grown up in Los Angeles speaking English, it might be that Candelaria is not as fluent as Joe is, either. Candelaria's stated lack of facility with Spanish—he claims to "speak English very fluently, Spanish very little, although [he] understand[s] a great deal of it" ("Nash Candelaria: An Interview" 120)—reflects a long history of language loss among Mexican Americans, and the typographical absences of accent marks make that loss paradoxically visible.[3] But the very fact that Candelaria's Spanish is limited does not make his narrative any less Chicana/o or any less representative of border literature; if anything, the frequency with which knowledge of Spanish is lost or at the very least threatened in border narratives and lived experience only makes it more so. Linguistic identity in flux is both the subject of the narrative and a conditioning factor of the writing of that narrative: it materially registers the threat of Spanish loss, of its subordination to English, without insisting that such linguistic experience is itself homogenous.

This multiplying effect of linguistic experience, whereby readers encounter a variety of narratives of language acquisition, subordination, and loss on the part of both characters and author, is also reflected in the question "Eres Mejicano?" Such a question is significant not only due to Joe's changing responses, which demonstrate his own changing linguistic experiences, but also due to its lack of italicization and its punctuation: traditionally (or at least as far back as 1754), interrogatives in Spanish have been preceded by an inverted question mark (¿), but here the typographic reminder of spoken Spanish is absent. Cutter parenthetically notes in her argument, "No Spanish-language accent marks and punctuation are used in Candelaria's novel" (191); thus José is actually Jose. Likewise, in an early review of the novel Paula Shirley writes, "Candelaria has the requisite ear for both Spanish and English to make Hispano and Anglo dialogue sound authentic. There are occasional misspellings ('abrazzo,' 'pidgeon Spanish') which are likely due to the fact that Cibola Press is a new publishing house. But these few lapses in spelling or punctuation do not interfere with one's reading" (101). Just as italics are both invisible processes that point out visible distinctions, both the reviewer and the critic feel compelled to point out the typographical inconsistencies—as though these elements are unavoidably visible and therefore at least slightly jarring—as they assign blame to sloppy proofreading in an attempt to sort out why the text comes to us in this form. But if we go further in our interrogation of the typographical issues that normalize the presence of Spanish on the page, we can see that, on a visual level, the Spanish language inadvertently preserves the hierarchy and rules of the "host" language and orthography.

At first glance, the lack of italicization traditionally associated with the presence of foreign words in English-language texts works to level the playing field, erasing visual distinctions between the standard English language and the intrusive Spanish. And many contemporary Chicana/o border writers, and Latina/o writers more generally, have increasingly published texts that consciously eschew italicization in favor of such leveling effects. For example, Rolando Hinojosa's *Klail City* (1978) employs italics for nearly all Spanish words, while Norma Elia Cantú's *Canícula* (1995) alternates between italicizing the Spanish and leaving it romanized. Ana Castillo's border novel *The Guardians* (2007) avoids italicization entirely. Even presses themselves express opinions about italicization; readers can expect books published by Arte Público Press to italicize Spanish words, while Karen Van Hooft, the executive editor at Bilingual Press (which eventually took over the distribution of

Memories and published all of Candelaria's later works), explains that their house style involves "rarely italiciz[ing] Spanish words in creative literature we publish (unless the author insists) because we consider code-switching to be a valid literary language" (Van Hooft, "Re: Candelaria").

But in Candelaria's text, the assimilation of Spanish into an English standard of typography, when coupled with the lack of Spanish orthography and diacritical marks, runs the risk of assimilating the language of the text into English on a linguistic and visual level. Candelaria's narrative may be advocating a politics of identity that embraces difference and allows for room to reside in the spaces between cultures and languages, but the material borders of the text, the spaces between the narrative and the material forms on/in which that narrative is presented, reminds readers that the variety of linguistic experience on the border also includes moments in which an embrace of difference still subjects those who are different to the codes and structures of the dominant culture. Consider, for example, a scene in which José introduces his son Joe to a relative: "I want you to meet Senor Padilla. He's your second cousin. 'Mi hijo,' he said to Herminio. 'No habla espanol. Es agringado.' An Americanized Mexican. There was a touch of pride in his father's voice, tinged with a sense of an apology. Look at this new generation that can't speak the mother language, he seemed to say. But what can one do?" (94) Coupled with the narrative, these absent visual markers record the loss of Spanish language and literacy in process, attesting to the diverse linguistic experiences of Chicanas/os on the borders between languages. Careful readers of the narrative and its typography, then, are presented with multiple representations of the relationship between Spanish and English.

Even the choice of spelling presents readers with both narrative and visual evidence of the existence of not one experience of Spanish but many, in various states of transition to and distance from English. The phrase "Eres Mejicano?" again proves useful here, because the spelling choice of "Mejicano" over "Mexicano" reflects a long history of the phonetic evolution of the name of a place and its people. The word Mexico derives from Nahuatl, a language in which, as Baca notes, *ch* is pronounced as *sh*, which the Spanish transliterated as "Mexico" at a time when the *x* sound also mimicked the *sh* sound. By the end of the fifteenth century, *sh* also sounded like the Spanish *j* sound. Lack of standardization led to various spellings of Mexico and Mejico, and in the present day writers of Latin American and specifically Mexican Spanish tend to use Mexico, while those from Spain quite often used to, and still occasionally do, use Mejico. By opting for the minoritized but also European spelling "Mejicano," the text's narrator potentially speaks the language of Spaniards. Such a linguistic choice also reflects the unique character of New Mexican Spanish: after "the original settlers . . . brought with them a sixteenth-century Spanish that was fundamentally rural Castilian" (Cobos), New Mexican Spanish developed in relative geographic and political isolation from both Castilian and Mexican Spanish, resulting in the use of some archaisms. Since the question comes from the mouth of a "Chicano from East Los Angeles . . . his nervous brown hand clasping and unclasping around a textbook" (92), readers witness a linguistic discord between the character asking the question and the narrator, each with a different relationship to the shapes, sounds, and spellings of the Spanish language: in effect, the narrative and its seeming "misspellings" grant readers access to the diversity of relationships to Spanish. The work of reading the "j" also calls into dispute the nature of the question itself: is asking "Eres Mejicano?" the same as asking "Eres Mexicano?"

With Joe's answer, the narrative and typography continue to tell multiple stories about language. Joe knows the identifier "was a derogatory word rather than a statement of fact—applied to the poor, the hungry, the unemployed, *the accented*, the powerless" (183, emphasis mine), and still he takes it up: he answers, when asked if he is Mexican, "Si [*sic*]" (92). In answering in the affirmative, Joe embraces the position of the accented. But in that moment, the typography literally erases the accent: the word "Si," as printed, is missing the accent mark that distinguishes the Spanish "yes" (sí) from "if" (si). The typography, by supplying the conditional conjunction instead of the simple affirmative, might even make Joe's Mejicano status "iffy." As a result, the narrative is changed by its appearance in print: the narrative sides with "the accented," while the typography erases it.

Certainly these gaps and inconsistencies in the representation of Spanish on the page could reflect the clash between a writer and his editor and/or publisher. Have Candelaria's narrative and identity politics been subordinated to those of a mainstream or big-five publisher whose goals and interests are not matched to his own? In this case, Candelaria never got quite that far: his very struggle to find a publisher for *Memories of the Alhambra* led him to self-publish the book. In his memoir, *Second Communion* (2010), Candelaria describes following the lead of fellow self-published Chicano author Raymond Barrio and establishing Cibola Press after facing rejection from New York publishers who blamed terrible markets or called the book "not [their] cup of tea" (188). In turn, he acknowledges that the publishing process itself "helped [him] overcome the flawed thinking that if a commercial publisher did not accept my book, then it was not worth publishing" (189). Thus, while Candelaria's and Cibola's house style reflect—intentionally or unintentionally—the goals and visual characteristics of English, they are very likely the result of the difficult and expensive prospect of printing accent marks in the 1970s without the aid of computers, as well as without the working knowledge of Spanish orthography that a dedicated copyeditor would have.

Besides, for a writer who acknowledges, "At times I feel guilty that I don't know Spanish better" ("Nash" 120), perhaps the lack of accents and occasional misspellings also testify to the author's admitted status as an "Anglicized Chicano" ("Nash" 119). But what they do not suggest is that Candelaria thought nothing of the materiality of his text. In fact, his detailed description of the production process indicates the opposite:

> I selected the typeface, designed the way the text fit onto the printed pages, and dealt with a typesetter supported in part by a grant from the National Endowment for the Arts. I pasted down the typeset pages, two pages per form, as required by the typical printer. One artist friend designed the book jacket while another did the oil painting illustration that appeared on the jacket. I dealt with a printing broker who placed the job with a Midwestern firm that specialized in short runs of books. I remember when the printed books arrived, box after box on pallets placed unceremoniously on the curb in front of our house. Where the hell was I going to store them? (*Second Communion* 191)

Candelaria's description bears evidence of the great care he put into making this book, the process whereby he shifted roles from author to typesetter, printer, and distributor. Even the problem of storage becomes one of simultaneous celebration and marginalization. And though he has argued that his troubles getting published were "the same publishing problems that all writers encounter" and that he doesn't think that "Chicano writers are at any special disadvantage in becoming writers" ("Nash"126–127), he describes the relative success of his book by noting that "it seems to show Anglos something in a way that does not make them defensive" ("Nash" 125). In some small way, the lack of italics and accents might contribute to that kind of success, meeting readers on unaccented grounds.

That somewhat peculiar typographic representation of Spanish would be repeated and solidified when Candelaria found a new publisher. Soon after the book came out, acquisitions editor Gary Keller at Bilingual Press, which specifically publishes works "by or about U.S. Hispanics," expressed interest, and Candelaria sold the press his remaining copies on consignment. But when the remaining copies were sold and the book was reprinted under a new contract, Bilingual Press "did not have the resources to hire someone to re-edit it, adding the diacritical marks. . . . In addition to re-editing we would have had to re-typeset the book, also adding to the cost and time involved" (Van Hooft, "Re: Candelaria"). Re-editing and re-typesetting the book would have cost both time and money, costs that would have kept the book from remaining continuously in print.

While the press made a choice that worked to keep the book in print, the long previous decisions of typesetters and typeface designers and manufacturers contributed to that choice in nearly invisible ways. Similar in a sense to the recently described "willful obliviousness" (McFadden) of the inventors of color film photography, who used a pale-skinned white model to calibrate skin tone and light in pictures, which resulted in film whose dynamic range "was biased toward white skin" (Del Barco), typeface professionals have noted the way that typesetting and its associated machinery have traditionally set the unaccented as the standard, thereby making accents more costly in terms of time and money. Writing in 1978, Hans H. Wellisch notes, "The use of diacritical marks has always been a headache for printers, typographers, and graphic artists" (53), in part because "modified letters are more costly to produce" (53). But as David Brezina argues, "Even though accents are often detached from the basic letterforms, it does not mean they are any less important" (n.p.): for Brezina, accented letters are not modifications of other letters but closer to letters unto themselves. Even in the digital age, while typographers have developed more cost-effective typefaces that acknowledge linguistic variations in the Latin alphabet, they note a real need for developing "multi-script typography" (Balius), or typography that incorporates a variety of alphabets that extend beyond Latin (such as Arabic, Chinese, and Japanese) in order to reflect our increasingly multilingual global society. At each stage in the development of typefaces and typesetting, such innovations require not only money but also a reorientation in our understanding of the relationships between languages. Candelaria's narrative, in which José becomes Jose, for instance, materially and narratively suggests that there is a price to pay for having an accent; it also, and perhaps more important, asks readers to consider their own orientations to the relationship between Spanish and English.

In Candelaria's novel, border textuality renders visible a multiplicity of narratives illustrated by the language of the story and the physical nonpresence of italics as well as diacritical marks, asking us to question and interpret their absence. Because the narrative and the typography are each telling stories about language, those narratives include both the celebration of linguistic and cultural diversity and the occasional and unintentional subordination of such linguistic diversity to English. And because the author self-published his work, we might be led to ask how to solve the problem of the text as it stands, when what border textuality demands is that we as readers recognize the very existence of multiple narratives as essential to any construction of the border. It also requires us to be attentive to the material realities of self-publishing, especially as those realities shape narrative in unexpected and nearly invisible ways. Here, the typography attests to the steep costs—both literal and metaphorical—of accents.

Throughout *Memories of the Alhambra* Joe is ridiculed by his extended New Mexican family for his "unaccented English" (96, 128), but despite his increasing success at using Spanish throughout the novel, and in turn celebrating linguistic and cultural difference, the visual figures on the page tell another, more complicated story. The typography narrates a Spanish more spoken than written, at one and the same time a Spanish in stasis, a Spanish in the process of change, a Spanish becoming English, even a Spanish under erasure. These are Chicana/o and border-linguistic realities: multiple, competing, conflicting. A border text like Candelaria's novel, with all of its typographical imperfections, also unintentionally but nevertheless forcefully calls attention to the multiplicity of stories being told about language, about the multiplicity of experiences of Spanish, and about the relationship between Spanish and English, both narratively and materially. Readers who are careful to attend to not one but many of these stories contained within a single novel have the opportunity to experience border textuality by negotiating that materiality in the process of reading the narrative.

Richard Yañez and the Physicality of Language

In his conclusion to *Out of Sorts: On Typography and Print Culture*, Joseph Dane distinguishes between an abstract text and a typographical text: "an abstract text is something to be read, not seen; it thus can be reproduced on a keyboard; a typographical text is what can only be reproduced as an image. It can be read, but it cannot be reproduced in different visual forms or shapes" (195). In the case of Candelaria's novel, we might argue that the novel is an abstract text, that the typographic erasures of accent marks, as well as the lack of italicization, are simply a practical matter easily corrected or even avoided as the subject of study. It's the story that counts, not the letters that tell the story. A more contemporary example might help highlight the competing claim that every border text—or at least every border text that aims to incorporate Spanish into a predominantly English-language narrative—is also a typographical text. While Candelaria's narrative and typography appear to work at cross purposes, in Richard Yañez's stories the lack of italics seems to work hand in hand with the narrative: typographic choices become intentional and purposeful, a subtle insistence to readers that they pay attention to the materiality of language. Lourdes Torres notes, "Recent Latino/a writers who experiment with language in more modest ways . . . have created a space for the publication of books that challenge linguistic norms for texts published in the US" (87); Yañez's work demonstrates the significance of these "more modest" and more clearly intentional experiments with italicization and typography in a text that insists on the importance of print.

"Desert Vista," the opening story of Yañez's collection, *El Paso del Norte: Stories on the Border* (2003), complicates what we might consider to be the traditional border narrative by turning attention away from the divisions between nations (Mexico and the United States) and ethnicities (Mexican and Anglo) and instead toward internal division: in this case, divisions that are primarily class-based. Claudia Sadowski-Smith, in her study of three contemporary border narratives, argues that Yañez's collection demonstrates the way "economic, gendered, and political divisions" among the Mexican population of El Paso "become spatialized in residential segregation or . . . in the multiplication of Latina/o-Chicana/o communities" ("Twenty-First-Century" 729). While "Desert Vista" is set in El Paso, with readers reminded that "minutes away the Río Grande separated us from another country" (10), more important, Yañez's characters navigate the literal barrier erected between the middle-class and working-class sections of Desert Vista, a subdivision in Ysleta where the protagonist, Raul, and his family live. Raul's family moves onto the middle-class side of Nottingham Drive, while his first friend in town, Santiago, lives on the other side of the barrier. Described in terms of what appears on the lawns—"busted Big Wheels. Crooked swing sets. Kids in diapers" (17)—and what doesn't—"No basketball courts. No birdbaths. No mulberry trees" (17), the other side of the barrier is a space Raul crosses into hesitantly in order to confront the friend who stole his girlfriend. This literal barrier carries symbolic weight, then, in its representation of Raul's negotiations of the boundaries of class, friendship, and adolescent desire within a Mexican American community.

As Raul attempts these negotiations, readers are time and again brought to understand his sense of dislocation in terms of language. Yañez has cited as an inspiration for this story Luis Alberto Urrea's description in *Nobody's Son* of "the borders of my mouth": "I remember being fixated on this for weeks, listing words (English, Spanish, Caló) that negotiated space in my upbringing as the grandson of Mexicans and the son of bilingual Americans. I found inspiration in the sounds/rhythms of language I associated with going to jr. high in El Paso, where languages ebb and flow, borders be damned" (Yañez, "Re: Questions"). As we have seen, this fascination with language is not an uncommon narrative thread in border literature: Chicana/o and Mexican American protagonists are frequently represented as caught between languages, where they know too little / too much / the wrong kind of Spanish and where the process of identifying one's voice is inextricably linked to the process of identifying one's language. But Yañez modifies the discourse of borderlands language identity in two important and connected ways: first, he acknowledges the different and even competing physicalities involved in speaking and writing, repeatedly emphasizing the material aspects of language in order to demonstrate its malleability. And second, through a careful and "very deliberate" (Yañez) use of typography, he further underscores the materiality of language, highlighting the notion that speaking, writing, and even knowing a language rarely or fully grants a person full, stable access to the world. Yañez's use of typography is a formal innovation that participates in border textuality by using the material of the text to invite readers into an experience of linguistic borderlands. What that typography uncovers for readers is a sense of the slippage between signifiers and signifieds, a sense that language, even when we seem to know it, will always be shaped by the way it is written or spoken.

As a recently transplanted junior high school student, Raul represents the middle-class Mexican American experience not only in terms of setting but also in terms of language. Describing himself as someone who "only really used Spanish the few times we visited my grandparents in La Loma" (4), Raul perhaps reflects current statistics that show that only 17 percent of third-generation Mexican Americans speak Spanish (Portes and Rumbaut). But using statistics like these can be tricky, because they tend to flatten out regional distinctions. More specifically, the 2010 U.S. Census discovered that 72.8 percent of El Paso's population speaks Spanish at home. Further, by placing Raul in an Ysleta school district, perhaps best known for its groundbreaking use of two-way dual-language Spanish-English programs, Yañez gestures toward the diversity of linguistic experience for Mexican Americans across regions: making Raul a transplant, an outsider, a newcomer to this neighborhood and school creates space for understanding the acquisition and maintenance of language, but also Mexican American identity more broadly, as an uneven process shaped by environment, just as Candelaria's narrative materially multiplies narratives of linguistic experience.

While Raul knows and speaks some small amount of Spanish already (he doesn't pause to reflect on words like "mijito" or "menso"), his linguistic education in the time period of this story centers on slang. Like a toddler shouting his first expletive in the middle of a crowded restaurant, much to the consternation of his parents, Raul frequently doesn't know what the words mean even as he says them. Thus, words like "joto" and "pendejo" become favorites even as he admits that he "still wasn't sure what *pendejo* meant in English" (13). And not all of the slang Raul encounters is specifically Spanish: he notes that "kissing had its own vocabulary" (7). As he learns the art of kissing—as well as the art of talking about kissing—he is introduced to more unfamiliar language. Boys in school quickly teach him "*Frenched*," "*hickey*," and the term that combines Raul's lack of Spanish knowledge with his lack of sexual knowledge: "*chi chis*" (7). Raul is even subtly guided into rethinking the shape of the female body in the telling of his own sexual adventures: as he recounts his second encounter with Ana Garza, he tells Santiago that he put his hands on her waist. Santiago responds, "Her hips?" at which point Raul "correct[s] [him]self" (7). Santiago encourages Raul to alter his own narrative, corralling and correcting Raul's desire, and in turn Raul learns the internal linguistic difference between the erotic "hips" and the comparatively unerotic "waist" of the female body. Yañez blends the adolescent vocabularies of love, sex, and Spanish to demonstrate Raul's coming of age as directly tied to a growing mastery of language and to a process of making sense of the world.

More specifically, Raul ties his understanding of language acquisition to an understanding of ethnic and cultural identity. This occurs throughout the story as Raul struggles to understand the meaning of the word *cholo* much in the same way that Joe struggles to define an Anglo in Candelaria's novel. As an identity marker that works as both a slur and a celebratory term of power, cholo presents a linguistic puzzle for Raul. He begins by associating the word with a particular image: "a brown-skinned boy wearing a hairnet and a starched T-shirt and khakis, with a neatly folded bandanna drooping out of his back pocket" (2). The bandanna is both "neatly folded" and "drooping," suggesting a kind of calculated nonchalance that Raul imagines connects with a specific kind of behavior: throwing mud balls at strangers' homes (in this case, Raul's) or "flipp[ing] off the teacher" (3). When his brother questions his logic, asking, "And that makes him a cholo?" Raul responds, "Doesn't it?" (3). Raul also connects cholos to graffiti, specifically graffiti that uses Gothic lettering "like on the Declaration of Independence" (3), though he does not immediately connect cholos to Spanish. He claims "he didn't know that's what cholos talked" (3). But soon he comes to think in terms of "cholo vocabulary" (12), imagining himself saying, "C'mon, don't be a pinche. Why you messing up our house, ese [*sic*]?" (12). For the most part, the identity of a cholo is a figment of Raul's imagination. But the climax of the story is not only a realization of Santiago's betrayal of Raul—it turns out that Santiago has been kissing Ana Garza—but also the moment at which Raul comes to label Santiago: Raul, angered by this betrayal, sets off "chasing a cholo" (15). By the end of the story, cholos are not images in Raul's mind. Instead they are "strangers" and "ex-best friends" (17) who live on the other side of the barrier from Raul, who fling mud at other people's houses while Raul flings mangoes. As he increases his understanding of the word "cholo," as its meanings change across the narrative, Raul's desire or need to label Santiago as a cholo collapses his simultaneous desires for a stable linguistic, cultural, and fraternal identity.

Yañez deepens and complicates the narrative of Raul's linguistic coming of age by repeatedly underscoring the ways both written and spoken language carry a physicality with them that constantly alters meanings. Language becomes as erotic as kissing. While Raul begins a small obsession with biting into and "suckling" (2) mangoes in the wake of his first kiss with Ana Garza, he also appears obsessed with the feel of new words. He "liked the way 'cholos' sounded and how it opened [his] mouth, like if [he] was blowing a bubble" (3), he "enjoyed the way 'joto' blew out of [his] mouth" (5), he "crowded [his] mouth with o's. Cholo. Joto. Pendejo" (13). Further, he describes hearing the combination of English and Spanish on the school bus as "mouthwatering" (8). Just as Gloria Anzaldúa begins "How to Tame a Wild Tongue," a chapter in *Borderlands / La Frontera* on Chicana/o Spanish, with an anecdote about a dentist who repeatedly exclaimed to her, "We're going to have to control your tongue" (203), Yañez neatly weaves together the two oral fixations, kissing and language, in order to emphasize the intersections of his protagonist's dawning sexual and linguistic identities. Language, like sex, the story reminds us, is a physical experience. Speaking the language grants access to a quasi-erotic pleasure. When Raul chooses to launch a mango at Santiago's front door instead of a mud ball, he is collapsing the loss of the erotic pleasure of Ana's kiss with the loss of his friendship with Santiago. The only pleasure left to him is that of finally labeling Santiago a cholo: he speaks him into existence. The cholo itself has assumed a material form in the figure of Santiago, solidifying Raul's sense of knowing—really knowing—cholos.

Yañez also repeats the doubling of linguistic and sexual vocabulary-building by introducing two notes that draw attention to the materiality of written language. Raul receives one note filled with Spanish slang from what appears to be a gang member that he "carried and read . . . all the time" (4) and another from Ana Garza. This doubling of the notes gets Raul into trouble with his parents, further entwining the experiences of adolescent sexuality and language. During a dinner-time conversation, Raul's mother places a folded note that she has found in his pants pocket in front of him and asks him to explain it to his father; thinking it is the note "written in cholo" (11), Raul tries to explain. It turns out that instead the note is the one from Ana Garza, and Raul's mother is more disturbed by her son's having a girlfriend than by his being threatened anonymously to "watch your sorry ass" by a member of the VLK gang. By emphasizing the physicality of the notes, the language that Raul carries with him as he struggles to decipher it, Yañez further threads together Raul's adolescent sexuality with his class- and ethnicity-based understandings of identity. For instance, Yañez takes the time and page space to block out the note from the VLK gang member in all capital letters, creating room for the language that confuses Raul. And in both cases, it's the shape of the letters that matters as much as what the letters say: from Ana Garza's "round cursive" (14) to the "stilted print" (14) of a cholo and his own struggles to "stay within the lines" (9, 14), Raul is drawn to reflections on the way meaning is conveyed through the materiality of print. Furthermore, what he writes never matches what he says: the "neatly written sentences" he'd prepared to deliver to Ana Garza instead "pour out of [his] mouth like a mudslide" (14): language materially fails him when it changes containers. Time and again readers are encouraged to think of language acquisition, whether it be the language of Spanish, of adolescent desire, of friendship, of class, or of cultural identity, as physical and material. The notes, the mangoes, the graffiti "curved and bent like the ironwork of houses in Juárez" (4): the feel of words in one's mouth is repeatedly emphasized in order to remind us that language comes materially wrapped; language is shaped by its own vehicles, written or oral.

The shape and feel of words changes and is changed by our understanding of the meaning of those words. Yañez underscores this, and in turn makes this material for readers, by intentionally engaging in play with the italicization of the text. Unlike Candelaria's novel, whose lack of italicization and diacritical marks can be traced to the economic and time-related costs facing him as a self-publisher and Bilingual Press as a small publishing house, Yañez's story is the result of a conscious choice to "to play with the idea of what words are 'foreign' to the character" (Yañez) and the support of the University of Nevada Press. "From the first readers through the copy editing," he acknowledges, "they respected my decisions about italics" (Yañez). Yañez joins a growing group of Latina/o writers who acknowledge the rhetoric of italics: Dominican American writer Junot Díaz consciously publishes without italics, as does Cuban American writer Achy Obejas. Obejas describes the process of inserting italics into her earlier work as "utterly arbitrary" and says regarding her more recent work, which does not feature italics, "In my life, I'm constantly code-switching, and I'm not unique, and I wanted the language on the page to reflect that" (Obejas). But Yañez's "ideas about italics" set him slightly apart from other Chicana/o and Latina/o writers. Whereas many texts either italicize every Spanish word or elect not to italicize any words at all, Yañez's story, because it involves a complicated borderlands where ethnic and linguistic identity do not map neatly onto one another, negotiates those borderlands in a material way. For example, he applies italics not only to Spanish words but to all other unfamiliar words: the new sexual slang, the new identity markers Raul encounters. Thus the first time "cholos" appears in the text, it is italicized, marking its foreignness not just to readers but also to Raul. Musing about who could have been throwing mudballs at their home, Raul suggests, "maybe it's *cholos*" (2). His brother, who is seemingly more familiar with the term, asks, "Cholos? . . . What do you know about cholos?" (2). The italicization is dropped. The term loses its foreignness, at least in terms of its materiality: it is now no different from any other word on the page.

On the surface, this would seem to imply a simple one-to-one correlation: when Raul is introduced to a new word, particularly a word in Spanish, it's italicized. From then on, the word no longer needs to be italicized: no longer an unknown, no longer foreign, it slips into romanized font, blending in with all of the other known words. The experience of the monolingual English reader, then, is matched by Raul's own experience. The potentially new word demands attention in its physical shape: we as readers, just like Raul, are called to reflect on its meanings. Do we know what the word "cholo" means? Does it mean the same thing in this story? To each reader? To each character? Throughout the story, then, Yañez alternates between italics and romanized font, striving to give material shape to language acquisition both to Raul, who enjoys the feel of words, and to readers, who must encounter these words in their physical forms in order to make meaning of the story.

Yañez confirms that this complicated use of italics is deliberate, explaining that for Raul the italicization falls away "when the words become part of his developing vocabulary as a border child" (Yañez). But the lack of italics, and the corresponding developing vocabulary, also indicate the gap between language acquisition and knowledge. For instance, when Raul responds to his brother's question, he says, "I know cholos" (2): the word is no longer italicized, but does he "know" them? At this point in the story, what Raul knows of cholos is the image of a strutting young man in khakis. More insightful is Raul's brother's response: he asks not "who" but "what," and later, "how": "how do you know cholos?" (2). Raul's brother's last question is one that demands knowledge of experience. It's clear from the narrative that Raul doesn't yet have enough experience to know cholos, even though he claims to. Likewise, he's not experienced enough to know other Spanish words even as the italics drop away: "While I still wasn't sure what '*pendejo*' meant in English, I crowded my mouth with o's. Cholo. Joto. Pendejo" (13). Such words are becoming familiar to him—their physicality, their sound, their status as signifiers—even as his understanding of them is limited. As a result, instead of a simplified rendering of knowing (romanized font) versus not knowing (italicized font), Yañez's play with typography leads us as readers to question Raul's understanding of language and identity. If these words, of which Raul has only a limited understanding, can be visually assimilated into his vocabulary, what does that mean? The romanization, or normalization, of words does not suggest that Raul has achieved an understanding of language—of what, for instance, a "cholo" really is—but rather that the process of understanding, its always unfinished nature, can be hidden from view.

Of course readers, like Raul, have only a tenuous hold on language: meanings of words slip and slide and change, depending in large part on their written or oral containers, or their signifiers, and on context. Given the normalized appearance of these words, the fact that Raul uses language without full control over or understanding of it is potentially masked. But the key here is that we as readers also have an opportunity to see the mask being applied: through Yañez's manipulation of typography we watch as Raul fumbles toward an understanding of language, and we are shown the way that speaking, writing, or even knowing a word for certain turns into an elaborate, erotic, and powerful fiction. Raul assimilates words into his vocabulary as if their foreignness, their unknowability, their untranslatability could be permanently erased. Just as Raul struggles in the end toward some sort of label for his ex-friend Santiago, just as he decides that Santiago must be a cholo, given his behavior and Raul's current understanding of that no-longer-italicized word, he has already reinvented what that word means, changed its container, cross-referenced it with his erotic loss, his loss of trust in someone he thought of as a friend. "Desert Vista" is not about the sudden, dawning realization that Santiago is a cholo. Instead, the story is about the sudden, dawning realization that naming something or someone grants the namer a sense of power. Knowing that "one of their weapons is what they call you" (Candelaria, *Memories* 78), Raul designates Santiago a cholo. He leans on a weapon that categorizes Santiago as other, as different, as enemy, as "target" (17).

That power, whether Raul knows it or not at the end of the story, is temporary. Yañez underscores this sense of temporary power through his both narrative and typographic emphasis on the physicality of language. The physical, material container or signifier of a word at any given time, whether that signifier is printed italics, handwriting, or the shape it is given by a human mouth, shapes its meaning. But paradoxically, it cannot contain the word itself. The process of language acquisition, many sociologists and border narratives alike would have us believe, is a pathway to power. But just as glossaries can oversimplify the relationships between Spanish and English words, italics can oversimplify the beginning and end of that process. That's not the case in "Desert Vista": though there are *cholos* and cholos in this story, the cholos are just as likely to be unknown, just as likely to be untranslatable as the *cholos*.

Conclusion

In both *Memories of the Alhambra* and "Desert Vista," the narratives are consumed with questions of identity: What is a Mexican? An Anglo? A cholo? The answers to these questions are almost always temporary, or at least insufficient, and endlessly malleable. The malleability of such identifiers is underscored by typographic decisions that have a significant impact on literary interpretation. Often the visuals function at cross-purposes with the narrative, multiplying understandings of the relationship between Spanish and English on the printed page. This is the case in Candelaria's novel, where the perhaps unintended but intriguing effect is an amplification of the narratives of linguistic diversity—from near-erasure to affirmative recovery—experienced in the Chicana/o borderlands. That narrative of linguistic diversity, in which characters and the material text variously claim, deny, or even erase their accents, is perhaps all the more meaningful in a contemporary context in which, as of 2015, residents of California continue to be denied the opportunity to include diacritical marks on their birth certificates (Lapan). But increasingly, borderlands writers like Yañez take advantage of our expectations and assumptions about italicized language to reflect more critically on what it means to acquire or know a language.

In the cases of both works we have examined, the materiality of the text is as crucial to an understanding of the narrative as the story being told. That materiality can reveal the subtle and multiple narratives of linguistic identity offered by the narrative and the typography, or it can reveal the way typography supports and extends the complexity of linguistic identity as narrated in the text. It can also be visible evidence of the materiality of the publishing process: signs of the struggles to print, with accents and all, one's story on one's own terms. Alternatively, it can suggest the editorial control authors have seized with regard to typography, and also the opening up of possibilities by presses now better able to recognize stories as both narrative and visual. Yañez says that working with the University of Nevada Press "definitely improved my writing without compromising my Chicano vision" (Yañez). When the costs of accents or italics are no longer a concern, "Desert Vista," like *Memories of the Alhambra*, can narrate—albeit more intentionally—the complexity and diversity of linguistic acquisition, maintenance, and loss for its Chicana/o border subjects. While easily overlooked, typography—especially in the case of borderlands texts like these—can function as an essential element of border textuality.

This chapter has investigated some of the most minute aspects of Chicana/o border literature, mining typography for insight into how writers, publishers, and readers visualize and understand the relationship between Spanish and English. What it uncovers is a series of competing narratives of language: one is reflected in a normalized Spanish that erases accents and other diacritical marks in the interest of accommodating the host language. Such erasures can give readers the illusion of seamless transitions between English and Spanish, of an ability to move fluidly and invisibly from Spanish to English. A second narrative, often asserting itself in the very same text, recognizes language acquisition in process, both narratively and materially. As sites that often reveal the negotiations of authors and characters, paratextual elements and bibliographic codes inevitably shape border narratives at the same time that those narratives often take as their subject the negotiation of language. With regard to language, the texts reveal themselves to be materially and narratively unstable.

In Chicana/o border literature, responding to this instability is not merely a matter of choosing the right word, of finding a linguistic equivalent; it is another sign of the fundamental instability of border identity. Language is a political choice, as is the degree to which one wants or needs to translate. Rather than choosing one language or another, one culture or nation or another, those who embrace border identity also embrace, or are at the very least subject to, that instability. Furthermore, as critics we cannot ignore the ways that the material margins of a text affect the interpretation of border literature. Whether they impose an unwanted system or conception of translation on a text or serve as a space in which border authors and texts resist those systems, the literal and figurative margins—the opening and closing pages, the footnotes and glossary, and even the typeface—surrounding a border text represent a visual, material site on which political choices the narratives describe are enacted and rejected, whether by authors, editors, publishers, or even typesetters. Exploring the evidence of translating in the margins gives us greater insight into the struggles among author, publisher, editor, and reader over the construction and consumption of border identity.

4

"My Book Has Seen the Light of Day"

The Editorial Paratexts of Recovery Projects

> Even scholars read, and edit, with a mission. Editors make, as well as mend.
> —D. F. McKenzie

In the course of the past twenty years, perhaps no project in Hispanic, Chicana, and/or U.S.-Mexico border literature has had more of an influence on the field(s) than the Recovering the U.S.-Hispanic Literary Heritage Project, directed by Nicolás Kanellos. In 1993, Kanellos described the goals of the project as "locating, rescuing from perishing, evaluating, disseminating and publishing collections of primary literary sources written by Hispanics in the geographic area that is now the United States from the Colonial Period to 1960" ("Foreword" 13). The project has now compiled a list of over seventeen thousand publications (books and pamphlets) and published at least thirty scholarly editions of recovered texts, including the work of María Amparo Ruiz de Burton, Daniel

Venegas, and Maria Cristina Mena. It has also published nine volumes of essays, the first of which editors Ramón A. Gutiérrez and Genaro M. Padilla explain as "imagined and designed to provide both the expert and the neophyte with the most current and comprehensive assessment of Hispanic literature in the United States, illustrating its ethnic and national diversity, its regional variations, the scope of its genres, its canonic texts and its untapped potentials" (17). Its value to scholars interested in the cultural and literary production of Hispanic American authors prior to 1960 is immeasurable; its emphasis on the recovery and preservation of texts previously lost or forgotten is necessary for a more comprehensive understanding of American history.

And yet it did not take long before scholars began critiquing both the project and the publications deriving directly from it. In "Grappling with the Archive of Mexican America," José F. Aranda argues that the growth of the archive "represents the culmination of decades of dedication to the study of people of Mexican descent in the United States. While this fact is undisputedly good news, our newly expanded archive worries me, not for its content but for the fear that its content may languish for lack of attention for years to come" (67). Obviously the problem is not that critics find no value in the archive, only that its depth and breadth present real problems for critics interested in sorting through its contents. In an archive as vast as this one, what potentially inhibits critics from its use is confusion over what to do with it, how to organize the unwieldy amount of information contained within its broad reach. Of the attempt to order every element in the archive chronologically, for example, Manuel Martín-Rodríguez writes, "Chicano/a literary historians must be careful not to do violence to a text's multiple temporalities and historical contexts by ascribing it solely to its period of composition or publication" (*Life* 168). Martín-Rodríguez also suggests that the recovery of Hispanic and Chicana/o texts comes with the challenge to recognize the borders between very different historical moments—those of initial publication, loss, and recovery—and that critics interested in recovery must respond to that challenge, resisting the temptation to collapse those temporal borders. Attending to the "multiple temporalities" of a given text means locating it in a border zone between historical moments, complicating the archive by recognizing a text's social life as it circulates in a variety of material forms.

As solutions to such complications, critics have begun to advocate a self-conscious approach to working in the archive, one that strives to attend to the complicated history of Chicana/o and Hispanic literature by making those complications visible. Thomas Kinney argues for a sustained "practice of refutation," which "combines ideological awareness and ethical responsibility with the constant deconstruction of our values and assumptions" (67). Martín-Rodríguez is more specific, defining a "a rhizomatic literary history" that

> would allow the historian to start, if s/he so desired, with the Chicano/a Movement (or with any other point in time) and then move backward (to situate the newly recovered texts in their original time, for instance), forward (toward post-Movement literature), sideways (toward Mexican or other relevant literatures) [and to] insert the recovered texts (for example) in at least two different temporal junctures: that of their production and early reception and that of their reappearance in our present Chicano/a literary world. (*Life* 166)

This approach is sensitive to the complications of Chicana/o and Hispanic literary history, acknowledging rather than erasing its spatial and temporal multiplicity. It is also quite useful for thinking through the issues that surface in any exploration of the recovered texts of U.S.-Mexico border literature in particular, as these texts and their histories frustrate the construction of temporal, national, and historical borders, forcing us to ask difficult questions about what exactly has been recovered, and why.

Taking this call for attentiveness to the multiple and even conflicting histories of Chicana/o and Hispanic literary production one step further requires an exploration of the material elements of the recovery project editions themselves for evidence of their social lives, of their multiplicity, and of the effects of changing material conditions on interpretation. Exploring the social lives of these editions means studying the effects of editorial prefaces, introductions, and notes from translators for evidence of editorial decisions, as well as visual elements such as cover pages and organizational structures for evidence of how they negotiate textual, temporal, cultural, and historical borders. Following all of those critics who have (almost from the inception of the recovery projects themselves) subjected themselves and their endeavors to self-conscious critique, asking how their own work shapes and is shaped by contemporary political, cultural, and social concerns, I want to ask, How do the material texts of recovery projects suggest that we read them? How do those material elements alter the conditions for interpretation? Furthermore, how do critics, editors, writers, and readers use the paratext to negotiate or even obscure the fluid historical and temporal borders of their texts? And how do these recovery projects reflect our own present concerns with history, with language, with the archive, with the fight against loss, erasure, marginalization, forgetting? How do recovery projects participate in the social lives of texts?

This chapter offers a preliminary exploration of these questions by working in two directions: it begins with a study of perhaps one of the most successful and famous recovery editions in the Recovering the U.S.-Hispanic Literary Heritage Project archive: *The Squatter and the Don* (1885) by María Amparo Ruiz de Burton, recovered and edited by Rosaura Sánchez and Beatrice Pita in 1992. With regard to this novel, Sánchez and Pita have been subjected to nearly as much criticism as Ruiz de Burton herself. Critics demonstrate a concern for the specifically political ways in which Sánchez and Pita appropriate Ruiz de Burton and her text as "proto-Chicana" or subaltern. The history of responses to Sánchez and Pita's historical and critical introduction to the novel suggest that they derive from a concern that this introduction, in its material presence preceding Ruiz de Burton's narrative, definitively shapes the interpretive possibilities for every reader of this edition in a way that underscores specifically late twentieth-century understandings of Hispanic and Chicana/o heritage. The first half of this chapter reflects on their editorial practices, emphasizing in particular the way they deal with a self-censored portion of Ruiz de Burton's novel, and concludes by demonstrating how those practices are taken up or set down in the more recent Random House / Modern Library edition (2004). Such analysis reveals an entirely new set of interpretive possibilities afforded by different material margins, as well as evidence of the pervasive effects of Sánchez and Pita's editorial and interpretive work on this popular edition.

The second section of this chapter works to acknowledge recovery projects of post-1960 works—the end date selected by the Recovery Project—that have already been threatened with loss or erasure. The 2000 bilingual edition of Margarita Cota-Cárdenas's *Puppet*, originally published in Spanish in 1985, constitutes a recovery project text whose preservation for American and Chicana/o literature appears to have demanded translation, exposing the linguistic sacrifices as well as the linguistic politics at play in the recovery of Spanish-language texts. Again, the material elements (or bibliographic codes) of the text and its paratexts, including the allographic foreword as well as its cover, design, and typography, offer insights into the way the author and her translators think about language. Because of the bilingual nature of Cota-Cárdenas's original text—it shifts between Spanish and English in the original publications—the problem of how to treat a translation into English ultimately has interpretive consequences, and the edition itself occupies a sort of borderlands existence, the original and the translation mutually dependent on one another in ways that also blur the boundaries between the two.

By addressing recovery projects of both nineteenth- and late twentieth-century Chicana/o or Hispanic literary texts, we can begin to draw some useful distinctions as well as comparisons between how we approach the recovery of texts from different historical moments. The archive of "forgotten" or "lost" texts should not be closed off to those texts published in the years after 1960; instead, we must call attention to the narratives we have more recently marginalized, and ask the same self-conscious questions of these recovery editions of more recent texts—For whom are we recovering these texts, and why? And what effect does "recovery" have on interpretation?—as we have begun to do with those of much older texts.

Recovering María Amparo Ruiz de Burton

Between *The Squatter and the Don*'s original publication in 1885—first self-published under the name C. Loyal, then published by Samuel Carson & Company later in the same year—and its recovery, María Amparo Ruiz de Burton's name and work nearly disappeared. The novel itself is a historical romance that details the disappearing land rights of Hispano farmers in the face of encroaching Anglo squatters as a result of the 1848 Treaty of Guadalupe Hidalgo and the related Land Act of 1851. In the plot's romantic entanglement of Mercedes Alamar, the daughter of a Californio family, with Clarence Darrell, the son of a squatter family, the novel's characters act, as Anne Goldman describes it, "as representatives of an overtly historical struggle to (re)define borders" (129). These borders refer, of course, to the newly drawn boundaries between the United States and Mexico but also to the shifting borders between race and class as landed elite Hispanic characters find their claims to upper-class whiteness eroded and rejected. Punctuated with smaller, related narratives reflecting on the rise of the railroad monopoly in the West, the ineptitudes of a far-away Congress, and an unjust legal system that characterizes justice as not only blindfolded but "begrimed" by the political machinations of judges and lawyers, the novel is an embodiment of Mrs. Darrell's own early remarks about history: "Let us cry for the spilt milk, and remember how, and where, and when, and why, we spilt it" (55).

Thanks to the Recovering the U.S.-Hispanic Literary Heritage Project, a recovery of *The Squatter and the Don* appeared in 1992, with a second edition published in 1997. Remembering "the how, and where, and when, and why" of Ruiz de Burton's narrative and biography didn't end there: in addition, the editors of this novel, Rosaura Sánchez and Beatrice Pita, published *Conflicts of Interest: The Letters of María Amparo Ruiz de Burton* in 2001. In 2004, editors Amelia María de la Luz Montes and Anne Elizabeth Goldman contributed *María Amparo Ruiz de Burton: Critical and Pedagogical Perspectives* to the growing corpus of Ruiz de Burton criticism surrounding these primary sources. Ruiz de Burton's novel is now taught in a variety of literature courses and was excerpted most recently in the eighth edition of the *Norton Anthology of American Literature* as well as the seventh edition of the *Heath Anthology of American Literature*. While the novel has seemingly emerged from obscurity into critical and pedagogical acceptance, there is no doubt that the context in which the book is now taught and read is one vastly different from that in which it was published, not to mention faded from public view.

In particular, readers' access to primary and secondary source material, a wealth of critical commentary, and editorial introductions have shaped the potential for interpretation, demonstrating that Ruiz de Burton's novel belongs as much to the late twentieth and early twenty-first centuries as it belongs to the late nineteenth century. In terms of the specific paratextual choices made in publishing it, the edition of *The Squatter and the Don* published by Arte Público Press (both the press and Kanellos's Recovery Project are housed at the University of Houston) and edited by Sánchez and Pita offers readers an entry into interpreting the novel in a way that reflects the specific concerns of contemporary Chicana/o politics and literary scholarship. The material evidence of editorial decisions that aimed to merely recover and explain the significance of the novel at the time of its original publication also renders visible its participation in border textuality, as these paratextual issues are also border issues. They complicate constructed distinctions, developing textual identities from the spaces between the text and the world. The material textual border zones of a recovered text like this one are always under construction—they are never guaranteed to remain the same across editions—and they are always shaping interpretation of the text. A brief overview of those textual choices, focusing on the editorial introduction and footnotes, will demonstrate this border textuality in action.

As James Diego Frazier has noted, the first editorial decision a reader encounters in the recovered text of Ruiz de Burton's novel is the altered title: in labeling the novel *The Squatter and the Don*, the editors have eliminated the subtitle: *A Novel Descriptive of Contemporary Occurrences in California*. But the element of Sánchez and Pita's edition that perhaps most alters the conditions for interpretation is also the one that has received the most attention from literary critics: the editorial introduction to the novel. The forty-nine-page introduction presents a wealth of information regarding the history and circumstances of the novel's plot and its publication, as well as the politics at play following the Treaty of Guadalupe-Hidalgo. This type of introduction functions as a posthumous allographic preface, "recommending" the book to readers (Genette 267). Thus, as Sánchez and Pita also present a reading of the power relations in the novel based on A. J. Greimas's "semiotic square" as a method of "recommending" *The Squatter and the Don* to readers, they operate in the borders of the material text but also in the border spaces between author and reader, assuming characteristics of both. As readers they develop an interpretation that they author and attach to the beginning of the text. In their reading, Sánchez and Pita argue, "While [two] sets of oppositions are suggested in the novel from the beginning, . . . the focus shifts from the first set of oppositions (Squatter vs. Don) to the second set (monopolies vs. individual entrepreneurs) towards the end of the novel" (31). This exposition of the semiotic square is accompanied by a variety of structuralist diagrams that map the oppositions and borders between squatters and rancheros, corporate capitalists and individual capitalists, governments and workers, and Anglos and Californios (see fig. 3). Presenting this

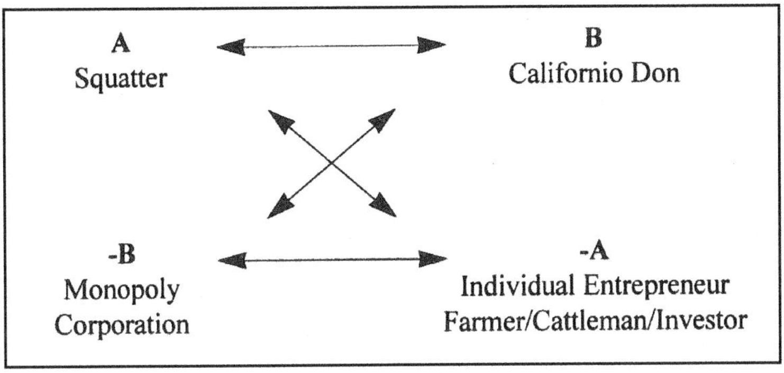

FIGURE 3 Illustration included in the critical introduction to *The Squatter and the Don.* (Reprinted with permission from the publisher of *The Squatter and the Don*, edited by Rosaura Sánchez and Beatrice Pita [©1992 Arte Público Press–University of Houston].)

analysis prior to the text has the effect of recommending the book to critics as worthy of reading, where worthiness is related to structuralist complexity. These diagrams, even as they acknowledge third terms (such as the Indian marginalized by both squatters and Californios), also solidify "opposition" as a key term in interpreting the novel.

Critics have been quick to point out—as early as 1993—that some of these editorial attempts to underscore the role of oppositions in the novel have led to an overenforcement of ethnic, racial, and national borders and to an oversimplification of both the novel and Ruiz de Burton's intentions. Critics have found particularly debatable Sánchez and Pita's claim that "Ruiz de Burton dialogues with a number of contemporary discourses—political, juridical, economic, commercial, and literary—both dominant and minority, all to voice the bitter resentment of the subaltern" (10). To begin, critics take issue with the idea of either Ruiz de Burton or her novel as subaltern given the author's own biography. Though she died in poverty, María Amparo Ruiz de Burton descended from the Ruiz family, who were "related by blood and marriage to some of the most prominent families in Alta California" (Aranda, "Contradictory" 556), and she married Captain Henry S. Burton, U.S. Army, who eventually became a brigadier general and died in 1869 after fighting in the Civil War. Furthermore, José Aranda notes, "As much as we, Chicano/a scholars and our allies, would like to read Ruiz de Burton as a prototypical Chicana feminist, resistance fighter, in-your-face Abraham Lincoln basher, and go-to-hell Supreme Court critic, she was none of these." A bit later he writes that "her biography indicates that she saw herself as part of a white, educated elite—aristocratic in its origins and with a history in Alta California as colonizers—not as colonized" ("Contradictory" 554, 558). Of course, biography is not destiny: Ruiz de Burton, in spite of or even because of her own upbringing, could very well have still penned the novel of the subaltern. But the general critical consensus is that the story she tells is far more complicated than that.

To the critique of Ruiz de Burton's biography, critics have added arguments that Sánchez and Pita incorrectly cast the narrative itself as evidence of a proto-Chicana voice (though the editors never use this word), the voice of the oppressed speaking out against Anglo oppressors. Jesse Alemán argues, for example, that the source of anguish in the narrative comes not from a critique of racial and class division but rather from a sense that the Californios have been mistakenly assigned to the wrong side: "In the end, the novel levels a scathing critique of US imperialism—not because it excludes Californios, dispossessing them of their land and livelihood, but because it does not include them in the privileged category of white class mobility in the first place" (67).[1] Rather than seeing the narrative or its author as "subaltern," Marcial González suggests, we might more readily attend to the ways "Ruiz de Burton's novels . . . initiate a tradition of novels that respond specifically to the racialization of Mexican Americans in the United States" (65). At the heart of many critiques is the concern that Sánchez and Pita's introduction tries too hard to make the narrative conform to what we now understand as Chicana/o literature. Of course, in order to legitimize the recovery of the text, it must do work we find valuable. But in labeling the novel as one that represents the voice of "a subordinated and marginalized national minority" (7), these critics argue, the editors are asking a nineteenth-century novel to perform according to the standards of late twentieth-century literature and theory, in turn simplifying the history of Mexican Americans in California. John-Michael Rivera suggests that such a move "presuppose[es] that these 'Proto-Chicano' works only 'speak' to other Chicano texts and that a cultural purity in the body of these texts can be reified through a resistance paradigm" (94). Editorial decisions that guide interpretation, as they do in this critical introduction, only emphasize that the recovery project is always already a political project.

These critical responses also attest to the significance of the placement of Sánchez and Pita's introduction: when Aranda says, "Sánchez and Pita's gesture toward present-day ethnic politics . . . with Ruiz de Burton as a figurehead is terribly misplaced and misleading" ("Returning" 15), he implicitly acknowledges that it is their words—placed before the text with the goal of leading readers through it—that must be read, perused, or skipped entirely in order to reach the text itself. At the very least, the introduction attempts to pin down a singular interpretation, offering the illusion of narrative (and political) stability by labeling it under one heading: subaltern. Such an illusion of stability as suggested by the placement and permanence of the introduction does a disservice to the complex, conflicted, and multiple political messages

Ruiz de Burton's text sends. By proposing an unbroken chain between Ruiz de Burton and Chicana/o authors of the late twentieth century, Sánchez and Pita's introduction invites readers to surrender to the fictive stability of genre, themes, class, and politics across centuries and generations of Mexican American people.

If their introduction shapes interpretation, other editing decisions made by Sánchez and Pita have had a lasting effect on the possibilities for readers' interpretation of Ruiz de Burton's text. Though these decisions have garnered less critical attention, they likewise shape how readers approach and think of Ruiz de Burton's text as a unified, stable text. While the introduction proposes the stability of "Chicana/o" literature, these editorial decisions seek to assign stability and even singularity to the versions of Ruiz de Burton's text. Although the introduction thoroughly records the history of the publication of *The Squatter and the Don*, even including evidence from Ruiz de Burton's letters regarding the difficulty she had in self-publishing her work, Sánchez and Pita's editorial decisions don't go as far as they could in highlighting for readers the differences between the self-published edition and that published by Carson.[2] For example, the Sánchez and Pita edition of *The Squatter and the Don* effectively makes a choice for readers about which edition—the self-published or the Carson edition—matters more and, more important, eliminates the opportunity for readers to re-create the other. This decision carries at least two implications: first, it creates the illusion of a textual singularity rather than a multiplicity, and second, it has influenced the shape of the "popular" edition issued in 2004 by Modern Library Classics, a division of Random House.

Archives and the texts we recover from them, including Ruiz de Burton's novel, give us glimpses into texts-in-process. Peter Shillingsburg notes that we can use archival materials either to search for "evidence of the single best form of the work with which the world at large should be presented" or to find multiple versions of the work to be "compared, analysed, and reported as distinct social, economic, and cultural instantiations of the work in a heritage of literary events" (41). In their edition of *The Squatter and the Don*, which was originally both self-published and published by Samuel Carson & Company in the same year (1885), Sánchez and Pita appear to opt for the former choice, presenting a single version of the text for readers. While this is certainly an acceptable option, one of the fundamental goals of textual criticism and the critical editions it generates is to assist readers in recognizing which version of a text they are reading, and how that version differs from others, by supplying enough information to allow them to recreate that other version. Jerome McGann explains, "When preparing a critical edition the editor chooses one particular version as the basis for his reading text, and he lets the critical apparatus carry all the information necessary for the reconstruction of the other possible versions and reading texts" (*Critique* 90). In the case of recovery projects in particular, this work is done out of a desire not simply for thoroughness, nor to give some antihistorical attention to the details of the ideal text, but actually out of quite the opposite desire: so that, when we catalog the versions of texts, we might discover the patterns of silence and exclusion imposed on the work of writers of color.

Regarding the differences between the editions of Ruiz de Burton's narrative, however, Sánchez and Pita include only the following footnote to their introduction:

> The two editions are substantially the same except for the introduction to Chapter XXXV. What began with a satirical portrayal of the image of the "Goddess of Justice" being defiled and prostituted by the likes of San Diego Judge Lawlack and lawyer Roper, is replaced in the second edition, published by Carson, by a less virulent and more general critique of bad judges. The first paragraph of Chapter XXXV in the Carson and present edition ends with a comment on the mockery of justice evident in cases in which judges, exposed for their corruption, sue their accusers for libel. This sentence probably reveals why Ruiz de Burton changed the opening page of Chapter XXXV. (346n23)

In the text of the narrative, then, Sánchez and Pita opt to offer the self-censored version. But such an editorial decision, coupled with the decision not to reproduce the original version, even in a footnote, can introduce a fairly high level of confusion over which version of Ruiz de Burton's text readers have in front of them, as well as erect a roadblock to readers seeking to put together the pieces of the multiple texts that make up what we now understand as *The Squatter and the Don*. By not offering readers a transcription of the self-published version of that first paragraph, Sánchez and Pita made a choice that obscures the other possibilities, even as those possibilities register the negotiations of what can and cannot be said, in the interest of a singular, stable narrative.

Sánchez and Pita's language about these two versions of the text also reflects how much their editorial decisions shape readers' relationship to the text. In this critical edition, readers cannot see the changes for themselves, so we must trust the editors' judgment that the two versions are "substantially the same." What is in that sentence that "probably reveals" the reasons for Ruiz de Burton's edit? Just how "virulent" is the original critique? Here are the two versions of the first paragraph of Chapter XXX:

> 1885 SELF-PUBLISHED VERSION
> If the Goddess of Justice could see how her pure white robes have been bespattered and soiled by his Honor Judge Gryllus Lawlack, she no doubt would feel grieved and affronted. Her eyes being bandaged, however, it is to be supposed

she is unconscious of the cruel manner in which the Judge has begrimed and blackened her garments, lowering her dignity to the dust, making her seem absolutely ridiculous, and all to please Peter Roper and John Gasbang. In her pitiful plight she looks as if she had been pushed down from her lofty place, under the judicial canopy beside the Judge, and made to accompany Roper to the San Diego taverns in one of his sprees, thence been pulled by him out into the streets, where he played with her 'Blind-man's buff' and reeled and hiccoughed into a gutter, bedraggling her in the mire.

But litigants must accept justice in that condition in San Diego as long as Judges like Gryllus Lawlack have the say as to her treatment and garb. The Supreme Court tries to rehabilitate the unfortunate Goddess by reversing the Judge; but the Judge retaliates by reversing the Goddess. Thus a painful game of see-saw is kept up between the Judge and the Goddess. The Supreme Court setting up the Goddess, the Judge tilting her into the dust again. (366)

1885 CARSON & COMPANY VERSION AND 1992/1997 VERSION

If those kind eyes of the Goddess of Justice were not bandaged, but she could see how her pure white robes have been begrimed and soiled in San Diego, and how her lofty dignity is thus lowered to the dust, she would no doubt feel affronted and aggrieved. And if she is so irreverently maltreated, can she afford any protection to those who must rely on her alone, having no riches to maintain protracted litigation or carry their plaints to higher tribunals? To the moneyless laity Justice thus defiled seems as helpless as themselves. She is powerless to accomplish her mission upon earth whenever a Judge, through weakness or design, may choose to disregard her dictates. At present the dignity of a Judge's personality is more sacred than the abstract impersonality of justice. Because the accepted theory being that Judges are always just and incorruptible (and generally the supposition is correct), there is a broad shelter for a Judge who may be neither just nor impartial. What mockery of justice it is in our fair land of freedom to say that a bad Judge can be impeached when impeachment is so hedged with difficulties as to be impossible—utterly ineffectual to protect the poor, victimized laity! Who is the poor litigant that would dare arraign an unjust Judge, well sheltered in his judicial ermine, and the entire profession ready to champion him? "*Libel*" would be the cry against any one who would dare hold the mirror for such Judge to see himself! Ah, yes, when the real libel is to distort the law and degrade the mission of justice on earth! (366)

In addition to naming names, the language of the original, self-published edition is markedly different in its attention to the attack on the personified Goddess of Justice. One can imagine that arguments about the role of the law in Ruiz de Burton's novel, such as those advanced by Alemán, who argues that the novel "plac[es] legalese in the context of fiction, and fiction in context of legalese . . . to affirm the discourse of the novel while it undercuts the legitimacy of legal rhetoric" (45), might be even further amplified by a reading of this version of the chapter's opening lines. The references to games, "Blind-man's buff" and "see-saw," and even the notion of "tilting [Justice] into the dust" cast the participants in the legal system as children (albeit violent children) ganging up on Justice, an idea absent in the revised or self-censored version.

But, more important, in that first version we see such games acted out between Justice and the lawyers and judges, with no mention of the citizenry, "the poor, victimized laity" (366). The comparison of the two versions, while it certainly reveals a new and longer critique of judges, also makes all the more apparent Ruiz de Burton's newly inserted mention of "those who must rely on her alone" (366). Perhaps Sánchez and Pita potentially saw her reference to "the moneyless laity," a simultaneous reference to the subaltern: whereas the first version metaphorizes Justice in the interest of pitting the moral good against the actions of men, the second version triangulates the battle by introducing those in need of justice, by acknowledging the odds stacked against them, by noting that the mechanisms designed to "speak" on their behalf are not only blindfolded but gagged, "as helpless as themselves." If Sánchez and Pita maintain an interest in a novel that voices such "bitter resentment," even as its characters cannot, their choice of the second version would make sense.

While the editors may have chosen the version of that excerpt that more clearly expresses a subaltern narrative, they paradoxically erase Ruiz de Burton's subaltern experience of authorial self-censorship. Giving readers a chance to read the politically motivated self-censorship Ruiz de Burton performed, perhaps in order to ensure literary survival, could in fact be strong evidence of Sánchez and Pita's opening argument, one that so many critics have challenged, that Ruiz de Burton's voice is in many ways a marginalized one. The editors have had to answer the question Which subaltern should speak? Ruiz de Burton, in her original and uncensored voice, or the narrative, in its revised version? Ultimately, they chose the self-censored version. And textual critics like Donald Pizer would likely support Sánchez and Pita's decision: arguing that a self-censored novel is one that "emerge[s] out of the personal tensions, conflicting motives, and cultural complexities of that moment" (149), and therefore can offer potential insight into the historical moment of its publication, Pizer sees value in upholding censorship in new critical editions of texts. But we need to see the censorship in order to understand it fully. We can learn, in other words, from witnessing what writers wouldn't or couldn't allow themselves to say.

In the end, either editorial decision—to print the self-censored or to print the uncensored version—could be a defensible one. But in a recovery edition such as this, when gaining access to original copies of the self-published edition or the Carson edition is difficult, if not impossible, some measure of reconstructability should be possible. Instead, Sánchez and Pita's edition performs the work of analyzing this textual decision for readers without also giving them an opportunity to debate that decision: it singularizes the history of publishing Ruiz de Burton's narrative, eliminating its political complexity. Editors of critical editions are no longer expected not to leave their fingerprints on their work, but they do a false service to their readers by not accounting for their choices.[3] It's important to consider why Ruiz de Burton wrote what she wrote when she wrote it and why she changed it, and also to have a clear explanation of why the editors deem one of those versions more accurate, authentic, or important than the other. These changes not only highlight the instability of the social text—something Sánchez and Pita's edition simultaneously reveals and conceals—but also tell us something about what they believe is important for us to read right now. In making these choices, Sánchez and Pita created an edition of *The Squatter and the Don* that joins Ruiz de Burton's self-published edition and the Carson edition as part of the complex net of versions that shape and are shaped by readers in many different ways.

In particular, Sánchez and Pita's critical edition appears to have shaped the "popular" edition of *The Squatter and the Don* released in 2004 by Random House under the imprint of Modern Library Classics. With regard to the changed paragraph, editor Jennifer M. Acker explains in the preliminary "Note on the Text," "As Rosaura Sánchez and Beatrice Pita write in their 1992 introduction and notes to the Arte Público Press edition of *The Squatter and the Don*, the two editions are essentially the same except for the first paragraph in Chapter XXXV" (xiv). Acker privileges the editorial decisions of Sánchez and Pita, adopting the less than precise language regarding the editions' being "essentially the same," though her editorial apparatus goes no further to support this claim. She goes on to write that this edition is "set from the second edition of 1885" (xiv), thereby making the same editorial choice as Sánchez and Pita. In this note, Acker both acknowledges the influence of Sánchez and Pita and perpetuates their oversight: despite extensive historical notes and a list of typographical corrections, the Modern Library Classics edition brings readers no closer to seeing the paragraph Ruiz de Burton eliminated from her first, self-published edition. Furthermore, the back cover of the paperback confuses matters by advertising its text as "set from the first edition of 1885." Since both the self-published edition and the Carson edition were published in 1885, such a statement confuses the textual situation, but it also contradicts its own editor. Faced with both of these statements, and with no opportunity to compare differences, what are readers meant to believe they are reading? In effect, the competing assertions of the jacket and the editor's note expose the instability of the text in a way the rest of the text seeks to conceal (or, at the very least, to downplay). In an instance of border textuality, the paratext insists on the fluidity of Ruiz de Burton's material, its errors reminding readers that more than one version of *The Squatter and the Don* exists.

The paratext of the Modern Library Classics edition of *The Squatter and the Don* also asserts itself as a distinct "version" of the text that distinguishes it from the more overtly critical scholarly edition edited by Sánchez and Pita. The Modern Library emphasizes its history in American publishing, claiming, "For decades, young Americans cut their intellectual teeth on Modern Library books. The series shaped their tastes, educated them, provided them with a window on the world" ("About"). They market their "Paperback Classics" as both scholarly and popular, top-of-the-line and affordable: scholarly endnotes are followed by reading-group guides, and the overall look of the text production highlights "values that emphasize superior quality and readability" ("About"). For this edition, identified as a "trade paperback," the list price of $13.95 reflects a slightly lower-than-average price for adult paperbacks. The text includes a biographical note on Ruiz de Burton, an introduction, the aforementioned note on the text, a facsimile of the first title page, the text, extensive historical and textual notes, and a short reading-group guide, and it concludes with advertisements for the Modern Library Classics imprint, suggesting dual impulses toward "scholarliness" and "readerliness." Such a duality is reflected perhaps most clearly in the choice of Ana Castillo to introduce the text of Ruiz de Burton's novel. In contrast to Sánchez and Pita, who offer strict literary and historical criticism, Castillo serves as a middle ground between scholarly and popular: novels like *Peel My Love Like an Onion* (1999) and *So Far from God* (1993) have made her familiar to a popular audience, while her critical work, *Massacre of the Dreamers: Essays on Xicanisma* (1994), as well as her more recent experimental work like *Psst . . . I Have Something to Tell You* (2005) and *Watercolor Women / Opaque Men* (2005), draw in more literary-critical audiences.

Recognizing and hoping to capitalize on Castillo's popularity, the Modern Library Classics edition works hard to make this Castillo's text as much as—if not more than—Ruiz de Burton's. Though Ruiz de Burton gets top billing on the cover, "Introduced by Ana Castillo" closely follows her byline. Castillo's name also makes an appearance on the spine, though in a smaller font than Ruiz de Burton's. On the back cover, however, Castillo's name is mentioned three times to Ruiz de Burton's one. Not only does the top of the back flap repeat that the text is "Introduced by Ana Castillo" but the summary blurb first quotes Castillo, then describes Ruiz de Burton's novel. And finally, after a paragraph break, instead of the traditional author summary, the publishers provide the following: "Ana Castillo is a poet, essayist, and novelist whose works include the recent poetry collection *I Ask the Impossible* and the novel *Peel My Love Like an Onion*. She lives in Chicago and teaches at DePaul University." There is no similar blurb for Ruiz de Burton; the entire back cover is an advertisement for Castillo. Taken together, the paratextual elements of the cover aim to make Ruiz de Burton's narrative contemporary by association.

As Ruiz de Burton's text undergoes a temporal dislocation from the late nineteenth to the early twenty-first century, the methods by which publishers justify its survival in print construct new conditions for interpretation. This move to make *The Squatter and the Don* more appealing to contemporary audiences collapses important historical and social differences between 1885 and 2004.

Thus, in place of Sánchez and Pita's claim that Ruiz de Burton "voice[s] the bitter resentment of the subaltern," Castillo opts for "Call it what you will, but I'd say the woman had *cojones*" (xvi). Lest it be assumed that Castillo's is a less rigorous introduction to *The Squatter and the Don*, however, I would rather argue that Castillo's goals in introducing the text are simply different from those of Sánchez and Pita. Whereas the Recovering the U.S.-Hispanic Literary Heritage edition contains a long exposition of the Ruiz de Burton text's relationship to the semiotic square, Castillo moves more quickly to address the aforementioned problem that numerous critics had with that introduction: its lack of sustained attention to the role of race and class. Calling Ruiz de Burton's novel "one truth among many of the social realities of that era" (xviii), Castillo spends a good portion of her six-page introduction examining the racist attitudes of the novel's heroes and tracing the complicated relationships among Anglos, Mexican elites claiming Spanish ancestry, and mestizos and indios. Writing, "No significant character [in the novel] seems above negating the basic human rights of people of color, in fact, in one or two instances, their very humanity" (xvi), Castillo insists that Ruiz de Burton's goal was never to write the history of the working class. Furthermore, Castillo won't waste time debating "whether or not its political theme really expresses the sentiments of the true underdog of that era, as has been debated by those interested in Chicano Studies" (xvii). Instead, Castillo recommends this book to readers in a way that asks them to consider its heroes and villains in light of a history more complicated than the dualities emphasized by Sánchez and Pita would imply.

But in a way that matches Sánchez and Pita in intent, Castillo continuously calls attention to her own historical moment, asking herself "how *The Squatter and the Don* speaks to the present" (xvii). In the midst of her introduction, such comments as "these are all logical questions for the student of democratic ideals today" (xiv) and "Currently, U.S. leaders are careful not to use the race card" (xiv) attempt to demonstrate the difference the distance of time has made. Elsewhere, her observations are less optimistic, such as her claim that the beliefs of manifest destiny are also "principles that, in 2004, the current leaders of the United States, projecting itself today as the model of democracy, have brandished as a means to an end" (xiv). Just as Sánchez and Pita use their introduction in part to make the case for Ruiz de Burton's inclusion in Chicana/o canons, Castillo more overtly emphasizes the significance of this text to contemporary audiences and to contemporary history, weaving in a critique of the Bush administration's foreign policy in the wake of 9/11. What we see in both introductions, then, is a working out of the politics at play in any recovery project. The Modern Library Classics edition of *The Squatter and the Don*, like the Arte Público / Recovering the U.S.-Hispanic Literary Heritage edition, is a text that is a product of contemporary concerns, recovered for its ability to speak to them from the past. Sánchez and Pita's concerns were for recovering a proto-Chicana text but also for engaging contemporary readers in making change happen: toward the end of their introduction, they argue that despite the novel's bleak conclusion, "there is also an implicit challenge in the novel, an interpellation of today's readers, as citizens, or as descendants of Californios, to resist oppression, to slay the monster who has not ceased to be victorious" (49). Castillo, meanwhile, recovers a text that foreshadows a contemporary moment in which "an indio today has no choice but to submit to the New World Order or be exterminated like a diseased mosquito as the Spanish feudal lord in California was in the nineteenth century. I do not declare these sad realities. I only observe them" (xviii). The vastly different outlooks of post-civil rights-era optimism that seeks out and celebrates evidence of resistance, subversion, and survival, on the one hand, and the post-9/11 cynicism that "only observes" the continued display of oppression and erasure, on the other, each shape *The Squatter and the Don* in their image.

In the closing lines of her introduction, Ana Castillo writes of *The Squatter and the Don*, "that it has resurfaced more than a century after its original publication is a testimony to its worthiness to be read" (xviii); this statement implies that the text simply resurfaced unaided, reappeared of its own accord, insisting on its own survival. But the fact is that the circumstances of its recovery are fairly dependent on the goals of the Recovering the U.S.-Hispanic Literary Heritage Project, which are founded on a desire to retrace the erased history of Mexican and Hispanic literature. Perhaps, then, Castillo does not give proper credit to those editors who did the work of resurfacing Ruiz de Burton's novel. Furthermore, the novel's "worthiness to be read" is continuously being reevaluated and reinvented by the editors and publishers who send it to press and the famous authors who introduce it. These editions teach readers how to read the novel, rescuing it from history for a variety of purposes. The recovery project itself conditions interpretation of the text, and both editions of *The Squatter and the Don* call attention to this fact.

Recovery and Translation in Margarita Cota-Cárdenas's *Puppet*

Border textuality manifests itself, shaping interpretation from the material margins of the text, adding to the text's instability even as editors attempt to conceal it, in recovery editions like Sánchez and Pita's or the Modern

Library Classics' *The Squatter and the Don* but also in much more recently lost and recovered texts. That a novel like Margarita Cota-Cárdenas's *Puppet* (1985) and others like it—for example, Aristeo Brito's *El diablo en Texas* (1976), presented in a recovered bilingual edition as *The Devil In Texas* in 1990—were published within the past thirty years and find themselves in need of recovery is perhaps telling in itself. While the 2000 edition of *Puppet* does not specifically label itself as part of a recovery project, much of the language of its allographic foreword by critic Tey Diana Rebolledo casts it as such. Rebolledo describes the book as both inaccessible to large groups of readers and an "underground classic" (xv) taught in Spanish-language classes, discussed at conferences and in critical essays, and widely anthologized. Thus, while the book appears to be well known in academic circles, until this recent edition "readership suffered" (xv) as the book struggled to stay in print. The parameters of an endeavor like that of the Recovering the U.S.-Hispanic Literary Heritage Project necessarily elide texts like these, but they also hide the fact that the problem of losing works of Latina/o literature more broadly, and of Chicana/o border literature more specifically, to lack of funds, distribution, and interest persists into the late twentieth and early twenty-first centuries. And in some ways, the problems appear the same: the question of what's worth recovering can't easily be answered by any chronological, encyclopedic, or national categorization system. Finally, the motivations for such recovery projects are likely similarly tied to preexisting interpretive models for Chicana/o and border literature: texts can be restored to print by scholars if and when they tell the stories that matter to those scholars. But the problem of language in the case of *Puppet* is likely the greatest challenge of all, as in this case it links the process of recovery, with its archaeological implications of merely dusting off and presenting, unchanged, a literary and/or historical artifact, with the fundamental linguistic changes to the text required of any translation. The choices made in the presentation of a bilingual recovery edition—"bilingual edition" meaning it contains versions of the text in both the source and target languages—ultimately highlights specific textual interpretations over others, and those choices guide us to ask questions about which audience the recovery project itself exists for, and why. Throughout, the paratext generates border textuality wherein both the narrative's protagonist and the material text of the recovery edition struggle to live between languages.

Puppet is not only narratively but also formally fragmented in a number of ways. Composed of fifteen vignettes, the narrative centers on the story of a professor named Petra/Pat Leyva who attempts to write the story of Puppet, a young Chicano wrongfully killed by police.[4] Petra/Pat's double name most clearly attests to the internal conflicts she experiences in her relationship with the Chicana/o community while caught between action and inaction regarding the police cover-up of Puppet's death, but the project itself is characterized by false starts as Petra debates whether and how to tell that story: "You start to write a new objective version of Puppet's life. You start but you don't finish because you don't know where. You could write about his death first since it was the most shocking . . . you throw out that idea because then it would be giving it a meaning that it didn't have, so sad and meaningless that end, making no sense" (2000, 37). Cota-Cárdenas's style is fragmented and disjointed, and Petra's narration shifts forward and backward in time, incorporating fantasy and classroom discussion, playing with language and even typography as it aims to represent the chaos of Petra's internal state as well as that of the Chicana/o community.

This material and narrative fragmentation emphasizes the novel's border status from a variety of vantage points: first and foremost, it's no accident that Pat's own introduction to the political ramifications of being between languages occurs on the physical, geographic, national border between the United States and Mexico: "my first words in English were back in Mexicali when my parents got to the border checkpoint . . . 'American-born'" (14). But because of the novel's narrative shifts between first and second person, its shifting between languages, its shifting between the living and the dead, Ana María Manzanas Calvo argues, "The border in *Puppet* is not restricted to a geographical location, or a declaration of citizenship, but is deterritorialized to mark the 'color line,' as Du Bois would put it, that crisscrosses the Americas" ("Mestiza" 54–55). A folding in of the material and the metaphor, "the fungibility of borders," as Mary Pat Brady would describe it, characterizes this and so many other Chicana/o border narratives.

And the story of publishing Puppet's story is fragmented as well: Carmen Salazar notes that "some fragments [of *Puppet*] were published earlier," including the poem "Lápida para Puppet," which appears in her 1975 collection *Noches*. Furthermore, Cota-Cárdenas explicitly emphasizes the material experience of writing *Puppet*: she explains, "Me puse a escribirla en serio en 1981 y no la pude terminar hasta 1985. Mi musa fue mi máquina antiquísima Underwood quien me ha inspirado sobre más de cuarenta años en mis creaciones. Le puse el nombre de *Mali* o Malinche" ("Conversando" 61). 'I got to serious writing in 1981 and I could not finish it until 1985. My muse was my ancient Underwood machine that has inspired me for more than forty years in my creations. I named it Mali or Malinche.' Naming her typewriter Malinche, historically (and, as feminists point out, problematically) remembered as translator to Hernán Cortés and simultaneous betrayer of the indigenous Mexican people, not only recovers the lost voice of Cota-Cárdenas's indigenous female heritage but grants agency specifically to the mechanical vehicle of print: Cota-Cárdenas's typewriter translates her ideas, her stories, her words, at the same time that it risks betraying her.

The lengthy writing process for such a short work that Cota-Cárdenas alludes to—the 2000 edition runs about 131 pages—only emphasizes the complexity of the story, while the story of its reception mirrors the difficulty of getting Puppet's own story heard. In both cases, language is a primary barrier. Tey Diana Rebolledo acknowledges, "Because it was written in Spanish and published by a small press, *Puppet* had its distribution problems from the start. With no wide distribution system for sending out books, readership suffered" (xiv–xv). Cota-Cárdenas published *Puppet* with Relámpago Books, a small press out of Austin, Texas, partly because, as Rebolledo notes, relatively few publishing houses would publish works in Spanish—neither Bilingual Press nor Arte Público would do it—leaving opportunities to publish in Spanish only to much smaller presses like Relámpago and El Norte Publications.

In spite of those diminished opportunities, Cota-Cárdenas pursued publication primarily in Spanish because she believed it was the language the story needed. Rebolledo notes in her foreword, "writing *Puppet* in Spanish was, at the time, a deliberate and, I might add, a political language choice for Cota-Cárdenas. When I asked her why she wrote *Puppet* in Spanish she said that for her there were many things she couldn't say in English, many things she would hear in her memory, the joke, the dicho (saying). It was also a resistance to what she felt was linguistic and cultural annihilation" (xiv). For Martín-Rodríguez, that cultural politics of language intersects with a politics of gender. In his reading of the 1985 edition of *Puppet*, he argues:

> Se trata de la creencia común de que las mujeres chicanas, "el soporte del hogar," son las encargadas de preservar y trasmitir el español, la lengua materna, y con él los valores tradicionales . . . en su elección del inglés las novelistas chicanas están, precisamente, rechazando ese papel tradicional que las relega al silencio público y las condena a la servidumbre casera. ("En la lengua" 68)
>
> One common belief is that Chicanas, "the support of the home," are the ones charged to preserve and to pass on Spanish, the mother tongue, and with it traditional values. In their choice of English, Chicana novelists are, indeed, rejecting that traditional role that relegates them to public silence and condemns them to servitude in the home.

Regarding Cota-Cárdenas, then, Martín-Rodríguez argues that her choice to publish mostly in Spanish is not regressive but instead a sign of an attempt to move both women and Spanish out of the home and into the public eye. He argues, "Ahora la mujer chicana tiene voz pública en español y no es una voz quebrada o disminuida, sino una voz plural y rica, autoconsciente" ("En la lengua" 71). "Now the Chicana woman has a public voice in Spanish, and it is not a broken or diminished voice, but a plural and rich, self-conscious voice."

But if Cota-Cárdenas's choice to publish a novella so heavily reliant on Spanish is meant to reflect the assertion of a rich, public, Spanish voice, how should/do we read the politics of a recovery project that included a translation into English? Does the translation force the Spanish back into the private realm, asserting that English will preserve the novel's public reputation? Had the past fifteen years dulled or even eased Cota-Cárdenas's fears about "linguistic and cultural annihilation," or does the 2000 bilingual edition represent the culmination of those fears? Perhaps the answer is not as dichotomous as those options would suggest. But whether indoors or "underground," as Rebolledo describes it, the Spanish of Cota-Cárdenas's 1985 edition at the very least appears to need the supplemental arm of English to see the light of day. Because the recovery edition of *Puppet* also turns the Spanish-language novella into a Spanish-English bilingual edition, we can surmise that fundamental to the desire to preserve, maintain, and reintroduce these border texts to readers is an assumption that longevity more likely rests with English. A bilingual edition ensures that the text can more easily migrate between Spanish- and English-language departments, courses, and syllabi; coupling the original version with a majority-English "translation" arguably only widens the scope of the audience and doesn't erase the significance of that original. But as the solution to the problem of keeping the book in print, as well as expanding its potential audience, the bilingual edition finds itself negotiating two audiences, caught between representations of Spanish and English.

Both textual and translation theorists have begun to explore the significance of how translations and bilingual editions a/effect interpretation. Luigi Reitani argues, for instance:

> In the bilingual edition, the translation loses its autonomy. Its aesthetic and cultural value is based rather on the correlation it manages to establish with the starting text. . . . Not only does the translation become functional to the reading of the "original," but the "original" may help give a better understanding of the choices made in the translation. The starting text therefore also loses its autonomy: in bilingual editions it "lives" by the translation. (591)

Thus the translated version of Cota-Cárdenas's narrative enables the continued existence of the otherwise marginalized Spanish-heavy text, but it "lives" only by virtue of necessity: the necessity of communicating with a monolingual English-speaking audience. Lance Hewson similarly argues that "the bilingual edition is a constant reminder of the differences between the source and target languages, and, paradoxically, of their apparent one-to-one equivalence . . . such an edition highlights the translation operation" (156). Materially speaking, the bilingual recovery edition of a border text like *Puppet* insists to readers that translation is a fundamental component of both the narrative itself and the persistence of that narrative in print. By including the original or "source" text, it aims not to erase it.

But what are the specific political ramifications of translating a predominantly Spanish-language text, especially one published in the United States, into English? And what are the politics of a recovery project that introduces translation into the process? Martín-Rodríguez addresses this issue specifically, arguing,

> If they are not to be accomplices to historical processes of marginalization, Chicano/a literary historians must strive for respecting the original language(s) in which the different works are written and consumed by linguistically proficient readerships. If translations into any other languages are needed, they should not take preference over the original; Chicano/a literary histories should not suppress Chicano/a multilingualism for the sake of an academic community of readers that is mostly monolingual. (*Life* 169)

It is worth pausing on his description of "Chicano/a multilingualism" here, because one further complicating factor in the recovery and translation of Cota-Cárdenas's work is the not-quite-entirely-Spanish language of her original text. In fact, that narrative blends a multitude of Englishes and Spanishes, as well as the mixture of the two, to depict the multilingual experience of border communities and individual characters. Even the characters themselves debate how best to tell the story, as when Memo, one of Pat's main sources of information, tells her, "The writer has to be witness, Petra. . . . La investigación? Ajá . . . Mira, look here, do you love your people, Petra? Bueno, then work on the story . . . or the relato . . . might be it'd turn out better in español." (28). That this last phrase appeared in the original version as "a lo mejor saldría mejor en español" (25) doubles over the question of how best—and in what language—to tell this story, both for the protagonist and the author.

For Petra and for Cota-Cárdenas, "translation" implies a "turning from" one language to another, but in a text that is bilingual to begin with, that turning becomes a gesture of reversing linguistic hierarchies. When applied to multilingual texts like *Puppet*, the original version's loss of autonomy is all the more complicated by the presence of the same exact words, sentences, and even paragraphs in both the original and the translation, as when the English strategically employed in the original text is carried over into the translation. Martín-Rodríguez's caution that critics and translators exhibit great care when presenting English-language versions of texts like *Puppet* can be tied both to the decisions made about how to translate and to those about how to materially present the process of those translations to a new readership. The material presentation of this new bilingual edition is in many (though not all) ways reflective of the narrative's own discourse on the relationship between Spanish and English, deconstructing the hierarchy even as it participates in it. After a brief discussion of the way language shapes characters and characters shape language within the narrative, I will turn to the bibliographic codes of the 2000 edition that shape readers' understanding of the relationships between the two languages, demonstrating how Petra's language problems become the readers' problems as well.

A preliminary distinction needs to be made between the understanding of identity espoused by Cota-Cárdenas's linguistic and formal choices and Petra/Pat's own understanding of her identity. Petra frequently finds herself caught between English and Spanish depending on her audience—as when she realizes that "when you pray, you pray in English" (107)—and her negotiations of linguistic borderlands are fraught with complications. Martín-Rodríguez helpfully draws the connection between Petra/Pat and the historical and legendary figure of Marina/Malinche, giving us an opportunity to reflect on the ways Petra exists between languages in a kind of reluctant embrace of mestiza consciousness ("En la lengua").[5] In some ways, Pat's experience of being between languages exemplifies Reitaini's claim about bilingual editions of texts: in the act of seemingly constant translation, Petra "loses [her] autonomy." As she loses herself in a sea of "I" and "you," English and Spanish, growing increasingly disoriented, she shouts at herself, "ARE YOU MALINCHE MALINCHI? WHO ARE YOU? AM I MALINCHI?" (105).

Desirée Martín goes further in interrogating the distinction between the politics of identity advanced by the form of the novel and that advanced by Petra herself. Martín describes Pat as in search of an "authentic" Chicana identity at the same time the narrative highlights the impossibility of constructing a stable identity. She claims, "While contradictory subjectivities and in-between spaces are explicitly rejected by most of the characters in the novel—especially by Pat herself—the language, form, and style of the novel explode strict boundaries at every turn, symbolically reflecting the transnational condition of Chicano/as in the United States" (92). The narrative bilingualism employed by Cota-Cárdenas throughout the novella, then, is often at odds with the characters' own desires for stability: it refuses to make a singular choice. Readers, in their attempt to follow Pat in her quest for a fixed identity, must navigate a narrative that espouses what Xochitl Estrada Shuru calls "a poetics of hysteria" (1) that refuses such fixity. For Shuru, the confusion, the difficulty, even the anxiety produced in the reading of this novel is part of the point: they give readers lived access to Petra's own experiences. Both Martín and Shuru implicitly or explicitly highlight the visceral experience of the reader as integral to interpretation of the text, acknowledging that the experience of abrupt shifts between languages as well as forms and styles compel readers to experience some sort of instability that mirrors Pat's own experience.

That visceral or material experience also changes depending on which edition and, furthermore, which language, the reader selects. The bilingual edition complicates matters of reader response most clearly in its liberal use of the word "translation." In fact, Martín does make note of the unique effects of *Puppet*'s translation, explaining, "While the bilingual edition of *Puppet* incorporates an English translation of the Spanish which remains interwoven throughout the text, both the version primarily written in Spanish and the English translation *are* and *are not* translations, since both are thoroughly multilingual" (93, Martín's emphasis). The original version of Cota-Cárdenas's 1985 novella incorporates vast amounts of English, while the 2000 translation also leaves phrases and sentences in Spanish. For example, compare the following excerpt, first as it appears in the original, then in translation:

> Eres tú, Pat? Pues no más quería 'ijirte que encontraron al papa del Puppet, con to'a y la familia. . . . Ya vienen en camino. . . . Al batito, lo vamos a interrar encima de la mamá . . . pues no podemos comprar otro plot. . . . Puppet and his uncle had carved out a cross for the grave . . . pues a Puppet se le hacía feo que su mamá no tuviera . . . cómo se llaman? *Lápida*, that's right. . . . Pues, qué se le va a hacer . . . pues, con la misma cruz. . . . A lo mejor el papá le va' querer comprar una piedra . . . *lápida* . . . dijieron que he took it real hard. . . . Veremos, verdad? (16)

> Is that you, Pat? Pues, just wanted to tell ya that they found Puppet's dad, con to'a y la familia . . . his family is on the way. . . . We're going to bury the kid on top of his mom. . . . We couldn't buy another plot. . . . Puppet and his uncle had carved out a cross for the grave. . . . Pues Puppet couldn't stand it that his mother didn't have . . . what are they called . . . *lápida*, a gravestone, that's right . . . well what can you do . . . well with the same cross or maybe his dad'll wanna buy him a stone . . . *lápida* . . . they said he took it really hard . . . we'll see, huh? (17)

In the original version, English phrases like "Puppet and his uncle had carved out a cross for the grave," "that's right," and "he took it real hard" stand out by virtue of linguistic difference, and all remain in the English translation, though they no longer stand out when surrounded by other English words. Interestingly, the grammar of the initial version "he took it real hard" is corrected in the English translation to "he took it really hard"; another small shift in language use with the potential to alter our understanding of the character. Phrases like "con to'a y la familia" and the words "Pues" and "lápida" are transferred from the original version into the translation as well, gaining new emphasis by virtue of linguistic difference. And while Martin convincingly argues that both versions are "thoroughly multilingual," it's worth pausing for a moment on the different way multilingualism operates in the predominantly English version.

First, as this passage indicates, the amount of Spanish transferred to the translation is less than the English present in the original: there are eighteen English words in the original version, eight Spanish words in the translation. Additionally, the translated version provides a direct translation of "lápida"—a gravestone—not present in the original. In both cases, the speaker is at a loss for words, doesn't know what it is called, but in each version the reason he doesn't know the word potentially changes. In the original version, when the speaker asks, "cómo se llaman?" 'what are they called?,' and presumably learns the response, "lápida," he appears not to know the proper term for a gravestone. When he follows up with "una piedra . . . lápida"—either corrected by someone else or correcting himself—he is simply replacing the somewhat more vague Spanish term with a more precise one. However, when the conversation is narrated predominantly in English, the focus of this search for words potentially becomes one of how to say the word in another language. Coupled with the direct translation of "lápida, a gravestone," the presentation of "a stone . . . lápida" emphasizes a translation from English to Spanish rather than a shift from imprecise to precise terminology. Does the speaker know the word he's reaching for in any language, or is it a matter of translation? Each version provides different opportunities for answering that question, and thus each presents a subtly different interaction between characters searching for the right words.

The shift to a heavier incorporation of English inevitably changes the interpretive possibilities of Cota-Cárdenas's text in at least two other ways: it potentially jolts readers out of an immersive reading experience, and it amplifies the narrative discourse of being caught on the borders between languages, materially registering Pat/Petra's linguistic frustrations. First, as Rebolledo claims in her introduction, "The English version has uniquely incorporated some Spanish so that the reader finds the meaning through an immediate translation or by context. Thus, the reader is able to access Chicano cultural reality" (xv), but because the Spanish is used comparatively sparingly and is nearly always immediately translated in the new version, the version of "Chicano reality" to which readers gain "access" is specifically one that is mediated by these accommodating measures. This immediate translation of Spanish words, as exemplified by "lápida, a gravestone" occurs frequently throughout the English version of the novella, in many cases somewhat jarringly. While the monolingual reader is gratified by instant translation, the visual layout of the Spanish words followed by the English translation may disrupt the continuity of a conversation or a line of prose. Such as pause is not necessarily a bad thing: for instance, when readers encounter written code-switching, Laura Callahan argues, "the visible contrast between the two codes . . . focuses the reader's attention on the language itself" (102). The presence of direct translations certainly accommodates readers in a way that the original version does not, altering the linguistic responsibility one must take in order to understand the text. But the experience of these manufactured pauses can also heighten readers' consciousness of the interplay of languages: they present an opportunity for monolingual readers to reflect on their own relationship(s) to language and the text, on whose needs are being served by the translation. This is perhaps what Rebolledo means when she claims, "It is the reader who gradually, in the act of reading, begins to fill in and complete the words and sentences, becoming in this way a participant in the dawning of consciousness" (xxi). Yet this is a process afforded only to the readers of the translated version, demonstrating a fundamental departure from the original.

Second, in the translated version, the English reader's encounter with Spanish words on the page, followed by their direct translation, might encourage or amplify their understanding of Pat's linguistic hybridity. Particularly when it appears in the midst of dialogue, the direct translation serves to create an understanding of the bilingual experience of language as one in which the speaker or listener is perpetually translating words into English. If it annoys the reader to read that way, he or she must then consider how annoying—or confusing, or liberating, or maddening—it must be to live that way. Consider the narrative impact of this attempt to accommodate the monolingual reader: "TU NUNCA QUISISTE OIR, YOU NEVER WANTED TO HEAR, TE ACUERDAS? YOU REMEMBER? pues something bad is going to happen to you, SOMETHING BAD, ya verás, you'll see" (2000, 7). For a bilingual person to offer an immediate translation when speaking aloud to someone else is fairly common, but this is a narrative moment in which Petra—or some part of Petra, at least—is talking to herself, perhaps not even aloud. Do we as readers believe she would actually repeat herself, to herself, in English? Reading Petra's voice as one that is now constantly translating, even to herself, serves to amplify or even change our understanding of Petra's fragmentation. She, like so many other Chicana/o protagonists, negotiates two languages, but here the internal dialogue goes one step further in making her a translator of herself. And only in the translated version does she translate her own words to herself—the original reads, "TU NUNCA QUISISTE OIR. TE ACUERDAS? TE ACUERDAS? Pues te va a pasar algo, ALGO MALO, ya verás, ya verás" (7, 1985)—giving readers a different and even potentially deeper insight into her fragmented identity. In the translated version, Petra's own language issues are displaced onto the reader in a way that is materially different from that in the text of the original: the assumption of a bilingual audience (as in the predominantly Spanish version) or the pause for accommodation (as in the mostly English version) gives readers very different experiences of the borders between languages.

These linguistic choices in both the original and the translation each shape in different ways our understanding of what Rebolledo calls the "cacophony of narration that even Homi Bhabha would be proud of" (xviii) in Cota-Cárdenas's narrative. That cacophony is only amplified by the variety of typographic choices introduced into the narrative: for example, the novella frequently includes phonetic spellings, such as "braun ais" for "brown eyes" (34) or the gently mocking rendering of Puppet's lisp via the word *cabrón* as "CABLÓN" (51), further adding to the linguistic diversity of the Chicana/o experience. As in some of the previous examples, the text also "utilize[es] different fonts and typefaces, such as bold letters, capitals, italics, and indented type throughout the novel . . . [and] emphasize[s] emotion, memory, fantasy, and reality" (Martin 94). These other typographical choices work more subtly on the reader, and their power is paradoxically rendered most visible when changes are introduced into the translated edition.

For example, the novella materially fragments itself in different ways depending on which version you read. While the novella is divided into fifteen chapters, both versions of the 2000 bilingual edition further subdivide the text with what might be called an illustrated intertitle that mimics an illustration of a cross that appears only once in the 1985 edition, at the conclusion of the text. In the recovery edition, a similar cross appears above each chapter's title—gesturing at least in part to the discussion of Puppet's gravestone—and also occasionally separates two sections of the text. Given the book's fragmented style, in which voices blend into and intersect with one another, giving readers trouble distinguishing who is speaking and to whom, the cross offers readers a respite from the voices. It acts as a pause and a break, signaling a separation between what comes before and after it, an opportunity to separate voices and events. In the English version of the 2000 edition, one such cross appears in chapter 5, between Memo's conversation with Petra about their friend Félix's being urged to testify against drug dealers and a moment in which Petra lapses into poetry, thinking about the lost innocence of Chicano children. However, no illustrated break is present in the original version. Instead readers face only a single paragraph break, with no pause, no illustrated visual cue, no reference to the cross for bilingual readers. The translation accommodates readers by giving them a break that the original doesn't supply; it also forcefully separates Petra and Félix's conversation from Petra's internal reflection process.

Likewise, the use of boldface is not consistent in the Spanish- and English-heavy versions of the 2000 edition, altering the reader's experience as well as the interpretive possibilities. While the translated version frequently employs boldface type, and typically matches the original version, this is not always the case. For example, in the translated version of chapter 11, entitled "Malinche's Discourse" (originally "Discurso de la Malinche"), Petra leads a class conversation that includes a discussion of whether or not feminism has had a negative effect on the Chicano Movement. When the class ends, she says to herself, "You leave class humming 'Some day my prince will come . . .' and you laugh and you laugh and you laugh Cinder-Malinsheesh (What did I say . . . ?)" (97). This is slightly different from the original version, which records this moment thus: "Sales de clase humming 'Some day my prince will come . . .' and you laugh and you laugh and you laugh **Cinder-Malinsheesh** (What did **I say?** . .)" (91). The English-heavy translation eliminates those bold emphases, but why? And to what effect? The changes may seem arbitrary, but the differences suggest that each version of Petra, in this case, is speaking with different inflections each time, generating multiple versions of this speech act. The boldface type draws attention to the invention of a portmanteau word that blends Cinderella and Malinche, insisting more emphatically on the way Pat draws together these two subjects of feminine (not to mention racialized) mythology, simultaneously blending cultural inheritances of misogyny. Furthermore, the erased emphasis on the words "I say" in the translated version simultaneously erases the notion that Petra is less concerned with "what" was said than with who said it. "What did I say? . . . ," emphasizing the final two words, could suggest pride in the coinage of a term that draws together these female figures with an exclamation of feminist exasperation like "sheesh." Even the placement of the ellipsis might change the meaning: perhaps it is only by comparison that "What did I say . . . ?" seems to dreamily trail off toward the interrogative, suggesting a slow-developing befuddlement, while "What did I say? . . ." first registers the question and then pauses in search of an answer. To make matters all the more complicated, the 1985 edition does not include an interrogative at all. Cota-Cárdenas's text showcases linguistic and typographic variety as a means of reflecting the fragmentation of Pat's inner state, as well as the turmoil besieging the Chicano community. By altering the boldface emphases here and in other places throughout the text, the typography multiplies that narrative experience of fragmentation by making every emphasized or de-emphasized word new. The words on the page, even when they are exactly the same, do not mean the same thing in each of these versions of *Puppet*: linguistically and materially, the text of the bilingual edition suggests that readers should see the original and the translation not as copies of one another but rather as distorted echoes.

Because the 2000 edition functions as a bilingual text, in which the Spanish-heavy original version and the English-heavy translation coexist, such differences might be more visible if the text presented the Spanish and its translation on facing pages. But the University of New Mexico Press edition of *Puppet* does not employ facing-page translation; rather, the two versions of the text are entirely separated, with one after another, in separate sections. In some ways, this presentation minimizes the potential for reader interaction with and comparison between versions: readers must flip between large sections of the book to compare lines, paragraphs, or chapters rather than having ready access on the opposite page. But, in a novel approach to the presentation format of the edition, each version has its own front cover: read one way, the book, employing a layout occasionally seen in bilingual children's books, begins with Rebolledo's introduction and the translated version of *Puppet*. If readers turn to the back cover and flip the book upside down, the novella now begins with the original version of *Puppet*.[6] The original and translated versions of the text meet in the middle, a nice materially constructed metaphor for the contact between languages and versions. This construction also gives the illusion that each version of the text is deserving of being the first in line to be read at the beginning, and that each version lives by the other. The format more forcefully places the choice of where to begin in the hands of the reader, drawing him or her into a reflection on border textuality.

But despite this attempt to eliminate the hierarchy of a text and its translation, the format and shape of the 2000 bilingual edition of *Puppet* constructs a hierarchy that accommodates and privileges the translated 2004 version even as it insists on the equal importance of the original 1985 version. A few key elements reinforce the sense that the translation is the primary text. First of all, the copyright page and Rebolledo's allographic "Foreword" precede only the translation, while the reproduction of the original version simply begins without any intermediary commentary. Placing the foreword before the English version is not only practical, as it describes why the translation was needed, but it also functionally chooses the English version as the beginning of the text in a way that the cover pages refuse to do. The cover pages themselves are not entirely identical, either: the cover of the translated version has the words "Introduction by Tey Diana Rebolledo" vertically down the right-hand side of the page, where it meets with the words "Translated by Barbara D. Riess and Trino Sandoval," which are typed across the bottom of the page. While the reproduction of the original version's cover appears to contain the same layout and portrait of a graffiti-covered wall, Rebolledo's name is replaced with "Photografia por Delilah Montoya / Diseñado por Linda Mae Tratechaud" 'Photography by Delilah Montoya / Designed by Linda Mae Tratechaud.' Instead of translators' names across the bottom, the following is provided: "University of New Mexico Press / 1–800–249–7737 / www.unmpress.com." Both the inclusion of references to the designer and photographer, which are typically relegated to the back cover (in miniscule font) and the contact information of the publisher, help define the original version as the "end" of the book. Furthermore, the reproduction of the original version's "cover" contains the bar code and ISBN number, another staple of the back of a paperback. These minor details give weight to the translated version as the "real" beginning of the book. The spine of the paperback contains the words "Puppet" at the top and bottom, printed frontward and backward so that the title can be read at the top of each side of the book. However, in the middle, "Cota-Cárdenas" is printed only once, in the same direction as the "Puppet" of the translated version.

In addition, while the cover image—a photograph by Delilah Montoya—initially appears to be replicated on each title page, a closer look reveals that the photograph is actually a wide panoramic shot that stretches over one cover, across the spine, and over the other cover. The gray-scale graffiti covering a wall draws the two versions of the text together, joined by an image that is slightly different on each cover. Of course, because the image is wrapped around the book, it is also necessarily upside-down on one side: the side containing the original version. Anyone quickly glancing at the cover would miss this detail; most of the graffiti images on this cover are shapes, and the upside-down letters look like hieroglyphics or nonsense. But the very top of that side's cover image reveals that it shows the bottom of the wall, with a patch of weeds and grass leading up to it. The image on this cover is upside-down, particularly stark evidence of Reitani's argument that "the starting text . . . also loses its autonomy: in bilingual editions it 'lives' by the translation" (591). In many ways, the design choices seek to eliminate the presumed linguistic hierarchy of the original (Spanish) and translated (English) versions, but even those choices reinforce traces of that hierarchy: someone—whether it be the editor, publisher, or reader—had to choose where to begin. The original version now not only comes second in this bilingual edition but it is also upside-down, illegible to readers moving front to back.

One other change is made across the two different covers: the subtitle of the text, listed in 1985 as "A Chicano Novella," is also the subtitle listed on the cover and the opening pages of the 2000 translation. Cota-Cárdenas explains that she discussed the subtitle with Juan Rodríguez, founder of Relámpago Books, and that they agreed that the subtitle conveyed dual meanings: "It works as 'nov-ella,' a short feminist novel, and a 'novella'" (Cota-Cárdenas, "Subtitles"). However, this bilingual edition of the text has a slight change: the subtitle on both the cover and the opening page preceding the original text has been changed to "Una Novella Chicana." As a result, the original text bears a translated subtitle, while the translated text bears the original subtitle. It is indeed a subtle change from "A" to "Una," coupled with a slight reordering of adjectives, one that essentially doesn't change the meaning of the subtitle. But the move to translate the subtitle from its original English into Spanish—and, peculiarly, to do it only on the side that precedes the original text—ultimately makes that version as it appears in the 2000 bilingual edition even more reliant on Spanish than it actually was in 1985. The nature of the 2000 recovery text as a bilingual edition, built on the underlying assumption that one version is in Spanish and the other is in English, undercuts the bilingual nature of the original 1985 edition by erasing its English-language subtitle. As a likely unintended result, Spanish is more firmly planted on one side, English on another.

Cota-Cárdenas herself is aware of the impact of the packaging of her work on interpretation (and, of course, sales). In an interview with Cecilia Yocupicio Valenzuela, she notes that the changes between her 1985 text and the 2000 version were few:

> Con el original de 1985, ningún cambio excepto tal vez alguna correccíon tipográfica. En la edición bilingüe de 2000, cambios tal vez de presentación solamente. Vimos que al libro lo cubrieron con una tela de plástico, se supone que para proteger la cubierta. Así, el lector/comprador en una librería (no las bibliotecas que pedían el libro por ya tener publicidad o pedido oficial de antemano), no tenía la oportunidad de abrir el libro para saber de qué se trataba. Pero cambios al relato, no, no lo cambiaría nada. Vino de mi pura alma; y no dije alma pura. ("Conversando" 61)

> With the original in 1985, there was not one change except perhaps some typographic corrections. In the 2000 bilingual edition, there were only changes of presentation. We saw that they covered the book with plastic, supposedly to protect the cover. So the reader/buyer in a bookstore (not the libraries that requested the book before it was published or officially ordered it beforehand) did not have the opportunity to open the book to know what it was about. But changes to the story, no, I wouldn't change anything. It came purely from my soul; and I didn't say my pure soul.

Cota-Cárdenas easily recognizes that the shrinkwrap initially covering the 2000 bilingual edition might dissuade readers from buying a book they couldn't browse through; the presentation of the novella has a similar impact on how readers will interact with the novel. While the plastic cover that prevents browsing is a useful metaphor for all of the other paratextual elements that can interrupt a reader's engagement with Cota-Cárdenas's text, it should be noted that the bilingual edition's presentation of the two versions of the text and its attempts to dispose of the hierarchy of such editions are not simply negative effects that obscure the real or more important version of the text. Instead this bilingual edition usefully reflects the complexities of bilingualism, translation, and the literary market in a way that makes Petra's own navigation of language even more material to readers. It exemplifies border textuality by bringing readers into contact with the subject matter of the narrative—the borderlands experience of bilingual identity—through the visceral experience of the borderlands of the bilingual material text. For readers, the material text supplies another inhabitable border zone from which to question the relationship between a text and its translation, the inseparability of the Spanish and

English languages into discrete versions. Examining the material text for evidence of its social life, we can assess the changes this "American-born" novella had to undergo in order to have a better chance of being read as American literature.

Conclusion

The recovery of texts like *The Squatter and the Don* and *Puppet* is a major accomplishment for the future of Chicana/o, Mexican American, and border literature. Giving wider audiences access to these novels, editors and translators as well as those selected to introduce the text work in concert to restore what was once lost, whether hundreds of years or merely decades ago. But the choice of what to recover, and how to go about doing so, has lasting effects on the social lives of those texts. Those effects are visible in the material evidence of those recovery texts and the editions that have followed them. Often editors and translators try to minimize the visibility of their choices, pretending to get out of the way of the text, merely setting the contextual stage of the text's initial production and reception. At the same time, those introductory justifications, as well as the paratextual and editorial choices made in the text, can't help but shape the text into a new version. These new versions reflect the current historical moment and its politics as much as those of the initial historical moments of the texts. Jerome McGann makes an argument that resonates with some of the editorial choices made by Sánchez and Pita. For instance:

> The critical edition embodies a practical goal which can be (within limits) accomplished, but it equally embodies an illusion about its own historicity (or lack thereof). According to this view of itself, the critical text is reproduced with a minimum of interference by contemporary concerns on the one hand, and a maximum of attention to the historically removed materials on the other. The rules for producing critical editions place such emphasis on these matters that editors cannot be encouraged to reflect upon the contemporary motivating factors which operate in their work. (*Critique* 94)

Sánchez and Pita's own critics were quick to point out those "contemporary motivating factors," highlighting the way a perceived need to justify Ruiz de Burton to the Chicana/o canon shaped their interpretation. In turn, that interpretation shapes new readers' interpretation of the novel by preceding it. That Sánchez and Pita's edition, as well as the Modern Library Classics edition, comes under scrutiny here is not meant to condemn their editorial choices; the goal is rather to emphasize how any paratextual choice has a shaping effect on the text. These particular editions reveal their own instability, exemplifying border textuality even as their editors attempt to conceal it.

The same is true for the more recent recovery projects that add the further complicating factor of translation. Margarita Cota-Cárdenas and her translators have produced completely new versions of her novella that even more emphatically and materially demonstrate the effects of multiple languages on border identity and texts. The multiple versions of *Puppet* also exemplify the impossibility of full translation, instead dramatizing both the benefits and the dangers of narrative and linguistic multiplicity for the characters who inhabit the Los Angeles of the narrative and for the texts through which we meet them. Examining choices of paratextual presentation, we can begin to locate the politics at stake in these recovery projects, the hierarchies of language more or less concealed, the sacrifices required for survival. Bilingual editions like Cota-Cárdenas's reach a wider audience of readers, and in the act of recovery are fundamentally changed. The evidence of these changes is apparent from the margins and borders of recovery texts. The cover pages, introductions, footnotes, and other critical apparatus speak to readers of the complicated social life of the text that these versions now participate in. Writing of editors in a way that should also speak to translators, recovery scholars, critics, and readers, Gary Taylor claims, "All such intermediaries pit transmission against transience; they mediate between the past and the future, the present and the distant, but attempt to do so in ways that render invisible their own acts of mediation and remediation" (96–97). And in their contradictions, their errors, erasures, and evasions, of which we find evidence in the material margins of texts, they reflect border textuality: they give readers a visual and material reminder of the instability of border politics, identity, and history.

5

In the Margins

Readers Writing on *The House on Mango Street*

> Marginality as site of resistance.
> Enter that space. Let us meet there.
> Enter that space.
> —bell hooks, "Choosing the Margin as a Space of Radical Openness"

Since its publication in 1984 by Arte Público Press, Sandra Cisneros's *The House on Mango Street* has climbed the ladders of critical and popular success, and it is now frequently taught across elementary, high school, and college levels. Most recently reissued in a twenty-fifth anniversary edition from Vintage Contemporaries, a division of Random House, Cisneros's story cycle has become one of the most canonical examples of Chicana writing, engaging readers across decades. In her introduction to the 1994 Knopf edition of *Mango Street*, Cisneros reflects on the book's popularity, writing, "The raggedy state of my books that some readers and educators hand me to sign is the best compliment of all" (xix). "Raggedy" books offer material evidence of reading—warped or dog-eared pages, torn covers, or notes in the margins—indications that readers have engaged with her work in an active way. The evidence of annotators across the country demonstrates that readers put *Mango Street* to a wide range of uses in their attempts to comprehend, interpret, and interact with it. This evidence, coupled with Cisneros's openness to such readerly (mis)handling of her work, offers an opportunity to consider more broadly the ways *Mango Street* constructs its material borders as a space of communication and identification.

And borders are fundamental to an understanding of Cisneros's most famous work, though there is some debate as to whether we might, in fact, call it border literature. Critics often disagree about categorizing *Mango Street* as such, since it is set not on the U.S.-Mexico border but in the Chicago Puerto Rican neighborhood of Humboldt Park.[1] But Cisneros herself argues that proximity to the border is not a condition of border identity: "In Texas, they are physically closer to the border, but emotionally they're very far away. We in Chicago were physically farther, but emotionally closer" (Interview 295–296). The narration of the protagonist, Esperanza, also hints at the haunting presence of border geography even at a distance. The border looms in vignettes such as "Geraldo No Last Name," in which the first-person narration drops away almost entirely to reveal hints of the story of Geraldo, "another *brazer* who didn't speak English. Another wetback" (66). Geraldo may be at a far remove from the border, but Cisneros, in very few words, insists on the importance of place. Here she outlines the urban geography of border existence: "They never saw the kitchenettes. They never knew about the two-room flats and sleeping rooms he rented, the weekly money orders sent home, the currency exchange" (66). The repeated insistence on Geraldo's invisibility, unknowability, the absolute loneliness of an unmourned death, wrenches the politics of undocumented immigration and the national border farther and farther north.

Attentiveness to space and place, particularly in studies of *Mango Street*, is useful not only when thinking about the national border but also when considering the impact of the material, textual borders on readers and writers. We can best examine that impact, and remain attentive to the politics of space and place, by exploring readerly marginalia. This is because the physical borders of the text function as significant contact zones: they narrow the space between authors and readers, and they are spaces where the malleability of narrative, power, and identity can be rendered visible.

This is certainly the case with Cisneros, who has marked up a copy or two of *Mango Street* herself. Far from "worthless," as Charles van Dyke described some marginalia in *Books and How to Use Them: Some Hints to Readers and Students* in 1883, Cisneros's minor marginalia entries in the pages of the Arte

Público first edition housed at the University of California, Santa Barbara, act as faint but significant clues to the complicated publishing history of *Mango Street*, which has been virtually erased in the wake of its later and continued success. One such note appears on the final page of the book, where Esperanza concludes her narrative by writing of the people on Mango Street, "They will not know I have gone away to come back. For the ones I left behind. For the ones who cannot get out" (102). As Ellen McCracken describes it, "Underlining the entire last line of the book with the 'delete' editing sign and her initials, [Cisneros] wrote: 'interpolations by ed. Nick Kanellos without my permission! Sandra Cisneros'" ("From Chapbooks to *Chica Lit*" 20). Beginning with Arte Público's revised second edition in 1988 and going forward into the Random House editions, the final sentence instead reads, "For the ones who cannot out" (110). Because the last line of the 1984 edition includes only the words "get out," Cisneros's marginalia clearly suggests that she did not prefer the first edition's ending, and thus we can read the ending of subsequent editions and printings, which eliminate the word "get," not as an error but as an intention, a desire to correct the "overcorrection" (de Valdés 15).

Regardless of that intention, both versions of the final line continue to circulate. And though there are admittedly fewer copies of the version that includes the word "get," the competing closing lines give some readers pause. Scholars and educators who have not been privy to these marginal notes, for example, have made up their own minds about which version is the correct one using various other kinds of evidence: Catrióna Rueda Esquibel notes that although the second version could be seen as "a printing error . . . [she] prefer[s] to believe that Cisneros intentionally changed the line" (199–200n12), while educational resources for *Mango Street*, like the Jane Schaffer Writing Program, note in their overview of lesson plans for the text, "We have noticed what we think is a misprint in the Vintage edition, and we have corrected it wherever we included it. . . . Several articles have supplied the word 'get' that we believe was meant to be included" ("House"). Each version has different interpretive effects, and, as Marci McMahon suggests, the elimination of the word "get" changes the final line in significant ways. McMahon writes, "Cisneros's revised edition complicates agency and conveys . . . that the people in Mango Street are indeed 'trapped' and that they 'cannot out' on their own" (202n25). In the closing narrative moment, in which Esperanza most firmly develops a confident, writerly voice, the multiple versions of the last line testify to both narrative and material instability.

In addition to multiplying narrative meanings, the dual final line and that seemingly minor marginal note appended by Cisneros also offer a glimpse of the occasionally difficult relationship between Cisneros and her editor and publisher, Kanellos: not only does Cisneros take the time to mark her book with additional notes of "Interpolations here & elsewhere without my permission" (quoted in McCracken, "From Chapbooks" 20) alongside another apparent proofreading error, but she has also accused Kanellos of "assum[ing] a paternalistic attitude concerning his writers and ask[ing] us to allow him to make decisions regarding our work" (quoted in Kolker). To be fair, Cisneros also acknowledged a debt to Arte Público "for nurturing my work for years" (quoted in Kolker) as she traveled and developed *Mango Street* from an Iowa Writers Workshop exercise into the completed series of vignettes over the next several years, missing the first deadline and barely making the second (Cisneros, "Do You Know Me?" 79). But in 1987, when an opportunity arrived in the form of a sizeable advance contract for her next collection, *Woman Hollering Creek and Other Stories*, courtesy of her new agent, Susan Bergholz, and Random House, Cisneros jumped, becoming arguably the best-known and most highly paid Chicana writer in the United States in the process. In her attempt to take *Mango Street* with her, as the new contract included the rights to it, difficulties ensued in the form of "hard feelings and legal disputes" (McCracken, "From Chapbooks" 20). Kanellos and Arte Público were less than inclined to give away the rights to a book that had the potential to become so influential; in the end, Kanellos regretfully notes, "When challenged by the author's agent, we lost *The House on Mango Street* without a fight from the University [of Houston], university counsel refusing to defend the pro-bono contract" ("Chavez v Arte Publico"). Though the dispute was resolved in favor of Cisneros's new publisher, in the years leading up to and in the midst of these "difficult negotiations with Arte Público," readers and scholars found the book "difficult to obtain"(McCracken, "Sandra Cisneros" 232).

Most discussions of *Mango Street*'s rise to mainstream prominence elide or are unaware of this part of its trajectory: Manuel Martín-Rodríguez has to remind readers that as "recently as 1989" (*Life* 129), five years after its initial publication by Arte Público Press, *Mango Street* was nearly invisible. At the time McCracken called the book "difficult to find in most libraries and bookstores... well known among Chicano critics and scholars, but virtually unheard of in larger academic and critical circles" (quoted in Martín-Rodríguez, *Life* 129). Cisneros's attempts to correct the copy, as well as to break her existing contract, all complicate the simpler success story in which no one, neither publisher nor author, not to mention readers—as readers frequently express strong feelings when the ending of a book is changed—feels compromised by the way that success was achieved. To that end, McCracken notes with nearly equal sympathy for the writer and her former publisher, "The press had been a loving although perhaps overbearing midwife for the birth of her fiction, but needed to let her move on, just as we release our children when they no longer need our everyday nurturing, hard as this might be" ("From Chapbooks" 20). With the 1991 republication through Random House, Cisneros and *Mango Street* began their journey to the center of mainstream popular and educational reading circles. No longer a neglected gem, *Mango Street* is now introduced to readers as an unqualified success, a worthy read. While it enjoys continued popularity on school syllabi and in book clubs, including the city-wide One Book, One Chicago program in the spring of 2009, the story of how the book went from difficult to find to mainstream darling is written at least in part into the margins of the text itself: in this case, in Cisneros's own hand. Cisneros's marginalia are but one small reminder of the complexity of the publishing process.

If the margins of a border text like *Mango Street* can offer insight into Cisneros's relationship to the publishing process, it likewise grants access to her relationship to her readers, as well as readers' relationship to Cisneros. Just as Cisneros felt compelled to write in her own book, to assert a voice she felt had been misrepresented or, at the very least, misrecorded, readers take to the edges, responding, commenting, and questioning, and the resulting marginal notes contain insights into how and why her book is being read. The borders between text and not-text, like the international boundary line, are sites of both restriction and freedom, and some readers respond to the problem of space and place as depicted in Cisneros's text by manipulating the margins for themselves. For Esperanza, whose story revolves around the desire for a home, "a house quiet as snow, a space for myself to go, clean as paper before the poem" (108), and for readers who seek to identify with Esperanza and her story, the clean white space of the margins offers an opportunity to write back.

Just what is it about *Mango Street* that encourages readers to speak in and from the margins? Certainly this text is merely one of many that bear the marks of marginal annotation, and what might be said about marginalia in this text could be said about those in any number of texts. But because this book is actively engaged in telling the story of a young woman learning to speak from the margins—as a woman, as a Mexican American, as a representative of an urban lower-class neighborhood—its own material margins take on significant meaning for those who seek to engage with Cisneros's text. Reading the marginalia of *Mango Street* shows us how we construct and reconstruct this text as a space for engagement with an author, specifically a Chicana author, in order to negotiate identity. But its material uses as a border text are also due to the shaping forces of other interests. Cisneros's text is uniquely positioned to help us understand the way readers, publishers, educators, and scholars collaborate with authors in the production of texts that materially gesture toward the significance of borders. Publishers and book designers construct blank space that invites response. Teachers create contexts in which the book can frequently be framed as "accessible" or "representative," shaping the institutional uses to which it is put and even supplying the fodder for marginal notes themselves. And readers themselves make use of the book in unexpected ways, multiplying interpretations as they send their books back out into the world, marginalia and all. The narrative of *Mango Street* encourages us to reflect on liminal spaces—both metaphorical and material—and readers themselves continue to construct this book as a border text, as a space for readers to engage with an author and for identities to be negotiated, for better or for worse.

The collaborative production of Cisneros's text from the margins via the insertion of marginalia should also call attention to the problematic power differentials at stake: in this case, the textual margins function as sites of both potential oppression and resistance. Just as the margins reveal power struggles between author, editor, and publisher, when readers actively collapse the distance between author and reader in their responses to *Mango Street*, they do so in the pages of a text that is fundamentally concerned with questions of ethnic and gender identity, of power and powerlessness. The opportunity for readers to recolonize the pages of a Chicana text, to co-opt the marginalized voice, is a very real and problematic effect of producing such a border-conscious text. But, as bell hooks writes of those who attempt to co-opt minority discourse, the margins—figurative and literal—constitute the space where forces of dominance *and* resistance meet and where the potential for power is greatest and yet most dangerous as a space of near-erasure (152). As a result, the narrative registers the agency and danger of the borders between author, character, and reader: at times Esperanza's narrative opens up to readers, asking them to participate. And at others it resists that recolonizing practice, begging silence of those same readers. *Mango Street* models and makes possible the act of speaking from the margins, which generates potentially productive *and* destructive results.

This chapter maps some of those productive and destructive results, demonstrating both how the text encourages marginalia and what that marginalia show with evidence from fifteen marked copies of the text, as well as how the text concludes by insisting on—though not always achieving—readerly silence. *Mango Street* both invites and resists written engagement. The invitation to participate is offered via form: many of the choices of narrative structure and content of Cisneros and her editors and publishers encourage a written reader response. But the withholding, or the request for readerly silence, is modeled by Esperanza and demanded by the unfolding events of the narrative's final vignettes. *Mango Street* invites and rejects reader participation, expressing an uncomfortable embrace of readers in the material border spaces of the text. Such an embrace recognizes the democratizing potential of erasing the boundaries between author(ity) and reader but resists the silencing of Esperanza's developing voice by readers who might write over her.

In the more narrow and detailed analysis that follows, fifteen marked copies of *Mango Street*—from here on referred to by the city from which they were sold—were bought for examination through the used book marketplace on Amazon.com with an eye toward a large geographic range.[2] Such an argument follows that of Alison Wiggins, who has explored Renaissance responses to Chaucer, saying, "To call up each individual copy reinforces the point . . . that every printed book is unique" (7). While this study draws on an admittedly small sampling of marked copies of *Mango Street*—a book whose copies number in the millions—it also suggests that each differently marked copy is worthy of attention for the changes it potentially introduces to the narrative. This small-scale study demonstrates the worthiness of each copy for scrutiny, representing only the beginning of a much larger discussion of the shaping effects of the kinds of marginalia readers feel compelled to inscribe throughout their reading experience. Collecting these copies and cataloguing the marginalia within them opens a doorway into understanding how we collaborate in the creation of this text's meanings, a foundation from which further research into readers' annotative responses can be launched.

Of course, as Heather Jackson notes, "Marginalia of all periods would appear to be potentially a goldmine for scholars. And so they are, but they are a contested goldmine" (6). Contestation comes in the form of concern that readers' marks are unintelligible, unscholarly, and unreliable. While the annotations of a Samuel Taylor Coleridge or a David Foster Wallace or a J. K. Rowling—whose annotated first edition of *Harry Potter and the Philosopher's Stone* sold in 2013 for the equivalent of $228,000—seem more clearly valuable, it is comparatively hard to discern the value of marks by students and other readers, especially when the likelihood of another reader's encountering those notes is minimal. Add in the anonymity and near-untraceability of these particular annotations and we might begin to wonder whether such marks are not a kind of fool's gold. If we don't know who's sending the messages—their names, their backgrounds (gender, racial, religious, economic, and so forth)—and we don't know who, if anyone, is reading the messages in these marginal notes, how much can they really tell us about readers, or Cisneros's text, or anything at all?

In response to these concerns, Stephen Frosh and Lisa Baraitser argue, "The things that can be found in the margins may not be grand, but this could be their appeal . . . they bring down to a human scale the over-passionate gestures of intellectual (and other) saviors; they are sideways-on, ironic, fragmentary and silly. They are often irritating and niggling, but they do at least bring one down with a bump" (70). Though these annotations may not initially or superficially register as interpretations worth exploring, especially given their limited audience, the marginalia in *Mango Street* suggest imperfect readerships engaged in the process—rather than the scholarly result—of meaning-making. Engaging in a study of that process gives us a sense of the meanings that are more and less easily afforded by the text and its contexts, as well as insight into how readers make the leap from passive to active engagement. We can also benefit from an attempt at understanding the power at stake on the material edges of the page, especially when the narrative itself offers the perspective of a marginalized voice like Esperanza's. If Cisneros's annotators are nameless, what better place to explore their annotations than a narrative in which Esperanza ruminates on the power and powerlessness of her own name? If the annotations are merely condensed forms of someone else's—perhaps a teacher's—words, then what more appropriate space to register their impact than in a narrative in which Esperanza learns to value her own voice among the voices of many others? Examining these readers' notes may not tell us about the specific identities of the readers themselves, but they can and do offer an opportunity to register a diversity of reading and interpretive experiences including and beyond the scholarly. The goal in reading such marginalia, particularly because they might not be read by anyone else, is to "deal judiciously, sensitively, and sympathetically with the anonymous and the oblique" (Wiggins 14).

In what ways, then, do these copies of the text suggest that it encourages marginalia? This chapter provides an overview of its material and narrative structure, showing how both the publishers' and the author's decisions about the shape of the text encourage response. It then explores the educational contexts, which frequently encourage very specific kinds of annotation, into which *Mango Street* has been placed. This section interrogates the problematic contextualizations of the text as either literarily "accessible," which leads to oversimplification, or "representative," which leads to essentialism, and it also addresses the challenge of marginalia as note-taking rather than as spontaneous, creative production. The analysis then turns to the narrative content, demonstrating the ways Cisneros's narrative about a young Chicana writing herself into existence both encourages readers to write themselves into existence and requests that such writing not overpower her own. The subject matter also encourages readers to make border crossings of their own as they grapple with the (im)possibility of empathizing with Esperanza. It concludes with a reflection on the way readers multiply the meanings of the text, considering how a digital environment might shape the possibilities for sharing annotations. The result is a recognition that every actor, from author to publisher to critic to teacher to reader, participates in the continuous production of this border text. The unstable nature of that process, which suggests the permanent incompleteness of the text and the constant struggle over narrative meaning, marks the text as "radically open" to competing voices, even when those voices threaten to overpower the burgeoning female Chicana voice. That radical openness is made material in readers' annotations, and it mirrors the narrative instability of border identity, making *Mango Street* a prime example of border textuality.

Material and Narrative Encouragements of Marginalia

The very structure of *Mango Street*—the linked vignettes that comprise the narrative—invites readers to inhabit the material textual borderlands. Michelle Tokarczyk, for example, argues that the book's short story structure is appealing to working-class readers with little time for reading. Beyond recognizing and accommodating readerly attention spans and schedules, the short stories and vignettes also invite readers' response by virtue of the abundance of white space surrounding them. Even the Troy annotator notices this, taking the time to write, "usage of white space" twice in the margins. The 1984 edition, as well as the 1991, 1994, and 2009 Vintage editions from Random House, contain swaths of blank space: half and sometimes whole pages on which nothing is printed. While the Arte Público editions have more space between the chapter title and the text of the chapter, the Vintage editions allow the space to lead the page, placing some chapter titles, immediately followed by the text, as far as two-thirds of the way down the page. The effect in either press's editions, though, is to visibly and materially separate each chapter from the next, adding to the sense that each is self-contained but also providing ample room for readers' response and reflection. Stories that could fit on one page, such as "Hairs," "Papa Who Wakes Up Tired in the Dark," "Four Skinny Trees," and many others have incredibly large upper margins (as well as titles in fairly large fonts) in the Vintage editions, causing the text to spill onto the next page. Printing the short story/vignette on the page in such a manner allows generous space for readers to use as they see fit.

The readers' pencil comments fill the blank spaces above the beginnings of the vignettes, and the spaces below the ends, summarizing the plot and attempting to get a hold on the characters: their race, class, ethnicity. Readers in nearly every marked copy examined performed the same sort of manipulation of blank space: afforded the opportunity to elaborate, they expanded their comments across the page beyond the tentative question mark or two-word comment. The annotator of the Sherman Oaks copy, in particular, filled the entire space of nearly every chapter, sometimes summarizing the brief text with nearly as many words as the original. The brevity of the reading material, combined with the white space, allows readers' thoughts to occupy a large portion of the page. The ample white space, like "the page before the poem" of *Mango Street*, looks as shown in the Saginaw copy (see figs. 4 and 5).

The note above the title reads, "it seems like they live in a poor run-down Mexican/black neighborhood. She is just describing everyone that lives around her. Like a neighborhood that if you didn't know anything about, would be scary, like someone would jump you or something, but that's not really how it is (I don't think)." And beneath the end of the printed text on page 25 is written: "I think she is deprived of a lot of things because things like the bike and

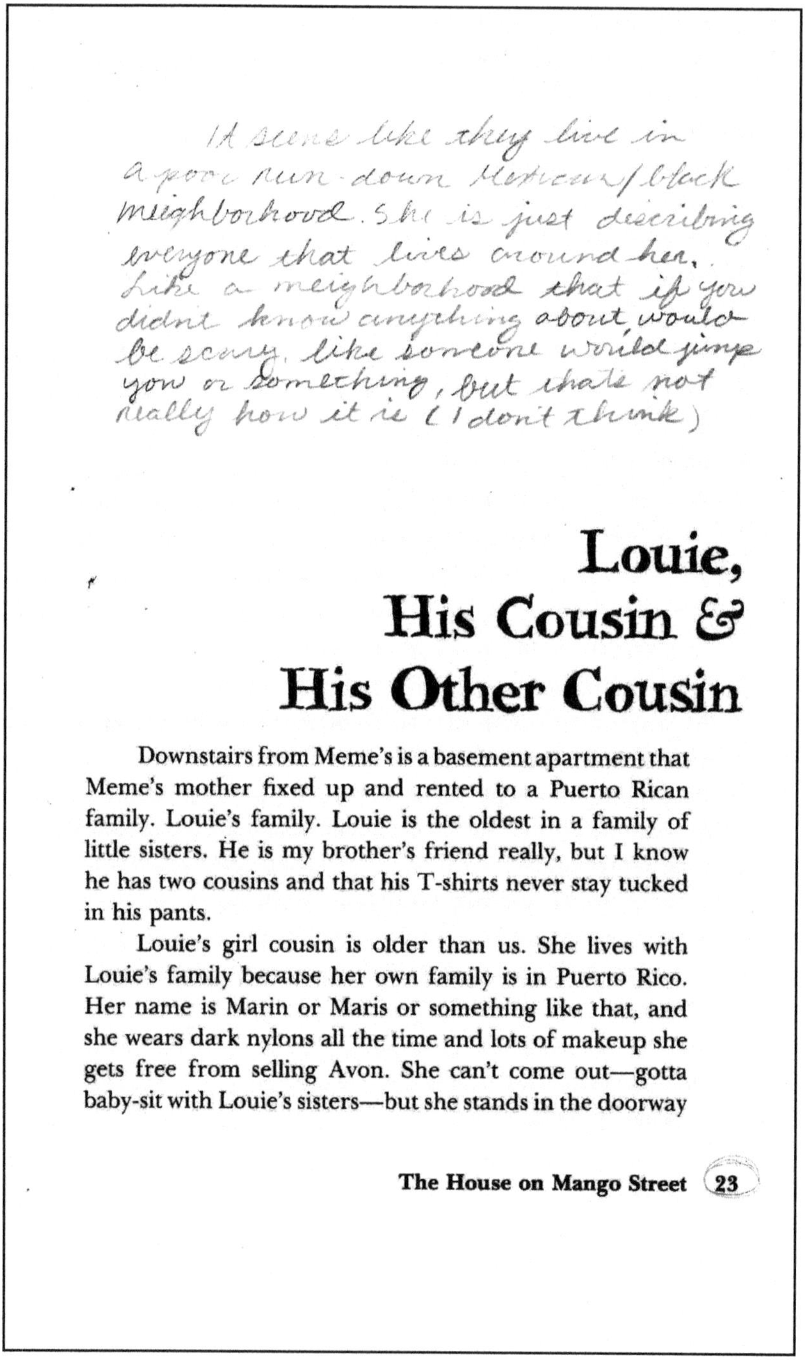

It seems like they live in a poor run-down Mexican/black neighborhood. She is just describing everyone that lives around her. Like a neighborhood that if you didnt know anything about would be scary. like someone would jump you or something, but thats not really how it is (I dont think)

Louie, His Cousin & His Other Cousin

Downstairs from Meme's is a basement apartment that Meme's mother fixed up and rented to a Puerto Rican family. Louie's family. Louie is the oldest in a family of little sisters. He is my brother's friend really, but I know he has two cousins and that his T-shirts never stay tucked in his pants.

Louie's girl cousin is older than us. She lives with Louie's family because her own family is in Puerto Rico. Her name is Marin or Maris or something like that, and she wears dark nylons all the time and lots of makeup she gets free from selling Avon. She can't come out—gotta baby-sit with Louie's sisters—but she stands in the doorway

The House on Mango Street 23

FIGURE 4 Marginalia in the Saginaw copy of *The House on Mango Street*.

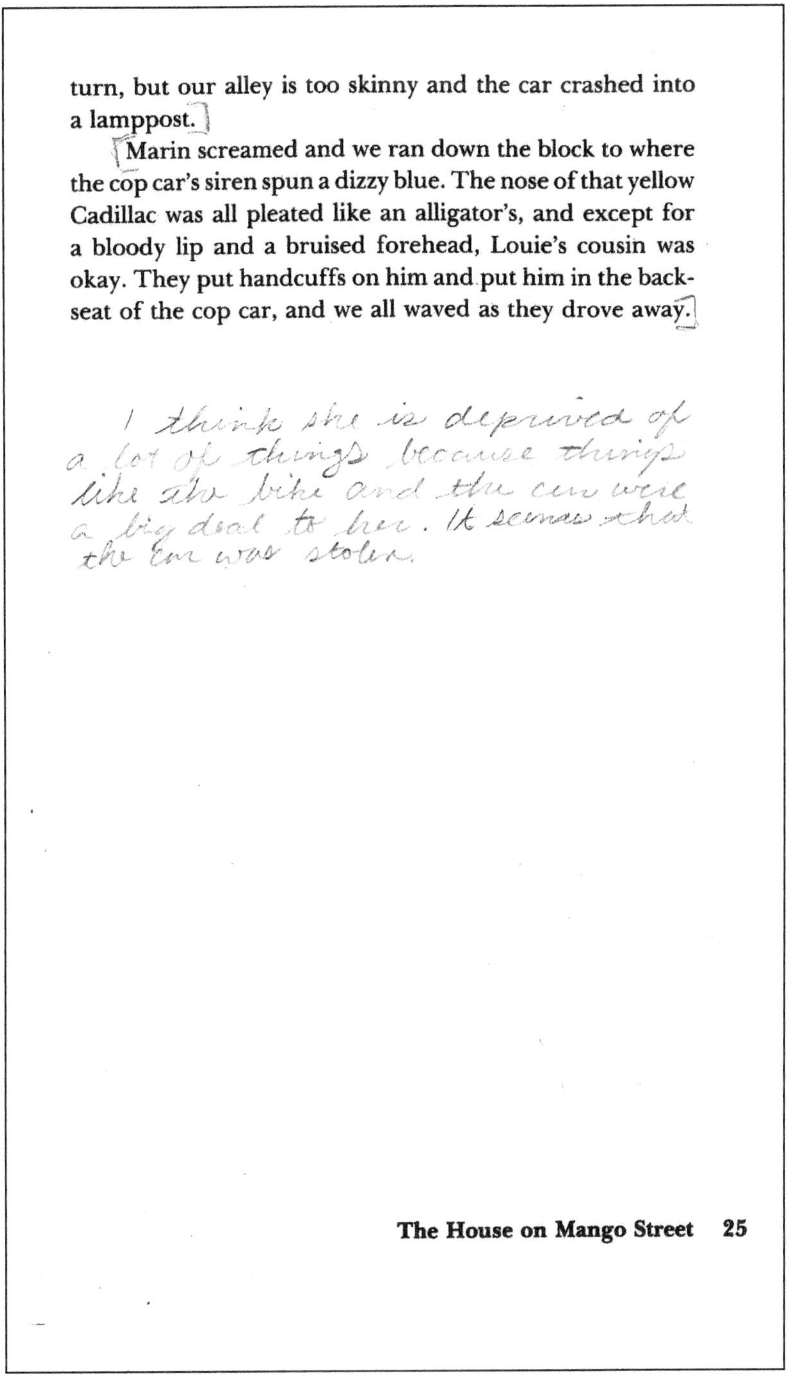
turn, but our alley is too skinny and the car crashed into a lamppost.

Marin screamed and we ran down the block to where the cop car's siren spun a dizzy blue. The nose of that yellow Cadillac was all pleated like an alligator's, and except for a bloody lip and a bruised forehead, Louie's cousin was okay. They put handcuffs on him and put him in the backseat of the cop car, and we all waved as they drove away.

I think she is deprived of a lot of things because things like the bike and the car were a big deal to her. It seems that the car was stolen.

The House on Mango Street **25**

FIGURE 5 Marginalia in the Saginaw copy of *The House on Mango Street*.

the car were a big deal to her. it seems that the car was stolen." While in the case of the Saginaw copy the marginalia are mostly summary in nature, we can detect a certain tentativeness—"(I don't think)"—in the comments, repeating the word "seems" above and below, as though the reader might be confident enough to occupy the margins of the text but not entirely confident in his or her own comprehension of that text.

There are a number of possible explanations for the blank space in this text. Offering a narrative connection, Martín-Rodríguez argues that the work is structurally shaped like a house, and "the question of whether to stay in a particular room or to occupy the entire house, so to speak, is entirely left up to the reader" (*Life* 74): the blank spaces lend a sense of division to those rooms. But from the perspective of Arte Público as a press, the layout not only adds a bit of bulk to an otherwise slim text but also acts a reminder that the press initially envisioned and "marketed the book as children's literature" (McCracken, "Sandra Cisneros" 237). In fact, Cisneros's first work with Kanellos was via her submission of the vignette "Chanclas" for a children's literature issue of *Revista Chicano-Riqueña*, the journal also published under Kanellos's editorship. Thus the wide margins and ample page space mimic the pages of many books for young readers, especially those referred to as "chapter books." As Barbara Seuling notes, in chapter books "text is divided into many short chapters, so that readers can feel accomplishment with each chapter read" (85). While this allographic peritext potentially makes the text more consumable for a wider audience—those in middle school, high school, and beyond—these narrative choices also reflect a sort of verisimilitude. If Esperanza is in fact the writer of this text, as is implied when readers witness her writing the first chapter of the story in the final chapter of the book, the brevity is another layer of realism. When Random House imports the wide margins from first edition to 25th anniversary edition, readers inclined to add their own private notes benefit.

This mingling of the author's words and the reader's words on the page also calls attention to Cisneros's manipulation of the genre of the story cycle, another structural decision that invites readers' written response. Though there is some debate as to the genre of this text, describing *Mango Street* as a story cycle, Delia Poey argues, allows "the text to 'poach' elements from the *Bildungsroman* while participating in a counterhegemonic discursive tradition which works to subvert the ideology of individualism" (213).[3] In other words, the nature of the story cycle, with each of its chapters featuring glimpses into a variety of lives in Esperanza's neighborhood, insists that *Mango Street* is about both the protagonist Esperanza and the community in which she lives. The chapters, which focus in turn on different neighbors and characters on Mango Street, speak back and forth, as though they are calling to each other from the windows of their homes, even as the narration remains in first person. The text invokes the generic bildungsroman in order to undermine it by emphasizing the importance of community, the fact that Esperanza is both an individual and Mango Street. As Janet Zandy writes, "The fictional or autobiographical working-class bildung leads not to separation and alienation, but to a consciousness of connective tissue and multiple histories and lives that comprise the self" (quoted in Tokarczyk 117–118); Esperanza is a product of all of those histories and lives on Mango Street.

Thus both the layout and the genre Cisneros's text creates a community of stories, elements that might further encourage readers to add their voices to the mix. Even if their notes are never shared, by joining their private thoughts with those of the narrator and characters on Mango Street, annotators further complicate the delicate negotiation of the individual and the community represented in the text: as Jerome McGann argues, "Every text, including those that may appear to be purely private, is a social text" (*Textual Condition* 21). For instance, the Disputanta annotator responds to the vignette "Hips," "the girls are ready to grow up; they want hips—i say wait and enjoy being little" (51). With this relatively innocuous comment, the reader takes on the role of advice-giver, of someone old enough to recognize the value of childhood. In this expression of personal opinion we see an annotator respond as though the children of the book could hear him or her. Writing back to the text, the annotator behaves like another narrator of the text. Cisneros's revision of the story cycle, one that encourages readers to understand the balanced relationship between the individual and the community, also encourages annotators to participate. As individuals, they write themselves into the text, joining the community of characters living in the world of Mango Street.

Educational Encouragement of Engagement

If it is true that both the material and the narrative structures of *Mango Street* invite marginalia from engaged readers, what kinds of marginalia do we see? What do these annotations show us? Just as they show readers invited by the structure of the text to tentatively respond to an author on her own turf, they also demonstrate the book's institutional uses, as the educational context itself encourages specific kinds of annotation. This perspective requires us to think of *Mango Street* as both literary text and educational textbook. Catherine C. Marshall's studies of the relationship between public and private annotation suggest that a literary work assigned as a textbook is likely used in different ways than when bought for private enjoyment. Marshall argues that context matters: "An educational setting . . . is a nice (and, more importantly, accessible) example of a situation in which sustained attention and close reading is necessary, and annotation of materials is encouraged" (2). Evidence of educational influence on the annotation of *Mango Street* can be found when the margins of the text are used as sites for teachers' or lecturers' notes, blurring the distinction between public and private annotation. For instance, above the table of contents in the Disputanta copy, the annotator summarizes a few key points: "learns ways to be good/bad / book like beads on a necklace—put them all together you have a girls life story / she's telling about who she is." The annotator mentions the "book like beads on a necklace," which is a reference to Cisneros's own description of how the stories of the book "tell one big story, each story contributing to the whole, like beads in a necklace," an often-quoted summary found in her introduction to the 1994 Knopf edition (xvii). The annotation appears in a Vintage edition, which does not contain this introduction, so where did the language come from? The annotator does not identify the phrase as a quote but instead integrates it into his or her own notes. Perhaps read somewhere else or offered by a teacher, the phrase indicates exposure to secondary sources, though it is not entirely clear whether the annotator is aware of the origins. The reader's vocabulary expands to include these notes, increasing his or her comprehension of the text.

In this case, readers' responses frequently reflect the trajectory of the once marginalized *Mango Street* as it has moved to the center of educational culture. Héctor Calderón acknowledges the book's uses for a wide range of age groups, saying that it is "studied widely in secondary schools and across a variety of departments in the university curriculum" (171). Likewise, Felicia J. Crúz notes that the audience for *Mango Street* has "expanded beyond the pale of Chicano and Latino communities to include families and students of all ages and ethnicities" (912). Given the relative fame of this text and its popularity on school syllabi for a wide range of ages, we can detect from the marginalia evidence of two potentially problematic uses of Cisneros's text: one that oversimplifies it as an "accessible" textbook of poetic and literary form and one that essentializes it as a "representative" Chicana text. In both cases, the annotations form the basis for understanding what is—and perhaps what is not—taught in the classroom, as well as how that educational context inevitably shapes meaning-making.

As defined here, accessible annotation demonstrates the extent to which the text is used to focus on formalist matters of literary vocabulary as opposed to issues of thematic or political significance. The book's approachable language, length, and young protagonist are inviting to young readers, and its seemingly simple engagement with literary language encourages instructors and readers to zero in on the kinds of literary techniques Cisneros employs. As a result, a kind of accessible annotation frequently appears in the form of marginalia meant to identify and define terms. Most obvious are marks like the vocabulary list on the inside front cover of the Saint Simons Island copy, listing words such as "alliteration," "metaphor," "anaphra [*sic*]," and "rhyme," with corresponding page numbers containing good examples. The New Hampshire copy includes the note, "vignettes = snapshots" in the opening pages, and the

Miamisburg annotator includes the definition of "parakon: poison & cure at the same time" (10) next to a passage about the double meanings of Esperanza's own name. Using the text as a vocabulary list or a space for definition allows *Mango Street* to become a handbook of poetic language, a reference manual of sorts. Even writers not prone to extensive notes include bits of vocabulary: a copy from Seattle, barely marked at all save for a few pages, identifies examples of "compound," "complex," and "simple" sentences in the vignette "Linoleum Roses" (101–102).

The book is, in many ways, accurately described as accessible. But one of the problems of bringing a text both about and from the margins into the mainstream is one of oversimplification. While educators might lean toward emphasizing those accessible aspects and therefore simplifying its narrative, critics lean in the opposite direction, arguing that the text is much more complicated than it seems. They highlight the rewards of multiple readings as well as the depictions of poverty, undocumented immigration, and sexual violence. Felicia Crúz, for example, argues, "On the whole, no single group seems inclined to focus on the book's 'simple,' 'direct' language and messages as part of Cisneros's complex arsenal of sophisticated literary devices and nuanced rhetorical strategies" (926). Despite the book's occasional use in the classroom as a textbook of poetic terms, which often leads to an oversimplified reading divorced from the difficult realities of race, gender, and class politics it narrates, critics continue to argue for its complexity.

In what seems to correspond to the critical consensus that this text is in fact quite complex, readers frequently take to the pages of *Mango Street*, (mis)translating, expressing confusion, asking questions, and even creating study guides, suggesting that the text functions in many ways to incite curiosity and invite response. This suggests that while the institutional context sometimes frames the text as simple and accessible, readers in those contexts reshape the text as far more complex with their questions and confusions. Annotators engage in asking a variety of questions from the margins of the text: is Cathy "friends with Esperanza?" (Disputanta 22); "Is Alicia crazy or something? I'm confused about the whole mouse thing" (Saginaw 32); "Earl has different ladies each night?" (Disputanta 70); "she not ready yet?" (Annapolis 52). Sometimes the questions are single words or phrases: "suicide?" (Los Angeles 30); "mentally retarded?" (Garland 43), or, most simply, "what?" (Garland 65). To whom/what are these questions being directed? Does the reader expect a response? Do these questions make it into the classroom, the book discussion, the conversation, or are they contained within these pages, safe from the possibility of embarrassing the writer? Regardless of whom the questions are meant for, they act as recorded participations in the text: the questions destabilize the singularity of the narrative, and they insist that this text is more complex than we might initially believe it to be.

Sometimes the annotations suggest a lack of awareness of the reader's own confusion: for example, in the relatively rare moments in which Spanish is used in *Mango Street*, annotators sometimes translate in the margins, such as when the Bowling Green annotator scrawls, "the spirits" in the margins alongside the word "los espiritus" (62). But, problematically, the Saint Simons Island annotator writes the word "wife" above "mamacita" (76) in his or her copy, a mistranslation that attempts to define the relationship between Esperanza's neighbors. Furthermore, because the annotator does not attempt to translate the term "mamasota," a term Esperanza thinks is "mean" (76), which appears in the next sentence, the play on words describing the very large woman in question is likely missed. The materiality of this particular text offers without correction a mistranslation of the text, suggesting that out there in the used book marketplaces other mistakes and mistranslations abound.

Annotations also give us a sense of readers in the process of learning, as when the Disputanta annotator responds to a vignette called "Hips," in which Esperanza and her friends talk about what hips are for. The passage reads, "One day you wake up and they are there. Ready and waiting like a new Buick with the keys in the ignition. Ready to take you where? 'They're good for holding a baby when you're cooking,' Rachel says" (49). The annotator has written near these lines: "Rachel thinks guys are there to be little helpers for you," followed by an arrow to another note: "oops talking about hips not guys" (49). Here we see the reading comprehension process at work, with comical results: on first reading, "they" are "guys" holding babies while women cook. The reader realizes on second reading that "they" refers to hips. The reader, by assuming something about who is doing the waiting—"guys"—in turn recasts the narrative in terms of a judgment about gender roles: does the idea of men as "little helpers" seem humorous to this reader? Perhaps to the reader it demonstrates Rachel's naiveté. These annotative questions and responses reinforce the notion not only that these readers are tentatively engaging in dialogue with the text and its author but also that the accessible text is not proving quite so accessible for these readers.

Nearly opposite to institutional contexts that present the text as accessible, which frequently erase the political specificity of the text, are the contexts that use Cisneros's text as "representative," or as a stand-in for the whole of Chicana/o literary production. Writing about both Cisneros and Rudolfo Anaya, Delia Poey argues, "It is their acceptance as representative that is troubling, given that they do provide opportunities for easy incorporation which erases their transformative possibilities" (215). Poey is more specifically noting that the very canonization of Cisneros's text as representative of Chicana/o literature, particularly in classrooms or contexts in which it is the only text by a person of color being offered, tends to obfuscate the narrative's culturally specific and complex narrative. Martín-Rodríguez, who argues that publishers play a large role in shaping the reception of a multicultural text, explains, "The tension between marginalization and commodification . . . is further problematized when books like *Mango*, originally celebrated for its contestatory and counterhegemonic impulses, are subsequently repackaged and reprinted for a larger market" (*Life* 129). When *Mango Street* is offered as the representative text of Chicana/o literature in the classroom, readers bring to the text expectations regarding its content, and in turn they are shaped by the text in ways that condition their expectations of all Chicana/o literature.

Many examples of readerly dialogue with this text demonstrate that while readers seem quite capable of identifying literary terms, their questions and silences about the text's more difficult issues, like poverty, undocumented immigration, and sexual violence, support Crúz's and Poey's arguments that the text is much more complex than it is frequently given credit for. Furthermore, these annotations bring to the text problematic perspectives that should be the starting point for conversation: they reveal biases, assumptions, and stereotypes that might be pressed or unraveled. Sometimes these annotations underscore readers' insistence on categorizing characters in problematic ways: to the Disputanta annotator, Esperanza's name "sounds Hispanic" (11), while the Garland annotator says the name "Lois" "sounds white" (73). Despite labeling characters racially him or herself, this same annotator appears to be bothered by the book's focus on race and ethnicity, highlighting the places where the narrator identifies a person by race. At first, the Garland annotator notes that "race is important" (20), then "mentions race" (23) regarding a Puerto Rican character, and then "mentions race first, as usual" (54) near an identification of an "Oriental" (54) shop owner. These annotations demonstrate a concern for matters of race and ethnicity, if not a sense of what to do with that concern.

To take another example, the annotator of the Bowling Green copy is particularly zealous about symbolism: responding to the vignette "Louie, His Cousin, & His Other Cousin," in which a young man steals a car and takes Esperanza and her neighbors for a joyride, the annotator has circled the phrases "white rugs" and "white leather seats," which describe the car, as well as the description of the "little white cat in the back window whose eyes lit up when the car stopped or turned" (24). In the margins, the annotator writes a one-word question: "cocain [*sic*]?" Such a move not only demonstrates an unsupportable interpretation but also potentially provides insight into the way this annotator has been reading the text, expecting that the barrio described on Mango Street would include drugs. In the next vignette, "Marin," the same annotator underlines the statement "Marin says . . . she's going to get a real job downtown" (26) and circles the words "real job," asking in the margins another question: "prostitution?" This annotation reveals the expectations of exoticism, violence, and drama that a reader brings to *Mango Street* and also reveals circulating stereotypes in a way authors and even teachers cannot control. The annotator introduces onto the page topics Cisneros herself does not engage, thus altering discourse surrounding the text by fitting the narrative into preconceived ideas of the setting. The annotator's guesses are not entirely supported by the text, and they reveal more about the reader's frame of reference, the expectations he or she brings to the text. Those expectations are shaped by context, in particular an educational context, which frequently and sometimes problematically casts this text as accessible or representative, if not some combination of the two.

Engaging and Distancing Readers: Esperanza as Emerging Writer

In many ways, the narrative itself joins the book's structure and context in encouraging readers to write back to the text. And, if we shift our attention to the way we understand the narrator of Mango Street, we can also reframe our understanding of those questions asked by the Bowling Green reader. The question marks following each of those comments—"*cocain?*" "*prostitution?*"—suggest a tentativeness, a hesitant and uncertain trying on of identity given the uncertainty of the narrator herself. Annotations that demonstrate interpretive confusion imply more than a mere failure of reading comprehension or an inability to imagine a Latina/o community outside of stereotype: these instances of uncertainty about the events of the text and their meanings suggest that readers faced with the ambivalence of *Mango Street* struggle to fill them in, to give voice to the story's silences. In turn, *Mango Street* both encourages and discourages such readerly desires to complete the picture Esperanza paints: on the one hand, the narrative expects that the careful reader will fill in narrative gaps Esperanza supplies, but on the other, the very construction of those gaps suggests a modeling of silence as a method of confronting and surviving traumatic events. Readers are therefore invited to respond but also, equally and in opposition, invited to fall silent as part of the negotiation of the radical openness of the margins.

Part of the complexity of the text, or the push and pull between voice and silence, is that readers must navigate those silences that surround Esperanza's youthful understanding of the world: her understanding of what it means to be an adult, what it means to be a woman, what it means to be a Mexican American. Helene Weldt-Basson describes the silences in *Mango Street* as "a form of textual voice that creates meaning through the blank space, the empty page or precisely what is said or is omitted" (201). Thus it is the Disputanta and Atlanta annotators and not Esperanza who respond to the end of "The First Job," in which Esperanza's first employer behaves lasciviously toward her, by jotting: "Ah, that old guy is a pervert" and "perv old man," respectively (55). The annotators say what Esperanza cannot. These silences are even more clearly demonstrated in readers' responses to "The Red Clowns." In this vignette, Esperanza is violently assaulted, though the language and details of the incident are not entirely explicit. The brief vignette begins with "Sally, you lied. It wasn't what you said at all. What he did. Where he touched me. I didn't want it, Sally. The way they said it, the way it's supposed to be, all the storybooks and movies, why did you lie to me?" (99). Later, Esperanza narrates, "Sally, make him stop. I couldn't make them go away. I couldn't do anything but cry. I don't remember. It was dark. I don't remember. I don't remember. Please don't make me tell it all" (100). With its repeated "I don't remembers" and its evasive nondescription of the event, the vignette creates confusion for a number of readers, who seek not only to summarize a story but interpret its meanings when they are not entirely clear. The gaps in the narrative depict Esperanza's unwillingness or inability to fully narrate her own trauma, demonstrating the illegibility of rape.

In response, readers use the page to answer the questions the text asks. For example, the annotator of the Miamisburg copy scribbles at the end, "Did she lose her virginity?" which is followed beneath it by an answer, "She got raped." Another note appended to the vignette, "The First Job," reads, "distance with man foreshadows chapter red clowns when Esperanza gets rape" (55), suggesting that the Ohio annotator returned to this chapter after answering that question, perhaps with the guidance of an instructor. Likewise, the annotator of the Disputanta copy effectively prefaces the vignette with the similar explanation, "She was raped," in the space above the beginning of the vignette, and the San Diego annotator similarly writes, "Esperanza got raped" (100). Other readers are hesitant to label the events as rape: the Los Angeles annotator writes, "first experience with boys—forced—not romantic—a lie" (100), while the Garland annotator simply writes, "not a good experience" (100). Regardless of who guides the marginalia, the fact that readers take the time to fill in Cisneros's constructed blank calls attention to that blank and suggests that perhaps some readers needed multiple readings (whether self-initiated or prodded) to determine what actually happened.

Sometimes marginalia can register multiple rather than singular interpretations of the text as readers develop new understandings and record them in the margins. In the example in which the Miamisburg reader first framed the scene in terms of Esperanza "los[ing] her virginity" and then changed it to "rape," we can begin to see the possibility of multiple interpretations developing in competition with one another. On the surface, the annotator's first choice of language might seem almost shockingly delicate, too poetic and ignorant of the violence involved, much like the Garland annotator's framing of the event as an "experience." Meanwhile, the appended "she was raped" is more direct and clinical, a more specific acknowledgment of the details of the event. Though many critical readings of this vignette suggest that Esperanza was raped, the introduction of this alternative reading offers an opportunity to consider the ways in which violence, shame, and fear are, for some, assumed as a given in the event of losing one's virginity.

For instance, we might consider the following: does the answer "she was raped" answer the original question, "Did she lose her virginity?" Given the instability of the word "virginity," especially among victims of rape and sexual assault, this question might encourage critics to read the scene in the context of a debate about various constructions of sexual identity, and it's possible that readers of *Mango Street* might bring complex understandings of virginity and sexual identity to the text. For example, in an essay on the subjective experience of virginity loss in the United States, Laura Carpenter presents her findings of a study of the influence of ambiguous definitions of sex on "conduct and identity" (127). In particular, she notes that a quarter of the female respondents in her study had been victims of forced sex and that none of them believed that virginity could be lost through forced sex (132). Readers of this text, these annotators included, bring to the text a variety of relationships to the concept of virginity; the question asked by one of them inadvertently, though no less meaningfully, creates an opportunity to reflect on the concept as well.

Additionally, the question of virginity could become another entry into considering Esperanza's conceptions of sexuality in light of the heavy significance of the sexual purity associated with the Virgin of Guadalupe, and also into considering whether "losing her virginity" might be considered more destructive than, if not as violent as, the term "rape." In "The 'Dual'-ing Images of La Malinche and La Virgen de Guadalupe in Cisneros's *The House on Mango Street*," Leslie Petty argues that for Cisneros, "being culturally defined by either of these two roles makes for an incomplete, frustrated life" (123). For contemporary Chicanas who seek to rescue Malinche from the long tradition of masculinist histories that would cast her as a traitorous descendent of Eve, perhaps we can read the Marianist question, "Did she lose her virginity?" as being answered by the Malinchista "She was raped." To read the question in this way is not to suggest that the annotator has knowledge of these critical or symbolic resonances: instead, it suggests that even instances of readerly confusion have the potential to produce new or more complex understandings of a borderized sexual identity as they are hinted at in the text. Cisneros's constructed narrative gaps encourage these kinds of questions, and future readers are further encouraged to agree or disagree, elaborating as they see fit. Even in their confusion, annotators offer interpretations that destabilize, undermine, and reshape future readings of the text in ways that are beyond the control of the author yet seemingly invited by the text itself. In this case, border textuality radically opens texts to both productive and destructive readings by calling attention to instability: the instability of border identity (its confusions, its silences, its erasures) as well as the instability of any given text.

But such instability should not be uncritically celebrated. Because the text suggests but never explicitly states that Esperanza was raped, annotations like these also negate the narrative reality that Esperanza's silences are hers to fill. From the margins, readers manipulate the textual center, their voices attempting to close the open text with their understandings of a difficult narrative moment. Studies of trauma frequently attest to the near-inevitability of silence in the accounts of survivors, suggesting that such silence might register a "yearn[ing] for a safe audience" (Sorsoli 138). In that case, Esperanza's silence or inability to define her assault might more accurately reflect her uncertainty about the reading audience. She may be telling the story of her transformation into a writer, but the story she is not telling is one about how she relates to us as readers. Her voice may be young and even naive, but her silences suggest she is also wary. In turn, as Lynn Sorsoli argues, readers are "listening to the impossibility of words to capture traumatic events, but also to the impossibility of many relationships, existing within this society and culture, adequately holding these stories" (138). As readers, we are invited into Esperanza's world and even encouraged to participate in it. But that relationship is not without its withholdings: when readers rush to fill in the gaps, not only are they not listening to Esperanza's silences but they are also failing to recognize the ways in which Esperanza feels unsafe in front of them. Doris Sommer acknowledges, "Even readers who share enough social space with a writer to claim privileged understanding may too hastily fill in the gaps these texts would demarcate" (8–9); this is the danger and responsibility of writing in the margins.

Readers can and do shoulder that responsibility in potentially productive ways as well, which we might record in the range of ways they respond to issues of race, nationality, and ethnicity. As readers struggle to identify, to sympathize, and to empathize with the Mexican American or even proto-Chicana voice of the narrative, they make border crossings of their own. For example, in a move that clearly engages with the politics at the heart of Cisneros's text, the Disputanta annotator asks, "American or Mexican, what comes first?" (10). Here the annotator asks a deceptively simple question that calls forth issues of ethnic identity, immigrant and first-generation nationalist loyalties, the hierarchy almost necessarily implied by the order of identification, double-consciousness, and borderlands identity. Perhaps this question arose from within the reader; perhaps it is the product of an instructor's lecture. Regardless, the pause to record such a question reflects the reader's growing awareness of the complications of identity. Most intriguing is the Nashua annotator's response to "Those Who Don't," a very brief vignette in which Esperanza describes the way outsiders view her neighborhood as something to be scared of, while she doesn't fear it at all. In turn, however, she narrates, "But watch us drive into another neighborhood of another color and our knees go shakity-shake and our car windows get rolled up tight and our eyes look straight" (28). The annotator writes: "difference/race/prejudice/make all of us a community" (28). Such a comment suggests that for the reader, community is shaped by the shared experience of racial difference and prejudice. And such a comment stands in sharp contrast to the numerous scholarly responses that focus on the way Cisneros's text celebrates community. Interacting with the text in a way that suggests that the question of identity is one not only for the characters on Mango Street but one for all readers, these annotations write back to the text and the audience.

If Esperanza models silence in ways that frustrate readers with regard to her testimony of assault, in other places readers adopt a silence that materially suggests a respect for the narrative voice. Thus the concluding vignettes of the narrative are also filled with annotative silences: silences that are encouraged by Esperanza's own status as a growing writer. Esperanza is first confused when her Aunt Lupe tells her, "You just remember to keep writing, Esperanza. You must keep writing. It will keep you free" (61). But by the end of the story cycle, as she sits down to write the very first chapter, she explains that when she writes, she "put[s] it down on paper and then the ghost does not ache so much" (110). In a demonstration of border textuality, *Mango Street* tells the story of a young woman writing herself into existence, a story that itself encourages other readers to write themselves into existence. But it does so in such a way that readers seem inclined not to monopolize or colonize the entire space of the text. The San Diego annotator acknowledges Esperanza's own desire to be heard in response to a poem she writes in "Born Bad," a vignette in which she mourns the loss of her Aunt Lupe. Next to a poem that Esperanza inscribes, the San Diego annotator writes, "one day we'll all hear her"; the writer simultaneously places herself in the narrative present, casting toward the future "one day," and the real-life present, in which Esperanza is in the act of being heard. Furthermore, in nearly all of the copies I obtained, there is little to no marking of the final two vignettes, "A House of My Own," and "Mango Says Goodbye Sometimes," suggesting that while the text encourages annotation, annotators also leave room for a narrator's developing voice. Materially, they express the value of silence. The disorienting clatter of the voices and stories of the people of Mango Street, combined with the underlining and highlighting and summaries and notations of "metaphor!" and "idea of postmodernism" strewn about, all eventually fall silent in the final two vignettes. For future readers, Esperanza's voice alone occupies the page—narratively and materially—as readers find her in the act of writing, and in fact writing the very book they're reading. Readers encounter Esperanza as a model for engaging in dialogue through writing, and through her they also learn to share the space of the page, just as her characters share the space of her narrative.

Conclusion

The annotators themselves continue to shape this border text. When readers turn their annotations into part of the text by selling them in the used book market, they intentionally or unintentionally join Cisneros and her narrator, the structure and the format, the publishers and the educational contexts in encouraging readers' response. When readers choose to underline, highlight, or respond in phrases or long sentences to the words on the page, they raise critical issues involving our understanding of the reading process as well as our understanding of the reader's role in the communications circuit (Darnton). Contemporary readers are buying and selling books across time zones and college campuses, their notes circulating nearly anonymously across a much larger geographic expanse. Jackson argues that in the twentieth century, marginalia have become "secret utterances" (145), but the sales of these marked copies indicate that to some extent readers continue to hold an understanding of their notes as "semi-public documents" (145). And the possibilities for exchanging such annotations are only multiplying in the digital age: Joanna Wolfe and Christine Neuwirth highlight the growing number of digital annotation tools and suggest, "As more and more readers take advantage of new annotation tools . . . many of these annotations will be housed in public (or semipublic) databases where they can be accessed and shared by subsequent readers of a text" (336). But even in print, annotators are already sharing their ideas with future readers, whether they mean to or not. For example, evidence of the circulation of this text—whether online or elsewhere—can clearly be seen in the San Diego copy, which contains three separate names written onto the inside cover. The cover lists "Bianca Fontanez" followed by "Gabe Simpson 09–10" and "John Beverly" as successive readers and annotators of the text.

But more compelling is the way each of these individual annotated copies changes the book itself, again making each printed copy unique. Some annotators can be sympathetic: "those trees are like her only friends" (Disputanta 75), and "it's easy to naturalize oppression when they are oppressed" (Miamisburg 100). Just as often readers are decidedly less sympathetic: "she could have been someone but she let poverty get in the way" (Saint Simons Island 90). These judgments are significant in that they speak what the text cannot or does not on its own. But they also change the shape of the text, each in a different way. For example, nearly every annotator offers up a reading of the clouds described in "Darius & the Clouds." Each of these annotators struggles to make sense of a somewhat dense vignette: a child whom Esperanza calls "sometimes stupid and mostly a fool" (33) points at a cloud and tells people it's God, which Esperanza finds wise. Beyond an opening description of how one can never have too much sky, readers are free to determine the meaning of such a statement with little to go on. Some, like the Annapolis annotator, simply link "sky—freedom," while the Miamisburg annotator merely lists "religion / hope." Others are more specific and see a negative connotation: the Disputanta annotator thinks "the clouds are her dreams floating away" and "freedom, hope, happiness (replace sky with these words)." The Nashua copy includes this note: "all the happiness in the world is trapped in the sky but there is not enough." The Sherman Oaks annotator shifts the focus off of Esperanza and onto Darius: "the sky to him is a comfort." The Saint Simons Island annotator sees the cloud as a "symbol that God is imperfect." Taken together, these annotations register the multiplicity of meanings generated at any one point in Cisneros's narrative, perhaps the clearest refutation of the charge that her narrative is simplistic.

Each of these annotations also offers interpretations that future readers may encounter, incorporate, reject, or ignore as they attempt to navigate the text for themselves. Future readers—even if they are few in number—confronted with these interpretations are then invited into dialogue, not only with the text but also with the ghost of another reader trying to make sense of the text. And each copy of the text, in turn, is made meaningfully and materially different. But even if no one purchases the marked-up copy, its placement on the market (rather than being tucked away in a personal library or even thrown away) blurs the line between public and private annotation by sending those marginalia—with their attitudes toward and thoughts about the narrative—into circulation. Continued scholarly engagement with these annotations not only widens the audience for them but also creates opportunities to reinvigorate the way we think about reading Cisneros's text.

By writing themselves into the text, and even in their silences, the annotators engage in interpretive dialogue with the author, the narrator, the structure, their teachers, scholars, and themselves. Their expectations are shaped not only by the material and narrative structure of the text but also by the educational or social context in which a reader is introduced to the text. In the case of *Mango Street*, ethnic revisions of the bildungsroman via a story cycle structure, a structural inclusion of blank or white space, and educational contexts that mark the text as accessible and representative produce a unique text that encourages annotation. Educators, as much as publishers and authors, encourage and shape the kinds of engagement available to readers, and it is likely that their words are filtered into the margins. The resulting marginalia are evidence of border textuality: of the possibilities as well as the limitations that those encouragements expose/impose. What can and can't be said in the margins of *Mango Street* is shaped not only by Cisneros and Esperanza but also by the book's publishers, designers, advocates, and teachers. In the digital age, the possibilities for annotation have only multiplied: from programs that enable annotation (as well as the storage and sharing of those annotations) to review sites from Amazon to Goodreads, readers have ample opportunity to write back to texts. In turn, scholars have ample evidence of the imperfect but nonetheless valuable readings of texts that compel readers to write back.

Frosh and Baraitser suggest that we read marginalia "not in order to delve down through them to what is more true, but rather to harness their energy to examine what happens next—what these gaps allow to happen, what comes about as a consequence of a narrative's scratched surface" (75). In this case, marginalia reveal that beneath its scratched surface, *Mango Street* wants its readers to engage in the material margins, even as its narrative registers the dangers of such engagement. As educators and scholars we can benefit from the study of such marginalia, what they can teach us about the text and the way we interact with it, as well as what our students and readers are hearing from us and seeing for themselves. The full complexity of *Mango Street* can best be detected when we consider it in the context of its circulations, its passing through the hands of readers as they engage with all of its borders.

Conclusion

From the Edge opens the door to numerous questions surrounding the material history and social lives of border books; by approaching the broad topic of book history in border literature from a variety of vantage points and using different emphases, it offers glimpses at the wealth of material remaining to be studied. I conclude by exploring just a few of those possibilities.

Chicana/o border writers confront the complexities of authorship in a material way, and there is much for scholarship to attend to on this subject. Chicana/o literature is, like many literatures produced by members of historically marginalized groups, complicated by discourses of authority and power, of control over one's own work, and of the political ramifications of the poststructuralist death of the author heralded by the 1970s and 1980s. Examining the presence of authorial revisions is only one way to explore how border writers position themselves as authors. We can and should consider the lengths to which many writers go to ensure that their works get into and stay in print, even in the absence of publishers willing to assist them. Border writers including María Amparo Ruiz de Burton, Aristeo Brito, Nash Candelaria, and Raymond Barrio, for example, resorted to self-publishing their works in order to introduce them to the reading public or to keep them on the shelves. Studies of the historical conditions that produced these Hispanic and Chicana/o texts that survive in new forms in the twenty-first century seem paramount to an understanding of the material ways in which these writers claimed authorship and ownership of their work.

Linked to questions of authorship are issues surrounding those publishing institutions that have shaped Hispanic, Mexican American, Chicana/o, and border literatures by their decisions regarding who and what to publish, and for whom. There is a significant amount of work to be done to reveal just how influential these publishing houses are in guiding readers to an understanding of Chicana/o literature, cultivating audiences, and molding the work of writers into products worthy of consumption. Manuel Martín-Rodríguez, for example, has extensively explored Quinto Sol and its part in ensuring the longevity of writers including Tomás Rivera, Rolando Hinojosa, and Estela Portillo-Trambley. It is in combination with Arte Público press that Nicolás Kanellos's *Recovering the U.S.-Hispanic Literary Heritage* reaches readers in print, and Bilingual Press / Editorial Bilingüe is responsible for introducing Ana Castillo as well as Alma Luz Villanueva and Nash Candelaria and for publishing translations of Alejandro Morales. More sustained research into the role of Arte Público Press in Houston, Bilingual Press / Editorial Bilingüe in Tempe, Arizona, and Quinto Sol in Berkeley, which later divided into two presses—Editorial Justa and Tonatiuh International—as major publishers and promoters of Chicana/o and border literature will likely yield new perspectives on how authors and publishers worked jointly and perhaps at times at odds with one another to produce works of Chicana/o literature that are now nearly canonical. The negotiations between authors like these and their publishers, perhaps found in evidence from authorial and institutional archives, would likely reveal conversations about the shape of these novels that, in turn, affect the shape of Chicana/o literature as a whole.

By comparing these presses to other even smaller contemporary presses like Chusma House Publications (San Jose), Calaca Press (National City), and Wings Press (San Antonio), we can begin to recognize how a variety of publishing outlets continue to redefine this literature. Furthermore, an expansion of the scope of study to include the largest publishing companies and their respective "Chicana/o" or "Latina/o" imprints puts each of the presses in dialogue with one another, leading to questions regarding intentions and audiences and generating a more focused understanding of how publishing institutions, in their own diversity, contribute to the diverse conceptions of Chicana/o and Latina/o literature. What were the impulses behind Penguin Books' launch of "Celebra," "the first imprint to exclusively publish mainstream Hispanic personalities" ("Penguin")? How does Celebra define "mainstream"? And why do they define those personalities, as well as the target audiences for the line's books, as Hispanic? How are those impulses and intended audiences different from those expressed by "Rayo," the imprint of HarperCollins that produces Spanish-language titles from a variety of Latina/o authors? How is border, Chicana/o, and Latina/o identity written and revised in the literary production of these texts, and what roles do these intersecting and yet wildly different publishing institutions play in that production? Exploring the impact of publishing companies on our understanding of the texts they produce can help us develop a more nuanced view of the competing intentions at play.

In the border spaces between author and publisher, the material text often reveals those competing intentions. The second and third chapters of this book attend to the smallest nuances of print, arguing that the visual impact of paratextual elements like glossaries and the bibliographic codes of typography attempt to dictate our understanding of border literature. So many border and Chicana/o texts make use of other kinds of visual elements that are worth more actively pursuing. Fabiola Cabeza de Baca's *We Fed Them Cactus* (1954), for instance, features a series of line drawings by Dorothy L. Peters throughout the text, while more recently John Rechy's 2003 novel *The Life and Adventures of Lyle Clemens* features lettering and chapter illustrations by Donald Hendricks. Such illustrations, much like the drawings added to and deleted from Rolando Hinojosa's *Estampas del valle y otras obras / The Valley*, may not appear to affect the meaning of the words on the page, but closer study of the use of such drawings will likely illuminate their impact on interpretation. Other writers, like performance artist Guillermo Gomez-Peña, more actively press the boundary line between word and image, whether in essay collections that feature numerous photos of Peña in various costumes or in adaptations of the codex as seen in his *Codex Espangliensis: From Columbus to the Border Patrol*, co-authored with Enrique Chagoya and Felicia Rice. Sandra Cisneros presses on the significance of image in her children's-book-like *Have You Seen Marie?* (2014), illustrated by Ester Hernández, and Salvador Plascencia narrates a materially frustrated experience of the page in *The People of Paper* (2005). The emphasis on visual aspects of border texts serves not only to demonstrate the impact of such nonlinguistic features on interpretation but to reinforce the reach of border textuality, where texts narrate the struggle over border identity at the same time they render materially visible the struggle over literary production and reception.

The thread of "instability" that has been traced in this book represents an engagement with an ongoing conversation about the possibilities and problems such a term affords. In Chicana/o border narratives and in their social lives, history is frequently rendered not only as fractured and contingent but also as incomplete (though again, it is not always clear whether this is a status to be celebrated or subverted). Numerous works of border literature embrace incompleteness and changeability. In *Borderlands / La Frontera: The New Mestiza*, Gloria Anzaldúa writes of her childhood: "huddling under the covers, I made up stories for my sister night after night. After a while she wanted two stories per night. I learned to give her installments, building up the suspense with convoluted complications until the story climaxed several nights later. It must have been then that I decided to put stories on paper" (87). From telenovelas to the Klail City Death Trip Series and from story and poem cycles to comics like *Love and Rockets*, by Jaime and Gilbert Hernández, twentieth-century Chicana/o cultural production has emphasized the series and the serial, highlighting narratives that often remain partial or incomplete for years at a time. Such literature makes material its status as unfinished in order to render visible the conditions of incompleteness, fragmentation, and even seriality that are particular to the experience of Chicana/o and *mestiza/o* identity in diaspora.

Sometimes that incompleteness is imposed upon from without, as in the case of Jovita González and Eve Raleigh's "incomplete" novel, *Caballero: A Historical Novel*, along with González's "moderately unified set of literary, which is to say also fictionalized, sketches fashioned into a novel" (Limón xv), *Dew on the Thorn*. Both novels concern communities along the U.S.-Mexico border in the aftermath of the Treaty of Guadalupe-Hidalgo, itself a text that shifted the ground under many Mexican and "Spano-Americans'" feet from homeland to hostland, creating a diaspora that involved only the movement of national boundary lines. Both texts have, in their recovery, been edited and presented in as close to "whole" condition as possible by José Limón and María Cotera. Paragraphs, sentences, and in one instance a whole chapter, go missing in these recovery editions, and Limón details his struggles to put together a clear reading text of both novels. His editorial choices shape the meaning of the text but cannot fully complete it. As the archive grows increasingly larger, the possibility for debate about the politics and products of recovery projects—and how and whether to "complete" them—only widens.

In contrast, some writers, like Rolando Hinojosa and Gilbert Hernández, embrace the incomplete, insisting on seriality as a mode of expression. Hinojosa's various installments of the Klail City Death Trip Series now numbers fifteen, stretching from 1973 to 2006. The proliferation of texts of this series explores a diasporic community that is always coming into being, always being revised and reshaped, making that process material for readers. Employing the serial, the series, and the incomplete creates narratives in which, as Hinojosa argues, "the reader has to collaborate with the writer" (quoted in Jussawalla and Dasenbrock 274). This collaboration renders visible and material the unstable boundaries between author and audience, reinscribing the destabilization of national, racial, ethnic, and political authority, the unbalancing of power brought on by diasporic communities.

Similarly, Gilbert Hernández's work on the *Love and Rockets* comic book series, particularly the "Palomar" stories, demonstrates that a multitude of formats opens up a multitude of possibilities for the construction of narrative as well as its interpretation. In addition to being published in serial format, allowing the story to unfold alongside competing and complementary narratives written by his brother, the Palomar stories have also been published in a variety of other formats, including a hardcover collection entitled *Palomar:*

The Heartbreak Soup Stories and as part of a set of reissued softcovers that organize the writing chronologically, including the volumes *Heartbreak Soup, Human Diastrophism*, and *Beyond Palomar*, which all deal with stories of Palomar's inhabitants. Works like *Human Diastrophism*, which had previously been published as *Blood of Palomar* with co-author Jaime Hernández as a stand-alone graphic novel, add to the complexity of versions, all of which tell a different story of Palomar. The proliferation of material formats mimics the immense number of stories circulating that constitute the textual world of Palomar, allowing readers to experience different but always incomplete versions of the narrative. The materiality of the text shapes our understanding of that text, and in many cases, the incomplete and the serial render visible and palpable the sense of incompleteness that is common to the text and border diasporic identities.

In still other cases, we might register the "incomplete" as a characteristic of many, if not all, publishing processes, regardless of form. John Rechy's groundbreaking *City of Night*, for example, was published as a novel in 1963 by New York publisher Grove Press. But earlier excerpts had appeared in *Evergreen Review, Big Table, Nugget*, and *The London Magazine*, and Rechy writes that *Evergreen Review* "had largely created the interest in my work that others were responding to" ("*City of Night* Remembered" 116). Rechy reveals that after going through twelve drafts of most of the chapters, when the proofs arrived, he began to edit until, "by the time I had gone through the galley proofs, the book was virtually rewritten on the margins and on pasted typewritten inserts" (119). Research might explore the differences between the excerpted and shorter materials and their appearance in the novel, both how they differ and how the context of different kinds of publication venues changes the possibilities for interpretation. But more fascinating still might be to look at those galley proof manuscripts as a book written and rewritten from the margins, further evidence of the multiple versions of *City of Night* that complicate our understanding of the author, his publishers (who accepted the changes even at that late stage), and the text.

The experience of readers—whether of incompleteness, linguistic frustration, or confusion—is another thread woven through the book. But what changes for readers when the very shape of books as we know them is undergoing rapid change as well? What is the material experience of reading the border in the digital age? In recent years the development and adoption of e-readers and other digital delivery formats have caused scholars and journalists alike to consider how such technology will reorient our understanding of books and their material forms. Often written with a combination of nostalgia and anxiety, or what Bill Brown most recently called "the melodrama of besieged materiality" (26), essays and articles question the significance of textual materiality now more than ever. Meanwhile, Chicana/o border writers, scholars, and their texts are changed by and changing these new technologies. As with print, their relationships to new modes of writing and reading are nearly always political. At the beginnings of this digital revolution, writer and performance artist Guillermo Gomez-Peña argues in his 1997 essay, "The Virtual Barrio @ the Other Frontier (or the Chicano Interneta)," "The utopian rhetoric around digital technologies reminded me of a sanitized version of the pioneer and frontier mentalities of the Old West, and also of twentieth-century futurism" (257). Nearly two decades later, Chicana/o "artivists" like Judy Baca, "conscious of digital media's liberatory potential as well as its persisting exclusions" (Sandoval 83), continue to work to create digital narratives of empowerment.

Certainly digital technology and its impact on the material text present an opportunity to rethink the archive, to expand and to preserve works that might otherwise be lost. A recovery project like Chicana por Mi Raza: Uncovering the Hidden History of Chicana Feminism (1965–1985), organized by Maria Cotera, does just this by collecting and preserving the materials and oral histories of the development of Chicana feminist thought. But these technologies also threaten erasure in a way that is uniquely felt by border and Chicana/o artists: again, as early as 2000, Gomez-Peña writes of a laptop stolen in 1998, which led to the loss of "at least five years of work—poems, performance texts, film and radio scripts, essays, personal letters, and several chapters of my next book." This is from his "Letter to an Unknown Thief," in which he continues: "You don't have the least idea of what this means to a Chicano intellectual who has been fighting the erasure of collective and personal memory" (261). He writes of the lessons he learned from this experience:

> I am beginning to feel strangely thankful, for you have forced me into many harsh realizations. First, that my LIFE cannot be trusted to high-technology. That airports are no less dangerous than, for example, South Central Los Angeles. And that I must always, ALWAYS be prepared to reconstruct the humongous puzzle of my already fractured self, and to edit out entire chapters of my life without fearing that the whole structure will collapse. So . . . gracias ladrón. ("Letter" 262)

For Gomez-Peña, the act of writing is materially and inextricably linked to the construction of a Chicano self-identity that is always "fractured," and the loss of such material constitutes a challenge to that identity. The instability he senses in "high-technology" reinforces the instability of the story of his life.

But Gomez-Peña also demonstrates that his relationship to digital technology is not that different from the relationship of many works of border literature to their material or printed texts. He writes, "I resent the fact that I am constantly told that as a 'Latino,' I am supposedly 'culturally handicapped' or somehow unfit to handle high technology. Once I have the apparatus in front of me, however, I am uncontrollably compelled to work against it—to question it, expose it, subvert it, and/or imbue it with humor, radical politics, and *linguas polutas* such as Spanglish, Franglais, and cyberñol" ("Virtual" 248–249). Whether supported by digital technology or the technologies of print, Chicana/o border texts will continue to question, expose, and subvert their materialities in service of calling attention to the complex political histories that shape their production, publication, and reception. As scholars committed to engaging with the texts of border literature, it is imperative that we do the same.

Notes

Introduction

1 See her *Ambassadors of Culture: The Transamerican Origins of Latino Writing* (2002).
2 Rachel Saint John's *Line in the Sand: A History of the Western U.S.-Mexico Border* (2012), and Samuel Truett's *Fugitive Landscapes: The Forgotten History of the U.S.-Mexico Borderlands* (2008), are particularly illuminating examples.
3 For further exploration of this concept as it connects to citizenship, see Josue David Cisneros's *The Border Crossed Us: Rhetorics of Borders, Citizenship, and Latina/o Identity* (2014)
4 See Juan Velasco's argument that the direction of crossing changes the way we imagine, construct, and consume the border in "Automitografías: The Border Paradigm in Chicana/o Autobiography" (2004).
5 See, for example, Manuel Luis Martínez, "Telling the Difference between the Border and the Borderlands: Materiality and Theoretical Practice" (2002).
6 Works devoted to postnationalism in Chicana/o literature more broadly include Marissa K. López's *Chicano Nations: The Hemispheric Origins of Mexican American Literature* (2011) and Ellie D. Hernández's *Postnationalism in Chicana/o Literature and Culture* (2010).
7 See, for example, George Bornstein and Theresa Tinkle's *The Iconic Page in Manuscript, Print, and Digital Culture* (1998).
8 For an investigation of the horizons of marketing Chicana and Latina literature via stereotypical cover pages, see Ellen McCracken's *New Latina Narrative: The Feminine Space of Postmodern Ethnicity* (1999).
9 Leticia Garza-Falcón's *Gente Decente: A Borderlands Response to the Rhetoric of Dominance* (1998) illuminates the deployments of such counterhistorical narratives in the writings of a range of female borderlands authors.
10 For a compelling discussion of the writings of women from both sides of the border, see Debra Castillo and María Soccoro Tabuenca Córdoba, *Border Women: Writing from La Frontera* (2002). Likewise, see Sadowski Smith's chapters titled "Asian Border Crossings" and "Native Border Theory" in *Border Fictions: Globalization,*

Empire, and Writing at the Boundaries of the United States, as well as James H. Cox's *The Red Land to the South: American Indian Writers and Indigenous Mexico*.

Chapter 1 "A Touch-Up Here and There": Authorial Revisions and Their Paratexts

An earlier version of portions of this chapter appeared as "Damaged Pieces: Embracing Border Textuality in Revisions of Sapogonia," in MELUS *37.3 (Fall 2012): 167–88.*

1 Any textual quotations list the appropriate page numbers for both editions, in order of publication date, where applicable.

2 Those books include *Klail City y sus aldredores* (1976) and *Generaciones y semblanzas* (1977) (the same Spanish-language book with two different titles), *Korean Love Songs* (1977) (written in English), *Mi querido Rafa* (1981) (written in Spanish and English), and *Rites and Witnesses* (1982) (written in English). A sixth, *Claros varones de Belken* (translated by Julia Cruz as *Fair Gentleman of Belken County*), was already written and had been submitted to his publisher, but would not be published until 1986.

3 See, for example, Akers as well as Martín-Rodríguez.

4 The recently released edition, *The Valley / Estampas del valle*, pairs the English of the 1983 edition with the Spanish of the 1973 edition, brought out by Arte Público Press in 2014, testifies to this claim.

5 For a discussion of another Spanish genre, *costumbrismo*, on Hinojosa's Spanish-language version of the novel, see Calderón.

6 Martín-Rodríguez addresses a similar situation in a brief discussion of the competing versions of *The Mixquiahuala Letters* offered by Bilingual Press and Anchor-Doubleday (*Life*).

7 In the 1994 edition, the words "some months before" (121) are added to the end of the sentence.

8 In the 1990 edition, the sentence reads, "that everything in life was defeated, as if instinctively, the body, void of mind and logic, concluded that the failure to be fertilized each month meant failure in life" (109).

9 For competing arguments regarding Pastora's role as feminine hero, see Ibis Gómez-Vega, "Debunking Myths: The Hero's Role in Ana Castillo's *Sapogonia*" and Kelli Lyon Johnson, "Violence in the Borderlands: Crossing to the Home Space in the Novels of Ana Castillo."

Chapter 2 Translating in the Margins: Transcultural Glossaries

This chapter is a revised version of "Translating in the Margins: Attending to Glossaries in Latina/o Literature," Journal of Modern Literature *39.3 (Spring 2016). © Indiana University Press, 2016.*

1 For an insightful study of the history and changing literary usage of the figure of Malintzin/La Malinche, see Norma Alarcón's "Traddutora, Traditora: A Paradigmatic Figure of Chicana Representation."

2 I am following those definitions of acculturation and assimilation outlined by Herbert Gans: "Acculturation refers mainly to the newcomers' adoption of the culture (i.e., the behavior patterns, values, rules, symbols etc.) of the host society. . . .

Assimilation, on the other hand, refers to the newcomers' move out of formal and informal ethnic associations and other social institutions and into the host society's non-ethnic ones" (877).

3 For in-depth studies of the novel's consideration of the issue of ethnic assimilation, see Pablo Ramirez, "Resignifying Preservation: A Borderlands Response to American Eugenics in Jovita González's and Eve Raleigh's *Caballero*," and John M. González, "Terms of Engagement: Nation or Patriarch in Jovita González's and Eve Raleigh's *Caballero*."

4 See, for example, Maria Montes de Oca Ricks and Miguel Díaz Barriga.

5 Galarza's autobiography and attendant glossary was also published in a decade that saw the appearance of at least three Chicano slang dictionaries. See, for instance, "Zoot Suit: The Time and Its Temper," as well as Vasquez and Vasquez, *Regional Dictionary of Chicano Slang*, and Bow, *Chicano Slang*.

6 This joking translation also seemingly anticipates and undercuts the awe with which Rudolfo Anaya's *curandera* figure will be treated in his 1972 Chicano novel *Bless Me, Ultima*.

Chapter 3 Making Language Visible: Transcultural Typography

1 While some examples of italicization in Chicana/o border texts are actually simply oblique (meaning the words are of the same typeface, just slanted instead of changed into a different, more calligraphic font), the frequent critical and literary conflation of italicized and oblique fonts under the term "italics" is continued here. In both cases (oblique and italic), the letters of "foreign" words are slanted in order to differentiate them from the rest of the text printed in roman font.

2 More recently, the trilogy has expanded to a tetralogy with the publication *Leonor Park* (1991), which follows the family into the Great Depression, and perhaps even to a pentalogy given the subject matter of *A Daughter's a Daughter* (2008).

3 On Spanish-language maintenance and loss in the United States, see, for example, Rumbaut, Massey, and Bean, "Linguistic Life Expectancies" (2006) or Guerrero García's "Sorry, I Don't Speak Spanish: Hispanics Deal with the Loss of Spanish Fluency" (2013).

Chapter 4 "My Book Has Seen the Light of Day": The Editorial Paratexts of Recovery Projects

1 For additional thought-provoking studies of whiteness in this novel, see John M. González, "The Whiteness of the Blush: The Cultural Politics of Racial Formation in *The Squatter and the Don*"; Jennifer Tuttle, "The Symptoms of Conquest: Race, Class, and the Nervous Body in *The Squatter and the Don*"; and Vincent Pérez, "Remembering the Hacienda: Land and Community in Californio Narratives."

2 These references include Ruiz de Burton's letter to George Davidson on 9 June 1884, saying "I have been writing a book, so I hope you won't scold me for being indolent. I don't know whether I shall publish it under my own name, so *I want to keep the matter quiet yet*. Only two or three friends know I am writing it. I want to publish it this fall, in September" (*Conflicts of Interest* 505) and, after a number of references to difficulties, a letter to M. G. Vallejo saying, "El libro ya salío a luz. Pobre hijito feíto mío!" 'My book has seen the light of day. My poor little ugly child!' (*Conflicts* 507).

3 For a more transparent editorial approach to presenting incomplete material from the Recovering the U.S.-Hispanic Literary Heritage Project, see José Limón's editorial introduction to *Dew on the Thorn* by Jovita González.

4 For a thoughtful analysis of *Puppet*'s concerns regarding brutality directed at Mexicans, Mexican Americans, and Chicanos, see Ruben Murrillo, "*Ser o no ser*? Where Death, Violence, and Silence Intersect in Margarita Cota-Cárdenas's *Puppet*."

5 On this topic, see Ana María Manzanas Calvo, *Border Transits: Literature and Culture Across the Line* (2007).

6 See, for example, Mandy and Andy Books, Inc., whose tagline is "Books kids can flip over!"

Chapter 5 In the Margins: Readers Writing on *The House on Mango Street*

1 For scholarship that counsels against designating *Mango Street* as border literature, see, for example, Claudia Sadowski-Smith, *Border Fictions: Globalization, Empire, and Writing at the Boundaries of the United States* (2008). For criticism in favor of the border designation, see, for example, Monika Kaup, *Rewriting North American Borders in Chicano and Chicana Narrative* (2001).

2 The study includes one copy each from sellers in Annapolis (MD), Atlanta (GA), Blacksburg (VA), Bowling Green (OH), Disputanta (VA), Garland (TX), Los Angeles (CA), Miamisburg (OH), Nashua (NH), Saginaw (MI), Saint Simons Island (GA), San Diego (CA), Seattle (WA), Sherman Oaks (CA), and Troy (MI).

3 For a foundational discussion of Chicana/o repurposings of the bildungsroman, see Erlinda González-Berry and Tey Diana Rebolledo, "Growing Up Chicano: Tomás Rivera and Sandra Cisneros" (1985).

Works Cited

"About Modern Library." *Modern Library*. Web. 14 Feb. 2010.

Acker, Jennifer. "Note on the Text." *The Squatter and the Don*. New York: Modern Library Classics, 2004. Print.

Akers, John C. "From Translation to Rewriting: Rolando Hinojosa's. *The Valley*." *Americas Review* 21.1 (1993): 91–102. Print.

Alarcón, Norma. "Traddutora, Traditora: A Paradigmatic Figure of Chicana Representation." *Cultural Critique* 13 (1989): 57–87. Web. 15 Mar. 2011.

Aldama, Frederick Luis. *Brown on Brown: Chicano/a Representations of Gender, Sexuality, and Ethnicity*. Austin: University of Texas Press, 2005. Print.

Alemán, Jesse. "Historical Amnesia and the Vanishing Mestiza: The Problem of Race in *The Squatter and the Don* and *Ramona*." *Aztlán* 27.1 (2002): 59–75. Print.

Anaya, Rudolfo. *Bless Me, Ultima*. 1972. New York: Warner Books, 1999. Print.

Anzaldúa, Gloria. *Borderlands / La Frontera: The New Mestiza*. San Francisco: Spinsters / Aunt Lute, 1987. Print.

Anzaldúa, Gloria, and Cherríe Moraga, eds. *This Bridge Called My Back: Writings by Radical Women of Color*. 2nd ed. New York: Kitchen Table: Women of Color Press, 1983. Print.

Aranda, José F. "Contradictory Impulses: María Amparo Ruiz de Burton, Resistance Theory, and the Politics of Chicano/a Studies." *American Literature: A Journal of Literary History, Criticism, and Bibliography* 70.3 (1998): 551–579. Print.

———. "Grappling with the Archive of Mexican America." *English Language Notes* 45.1 (2007): 67–78. Print.

———. "Returning California to the People: Vigilantism in *The Squatter and the Don*." *María Amparo Ruiz de Burton: Critical and Pedagogical Perspectives*. Ed. Amelia María de la Luz Montes and Anne Elizabeth Goldman. Lincoln: University of Nebraska Press, 2004. 11–26. Print.

Arteaga, Alfred. "An Other Tongue." *An Other Tongue: Nation and Ethnicity in the Linguistic Borderlands*. Ed. Alfred Arteaga. Durham, NC: Duke University Press, 1994. 9–34. Print.

Baca, Damían. *Mestiz@ Scripts: Digital Migrations and the Territories of Writing*. New York: Palgrave Macmillan, 2008. Print.

Baker, Samuel. "Ana Castillo: The Protest Poet Goes Mainstream." *Publishers Weekly* 24.33 (12 Aug. 1996): 59–60. Print.
Balius, Andreu. "The Value of Typography in a Global Multilingual World." *ELISAVA tdD*. 2013. Web. 15 Aug. 2015.
Barriga, Miguel Díaz. "Vergüenza and Changing Chicano/a Narratives." *Changing Men and Masculinities in Latin America*. Duke University Press, 2003. 256–280. Print.
Bornstein, George, and Theresa Tinkle. "Introduction." *The Iconic Page in Manuscript, Print, and Digital Culture*. Ann Arbor: University of Michigan Press, 1998. 1–6. Print.
Bow, Ernie. *Chicano Slang: A Short List*. Santa Maria, CA: El Quetzal, 1978. Print.
Brady, Mary Pat. *Extinct Lands, Temporal Geographies*. Durham, NC: Duke University Press, 2002. Print.
———. "The Fungibility of Borders." *Nepantla: Views from the South* 1.1 (2000): 171–190. Print.
Brezina, David. "On Diacritics." *I Love Typography*. 24 Jan. 2009. Web. 9 Aug. 2015.
Brito, Aristeo. *El diablo en Texas*. Tucson, AZ: Editorial Peregrinos, 1976. Print.
———. *El diablo en Texas / The Devil in Texas*. Trans. David William Foster. Tempe, AZ: Bilingual Press, 1990. Print.
Brown, Bill. "Introduction: Textual Materialism." *PMLA* 125.1 (Jan. 2010): 24–28. Print.
Bruce-Novoa, Juan. "The Topological Space of Chicano Literature." *RetroSpace: Collected Essays on Chicano Literature, Theory, and History*. Houston: Arte Público Press, 1990. 146–156.
Bryant, John. *Melville Unfolding: Sexuality, Politics, and the Versions of* Typee. Ann Arbor: University of Michigan Press, 2008. Print.
———. "Witness and Access: The Uses of the Fluid Text." *Textual Cultures: Texts, Contexts, Interpretation* 2.1 (2007): 16–42. Print.
Cabeza de Baca, Fabiola. *We Fed Them Cactus*. Albuquerque: University of New Mexico Press, 1954. Print.
Caldéron, Héctor. *Narratives of Greater Mexico: Essays on Chicano Literary History, Genre, and Borders*. Austin: University of Texas Press, 2004. Print.
Callahan, Laura. *Spanish/English Codeswitching in a Written Corpus*. Philadelphia: John Benjamins Publishing, 2004. Print.
Candelaria, Nash. *A Daughter's a Daughter*. Tempe, AZ: Bilingual Press, 2008. Print.
———. *Inheritance of Strangers*. Tempe, AZ: Bilingual Press, 1985. Print.
———. *Leonor Park*. Tempe, AZ: Bilingual Press, 1991. Print.
———. *Memories of the Alhambra*. Tempe, AZ: Bilingual Press, 1977. Print.
———. "Nash Candelaria: An Interview." Interview with Bruce-Novoa. *De colores* 5.1–2 (1980): 115–129. Print.
———. *Not by the Sword*. Tempe, AZ: Bilingual Press, 1982. Print.
———. *Second Communion*. Tempe, AZ: Bilingual Press, 2010. Print.
Cantú, Norma Elia. *Canícula: Snapshots of a Girlhood en la Frontera*. Albuquerque: University of New Mexico Press, 1995. Print.
Carpenter, Laura. "The Ambiguity of 'Having Sex': The Subjective Experience of Virginity Loss in the United States." *Journal of Sex Research* 38.2 (2001): 127–139. Web. 10 Feb. 2013.
Carr, Peter. "Re-Borderization in the Novels of Ana Castillo and Cormac McCarthy." *Revista de Estudios Norteamericanos* 12 (2007): 21–37. Print.
Castillo, Ana. "Ana Castillo: Two Interviews." Interviews by Héctor A. Torres. *Conversations with Contemporary Chicana and Chicano Writers*. Ed. Torres. Albuquerque: University of New Mexico Press, 2007. 146–190. Print.

———. "Antihero." 1981. TS Series IV, Box 15, Folder 7. Ana Castillo Papers, California Ethnic and Multicultural Archives, University of California, Santa Barbara.
———. "Death of a Chicken." 1981. TS Series IV, Box 15, Folder 7. Ana Castillo Papers, California Ethnic and Multicultural Archives, University of California, Santa Barbara.
———. *The Guardians*. New York: Random House, 2007. Print.
———. "An Interview with Ana Castillo." Interview by Bryce Milligan. *South Central Review* 16.1 (1999): 19–29. *JSTOR*. Web. 21 June 2011.
———. "Introduction." *The Squatter and the Don*. By María Amparo Ruiz de Burton. Ed. Jennifer M. Acker. New York: Modern Library Classics, 2004. Print.
———. *Massacre of the Dreamers: Essays on Xicanisma*. New York: Penguin Books, 1994. Print.
———. *The Mixquiahuala Letters*. Binghamton, NY: Bilingual Press, 1986. Print.
———. *The Mixquiahuala Letters*. New York: Anchor Books, 1992. Print.
———. *My Father Was a Toltec and Selected Poems, 1973–1988*. Albuquerque: West End Press, 1988. Print.
———. *Peel My Love Like an Onion*. New York: Doubleday, 1999. Print.
———. *Psst . . . I Have Something to Tell You, Mi Amor*. San Antonio: Wings Press, 2005. Print.
———. *Sapogonia (An Anti-Romance in 3/8 Meter)*. Tempe, AZ: Bilingual Press, 1990. Print.
———. *Sapogonia: An Anti-Romance in 3/8 Meter*. New York: Anchor–Doubleday, 1994. Print.
———. *So Far from God*. New York: Norton, 1993. Print.
———. *Watercolor Women/Opaque Men: A Novel in Verse*. Willimantic, CT: Curbstone Books, 2005. Print.
———. *Women Are Not Roses*. Houston: Arte Público Press, 1984. Print.
Castillo, Debra, and María Socorro Tabuenca Córdoba. *Border Women: Writing from La Frontera*. Minneapolis: University of Minnesota Press, 2002. Print.
Chartier, Roger. *The Order of Books: Readers, Authors, and Libraries in Europe*. Stanford, CA: Stanford University Press, 1994. Print.
Chicana por Mi Raza Digital Memory Collective. University of Illinois Urbana–Champaign. 2015. Web. 26 Aug. 2015.
Cisneros, Josue David. *The Borders Crossed Us: Rhetorics of Borders, Citizenship, and Latina/o Identity*. Tuscaloosa: University of Alabama Press, 2014. Print.
Cisneros, Sandra. "Do You Know Me? I Wrote *The House on Mango Street*." *Americas Review* 15.1 (1987): 78–79. Print.
———. *Have You Seen Marie?* New York: Vintage, 2014. Print.
———. *The House on Mango Street*. Houston: Arte Público Press, 1984. Print.
———. *The House on Mango Street*. 2nd rev. edition. Houston: Arte Público Press, 1988.
———. *The House on Mango Street*. 1984. New York: Vintage, 1991. Print.
———. *The House on Mango Street*. 1984. New York: Knopf, 1994. Print.
———. *The House on Mango Street*. 1984. Intro. Sandra Cisneros. New York: Vintage Contemporaries, 2009. Print.
———. Interview. *Interviews with Writers of the Postcolonial World*. By Feroza F. Jussawalla and Reed Way Dasenbrock. Jackson: University Press of Mississippi, 1992. 286–306. Print.
Cobos, R. *A Dictionary of New Mexico and Southern Colorado Spanish*. Santa Fe: Museum of New Mexico Press, 2003. Print.
Cota-Cárdenas, Margarita. "Conversando con Margarita Cota-Cárdenas sobre *Puppet*."

Interview with Cecilia Yocupicio Valenzuela. *Explicacíon de Textos Literarios* 33.1 (2004–2005): 55–67. Print.

———. *Puppet: A Chicano Novella*. Austin: Relámpago Books, 1985. Print.

———. *Puppet*. Trans. Barbara D. Riess and Trino Sandoval. Albuquerque: University of New Mexico Press, 2000. Print.

———. "Subtitles: PUPPET." Message to the author. 2 July 2015. Email.

Cotera, María. "Feminism on the Border: *Caballero* and the Poetics of Collaboration." *Native Speakers: Ella Deloria, Zora Neale Hurston, Jovita González, and the Poetics of Culture*. Austin: University of Texas Press, 2008. 199–224. Print.

———. "Hombres Necios: A Critical Epilogue." *Caballero: A Historical Novel*. Jovita González and Eve Raleigh. Ed. José E. Limón and María Cotera. College Station: Texas A&M University Press, 1996. 339–346. Print.

Cox, James. *The Red Land to the South: American Indian Writers and Indigenous Mexico*. Minneapolis: University of Minnesota Press, 2012. Print.

Crúz, Felicia J. "On the 'Simplicity' of Sandra Cisneros's *House on Mango Street*." *MFS: Modern Fiction Studies* 47.4 (2001): 910–946. Web. 17 Aug. 2009.

Cutter, Martha. *Lost and Found in Translation: Contemporary Ethnic American Writing and the Politics of Language Diversity*. Chapel Hill: University of North Carolina Press, 2005. Print.

Dane, Joseph. *Out of Sorts: On Typography and Print Culture*. Philadelphia: University of Pennsylvania Press, 2011. Print.

Darnton, Robert. "What Is the History of Books?" *The Book History Reader*. Ed. David Finkelstein and Alistair McCleery. New York: Routledge, 2002. 9–26. Print.

Del Barco, Mandalit. "How Kodak's Shirley Cards Set Photography's Skin-Tone Standard." *Morning Edition*. NPR. 13 Nov. 2014. Radio.

Deleuze, Gilles, and Félix Guattari. "What Is a Minor Literature?" *Kafka: Toward a Minor Literature*. Trans. Dana Polan. Minneapolis: University of Minnesota Press, 1986. 16–27. Print.

Derrida, Jacques. "Living On: Borderlines." Trans. James Hulbert. *Deconstructionism and Criticism*. 2nd ed. New York: Continuum Publishing, 2004. 62–142. Print. x Drucker, Johanna. "Electronic Media and the Status of Writing." *Figuring the Word: Essays on Books, Writing, and Visual Poetics*. New York City: Granary Books, 1998. 232–236. Print.

Espadas, Juan, and Arvilla Payne. "Linguistic Variation in Two Works of Rolando Hinojosa." *Confluencia* 6.1 (1990): 65–74. Print.

Esquibel, Catrióna Rueda. *With Her Machete in Her Hand: Reading Chicana Lesbians*. Austin: University of Texas Press, 2006. Print.

Fernández, Roberta. *Intaglio: A Novel in Six Stories*. Houston: Arte Público Press, 1990. Print.

Firmat, Gustavo Pérez. "For a Bilingual Writer, 'No One True Language.'" Interview with Renee Montagne. NPR: *Morning Edition*. 17 Oct. 2011. Radio.

Flores, Lauro. "Chicano Autobiography: Culture, Ideology, and the Self." *The Americas Review* 18.2 (1990): 80–91. Print.

Fox, Claire F. *The Fence and the River: Culture and Politics at the U.S.–Mexico Border.* Minneapolis: University of Minnesota Press, 1999. Print.

Frazier, James Diego. "The Squatter and the Don: Title Page as Paratextual Borderland." *ANQ: A Quarterly Journal of Short Articles, Notes, and Reviews* 22.2 (2009): 30–37. Print.

Freistat, Neil. "Introduction: The Place of the Book and the Book as Place." *Poems in Their Place: The Intertextuality and Order of Poetic Collections*. Chapel Hill: University of North Carolina Press, 1986. 3–17. Print.

Frosh, Stephen, and Lisa Baraitser. "Marginalia." *Qualitative Research in Psychology* 5 (2008): 68–77. Web. 22 July 2015.
Galarza, Ernesto. *Barrio Boy. 1971.* South Bend, IN: Notre Dame University Press, 2011. Print.
———. *Merchants of Labor.* Charlotte, NC: McNally and Loftin, 1964. Print.
———. *Strangers in Our Fields.* United States Section, Join United States-Mexico Trade Union Committee, 1956. Print.
Gans, Herbert J. "Toward a Reconciliation of 'Assimilation' and 'Pluralism': The Interplay of Acculturation and Ethnic Retention." *International Migration Review* 31.4 (1997): 875–892. Web. 12 Sept. 2014.
García, Guerrero. "Sorry, I Don't Speak Spanish: Hispanics Deal with the Loss of Spanish Fluency." *Minero Magazine.* 12 Feb. 2013. Web. 1 June 2015.
García Márquez, Gabriel. *One Hundred Years of Solitude.* Trans. Gregory Rabassa. New York: Harper & Row, 1970. Print.
Garza-Falcón, Leticia. *Gente Decente: A Borderlands Response to the Rhetoric of Dominance.* Austin: University of Texas Press, 1998. Print.
Genette, Gérard. *Paratexts: Thresholds of Interpretation.* Trans. Jane E. Lewin. Cambridge University Press, 1997. Print.
Goldman, Anne. *The Squatter and the Don.* Review essay. *MELUS* 19.3 (1994): 129–131. Print.
Gomez-Peña, Guillermo. "Letter to an Unknown Thief." *Dangerous Border Crossers: The Artist Talks Back.* New York: Routledge, 2000. 261–262. Print.
———. "The Virtual Barrio @ the Other Frontier (or the Chicano Interneta)." *Dangerous Border Crossers: The Artist Talks Back.* New York: Routledge, 2000. 247–260. Print.
Gomez-Peña, Guillermo, Enrique Chagoya, and Felicia Rice. *Codex Espangliensis: From Columbus to the Border Patrol.* San Francisco: City Lights Books, 2000. Print.
Gómez-Vega, Ibis. "Debunking Myths: The Hero's Role in Ana Castillo's *Sapogonia.*" *Americas Review* 22.1–2 (1994): 244–258. Print.
González, John M. "Terms of Engagement: Nation or Patriarch in Jovita González's and Eve Raleigh's *Caballero.*" *Recovering the U.S. Hispanic Literary Heritage.* 4th ed. Ed. José F. Aranda and Silvio Torres-Saillant. Houston: Arte Público Press, 1997. 264–276. Print.
———. "The Whiteness of the Blush: The Cultural Politics of Racial Formation in *The Squatter and the Don.*" *Maria Amparo Ruiz de Burton: Critical and Pedagogical Perspectives.* Ed. Amelia María de la Luz Montes and Anne Elizabeth Goldman. Lincoln: University of Nebraska Press, 2004. 153–168. Print.
González, Jovita. *The Dew on the Thorn.* Houston: Arte Público Press, 1997. Print.
González, Jovita, and Eve Raleigh. *Caballero: A Historical Novel.* Ed. José E. Limón and Maria Cotera. College Station: Texas A&M University Press, 1996. Print.
González, Marcial. *Chicano Novels and the Politics of Form: Race, Class, and Reification.* Ann Arbor: University of Michigan Press, 2008. Print.
González-Berry, Erlinda, and Tey Diana Rebolledo. "Growing Up Chicano: Tomás Rivera and Sandra Cisneros." *Revista Chicano-Riqueña* 13.34 (1985): 109–119. Print.
Grant, Ulysses S. *Personal Memoirs of Ulysses S. Grant.* New York: Cosimo, 2006. Print.
Greimas, A. J. *Structural Semantics: An Attempt at a Method.* Trans. Daniele McDowell, Ronald Schleifer, and Alan Velie. Lincoln: University of Nebraska Press, 1983. Print.
Gruesz, Kirsten Silva. *Ambassadors of Culture: The Transamerican Origins of Latino Writing.* Princeton, NJ: Princeton University Press, 2002. Print.
Gutíerrez, Ramón, and Genaro M. Padilla. "Introduction." *Recovering the U.S.-Hispanic Literary Heritage.* Houston: Arte Público Press, 1993. Print.
Gutjahr, Paul C., and Megan Benton, eds. "Introduction." *Illuminating Letters: Typography*

and Literary Interpretation. Amherst: University of Massachusetts Press, 2001. 1–17. Print.
Hamilton, Patrick. *Of Space and Mind: Cognitive Mappings of Contemporary Chicano/a Fiction*. Austin: University of Texas Press, 2011. Print.
Hernández, Ellie D. *Postnationalism in Chicana/o Literature and Culture*. Austin: University of Texas Press, 2010. Print.
Hernández, Gilbert. *Beyond Palomar*. Seattle: Fantagraphics, 2007. Print.
———. *Heartbreak Soup (Love and Rockets)*. Seattle: Fantagraphics, 2007. Print.
———. *Human Diastrophism*. Seattle: Fantagraphics, 2007. Print.
———. *Palomar: The Heartbreak Soup Stories, A Love and Rockets Book*. Seattle: Fantagraphics, 2003. Print.
Hernández, Jaime, and Gilbert Hernández. *Blood of Palomar*. Seattle: Fantagraphics, 1996.
Hewson, Lance. "The Bilingual Edition in Translation Studies." *Visible Language* 27.1–2 (1993): 139–162. Print.
Hinojosa, Rolando. *Becky and Her Friends*. Houston: Arte Público Press, 1990. Print.
———. *Claros varones de Belken*. Berkeley, CA: Editorial Justa Publications, 1981. Print.
———. *Dear Rafe*. Houston: Arte Público Press, 1981.
———. *Estampas del valle y otras obras / Sketches of the Valley and Other Works*. Trans. Gustavo Valdéz and José Reyna. Berkeley, CA: Quinto Sol, 1973. Print.
———. *Estampas del valle y otras obras / Sketches of the Valley and Other Works*. Trans. Gustavo Valdéz and José Reyna. 2nd ed. Berkeley, CA: Editorial Justa Publications, 1977.
———. *Estampas del valle y otras obras / Sketches of the Valley and Other Works*. Trans. Gustavo Valdéz and José Reyna. 3rd ed. Berkeley, CA: Editorial Justa Publications, 1980.
———. *Fair Gentlemen of Belken County*. Trans. Julia Cruz. Tempe, AZ: Bilingual Press, 1987. Print.
———. *Generaciones y semblanzas*. Berkeley, CA: Editorial Justa Publications, 1977. Print.
———. *Klail City*. Houston: Arte Público Press, 1987. Print.
———. *Klail City y sus alrededores*. Havana, Cuba: Casa de las Americas, 1976. Print.
———. *Korean Love Songs*. Berkeley, CA: Editorial Justa Publications, 1977. Print.
———. *Mi querido Rafa*. Houston: Arte Público Press, 1981. Print.
———. *Partners in Crime: A Rafe Buenrostro Mystery*. Houston: Arte Público Press, 1985. Print.
———. *Rites and Witnesses*. Houston: Arte Público Press, 1982. Print.
———. "The Sense of Place." In *The Rolando Hinojosa Reader: Essays Historical and Critical*. Ed. José David Saldívar. Houston: Arte Público Press, 1985. 18–24. Print.
———. *The Valley*. Tucson, AZ: Bilingual Press / Editorial Bilingüe, 1983. Print.
Hodgson, Richard, and Ralph Sarkonak. "Bi-Graphic Collisions: Languages in Con(tact)(flict)." *Visible Language* 21.1 (1987): 18–41. Print.
hooks, bell. "Choosing the Margin as a Space of Radical Openness." *Yearning: Race, Gender, and Cultural Politics*. Cambridge, MA: South End Press, 1990. Print.
"The House on Mango Street Curriculum Guide." Jane Schaffer Writing Program. 2012. Web. 20 Aug. 2015.
Huerta, Javier O. *American Copia: An Immigrant Epic*. Houston: Arte Público Press, 2012. Print.
Jackson, Heather. *Marginalia: Readers Writing in Books*. New Haven, CT: Yale University Press, 2002. Print.
Johnson, Kelli Lyon. "Violence in the Borderlands: Crossing to the Home Space in the Novels of Ana Castillo." *Frontiers* 25.1 (2004): 39–58. *Academic Search Premier*. Web. 21 June 2011.

Jussawalla, Feroza F., and Reed Way Dasenbrock. *Interviews with Writers of the Postcolonial World.* Jackson: University Press of Mississippi, 1992. Print.

Kanellos, Nicolás. "Chavez v Arte Publico Press: Reflections on Artists and Copyright on Campus." Houston: University of Houston Law Center / Institute of Higher Education Law and Governance, 2000. Web. 15 July 2015.

———. "Foreword." *Recovering the U.S.-Hispanic Literary Heritage.* Vol. 2. Ed. Erlinda Gonzales-Berry and Chuck Tatum. Houston: Arte Público Press, 1993.

Kaup, Monika. *Rewriting North American Borders in Chicano and Chicana Narrative.* New York: Peter Lang, 2001. Print.

———. "The Unsustainable Hacienda: The Rhetoric of Progress in Jovita González and Eve Raleigh's *Caballero.*" *MFS: Modern Fiction Studies* 51.3 (2005): 561–591. Print.

King, Rosemary. *Border Confluences: Borderland Narratives from the Mexican War to the Present.* Tucson: University of Arizona Press, 2004. Print.

Kinney, Thomas J. "Remapping the Archive: Recovered Literature and the Deterritorialization of the Canon." *Recovering the US-Hispanic Literary Heritage.* Vol. 4. Ed. José F. Aranda Jr. and Silvio Torres-Saillant. Houston: Arte Público Press, 2002. 58–73. Print.

Köhler, Angelika. "Determined to Indeterminacy: Pan-American and European Dimensions of the Mestizaje Concept in Ana Castillo's *Sapogonia.*" *Borderline Identities in Chicano Culture: Hrsg. Michele Bottalico und Saleh el Moncef bin Khalifa.* Venice: Mazzanti Editori, 2006. 101–114. Print.

Kolker, Claudia. "Family Feud." *Houston Press,* 29 June 1995. Web. 20 Aug. 2015.

Lapan, Tovin. "California Birth Certificates and Accents: O'Connor Alright, Ramón and José Is Not." *The Guardian* 11 Apr. 2015. Web. 21 Aug. 2015.

Larsen, Neil. "Foreword." *Border Writing: The Multidimensional Text.* By Emily Hicks. Minneapolis: University of Minnesota Press, 1991. xi–xxi. Print.

Leal, Luis. "History and Memory in *Estampas del Valle.*" *Revista Chicano-Riqueña* 12.3–4 (1984): 101–108. Print.

Lee, Joyce Glover. *Rolando Hinojosa and the American Dream.* Denton: University of North Texas Press, 1997. Print.

Limón, José "Introduction." *Caballero: A Historical Novel.* By Jovita González and Eve Raleigh. Ed. José E. Limón and Maria Cotera. College Station: Texas A&M University Press, 1996. Print.

———. "Introduction." *The Dew on the Thorn.* By Jovita González. Houston: Arte Público Press, 1997. Print.

López, Marissa. "Chicana/o Literature: Theoretically Speaking, Formally Reading Ana Castillo's *Sapogonia.*" *Aztlan* 32.2 (2007): 139–156. Print.

———. *Chicano Nations: The Hemispheric Origins of Mexican American Literature.* New York: New York University Press, 2011. Print.

Loyal, C. [María Amparo Ruiz de Burton.] *The Squatter and the Don.* San Francisco: n.p., 1885. Print.

Lynch, Joy. "'A Distinct Place in America Where All Mestizos Reside': Landscape and Identity in Ana Castillo's *Sapogonia* and Diana Chang's *The Frontiers of Love.*" *MELUS* 26.3 (2001): 119–144. Print.

Manzanas Calvo, Ana María. *Border Transits: Literature and Culture across the Line.* Amsterdam: Rodopi, 2007. Print.

———. "A Mestiza in the Borderlands: Margarita Cota-Cárdenas' *Puppet.*" *Atlantis* 34.1 (2012): 47–62. Print.

Márquez, Antonio. "Self and Culture: Autobiography as Cultural Narrative." *Discurso literario* 7.1 (1990): 51–66. Web. 15 Dec. 2009.

Marshall, Catherine C. "Annotation: From Paper Books to the Digital Library." *Proceedings of the Second ACM International Conference on Digital Libraries* (1997): 131–140. Web. 11 Nov. 2009.

Martin, Désirée A. "Multilingual Aesthetics and the Limits of Chicano/a Identity in Margarita Cota-Cárdenas' *Puppet*." *MELUS* 33.3 (2008): 91–109. Print.

Martín-Rodriguez, Manuel. "En la lengua materna: Las escritoras chicanas y la novela en español." *Latin American Literary Review* 23.45 (1995): 64–84. Print.

———. *Life in Search of Readers: Reading (in) Chicano/a Literature*. Albuquerque: University of New Mexico Press, 2003. Print.

Martínez, Manuel Luis. *Countering the Counterculture: Rereading Postwar American Dissent from Jack Kerouac to Tomas Rivera*. Madison: University of Wisconsin Press, 2003. Print.

———. "Telling the Difference between the Border and the Borderlands: Materiality and Theoretical Practice." In *Globalization on the Line: Culture, Capital, and Citizenship at U.S. Borders*. Ed. Claudia Sadowski-Smith. New York: Palgrave, 2002. 53–68. Print.

McCoy, Beth. "Race and the (Para)Textual Condition." *PMLA* 121.1 (2006): 156–169. Print.

McCracken, Ellen. "From Chapbooks to *Chica Lit*: U.S. Latina Writers and the New Literary Identity." *International Perspectives on Chicana/o Studies: "This World Is My Place."* Ed. Catherine Leen and Niamh Thornton. New York: Routledge, 2014. 11–23. Print.

———. *New Latina Narrative: The Feminine Space of Postmodern Ethnicity*. Tucson: University of Arizona Press, 1999. Print.

———. "Sandra Cisneros." *Latino and Latina Authors*. Ed. Alan West-Durán. New York: Charles Scribner's Sons, 2004. Gale Cengage Learning. 230–250. Web. 12 July 2015.

McFadden, Syreeta. "Light and Dark: The Racial Biases That Remain in Photography." Interview with Celeste Headlee. *Tell Me More*. NPR. 16 Apr. 2014. Radio.

McGann, Jerome. *A Critique of Modern Textual Criticism*. Chicago: University of Chicago Press, 1983. Print.

———. *The Textual Condition*. Princeton: Princeton University Press, 1991. Print.

McKenzie, D. F. *Bibliography and the Sociology of Texts*. London: The British Library, 1986. Print.

McMahon, Marci. *Domestic Negotiations: Gender, Nation, and Self-Fashioning in US Mexicana and Chicana Literature and Art*. New Brunswick, NJ: Rutgers University Press, 2013. Print.

Mendoza, Louis Gerard. *Historia: The Literary Making of Chicano and Chicana History*. College Station: Texas A&M University Press, 2001. Print.

Miner, Heather, and Robin Sager. "Beyond National Borders: Researching and Teaching Jovita González." *Teaching and Studying the Americas: Cultural Influences from Colonialism to the Present*. Ed. Anthony B. Pinn, Caroline F. Levander, and Michael O. Emerson. New York: Palgrave Macmillan, 2010. Print.

Montes, Amelia María de la Luz, and Anne Elizabeth Goldman, eds. *María Amparo Ruiz de Burton: Critical and Pedagogical Perspectives*. Lincoln: University of Nebraska Press, 2004. Print.

Montes de Oca Ricks, Maria. "Ernesto Galarza." *Dictionary of Literary Biography. Chicano Writers: Second Series*. Ed. Francisco Lomelí and Carl R. Shirley. Vol. 122. Detroit: Gale , 1992. 89–101. Web. 9 May 2013.

Moylan, Michele, and Lane Stiles. "Introduction." *Reading Books: Essays on the Material Text and Literature in America*. Amherst: University of Massachusetts Press, 1996. 1–15. Print.

Murillo, Ruben. "*Ser o no ser*? Where Death, Violence, and Silence Intersect in Margarita Cota-Cárdenas's *Puppet*." *Textxet: Studies in Comparative Literature* 68 (2013): 139–158. Web. 18 Apr 2015.

Murrah-Mandril, Erin. "Jovita González and Margaret Eimer's *Caballero* as Memory Site." *Arizona Quarterly* 67.4 (Winter 2011): 135–153. Print.

Neate, Wilson. "The Function of Belken County in the Fiction of Rolando Hinojosa: The Voicing of the Chicano Experience." *Americas Review* 18.1 (1990): 92–102. Print.

Obejas, Achy. Interview with Marika Preziuso. *Small Axe Salon*. 27 Oct. 2010. Web. 14 May 2014.

Paredes, Américo. *With His Pistol in His Hand: A Border Ballad and Its Hero*. Austin: University of Texas Press, 1958. Print.

"Penguin Launches Personality Driven Hispanic Imprint." *Authorlink* 6 Mar. 2008. Web. 26 Aug. 2015.

Pérez, Vincent. "Remembering the Hacienda: Land and Community in Californio Narratives." *María Amparo Ruiz de Burton: Critical and Pedagogical Perspectives*. Ed. Amelia María de la Luz Montes and Anne Elizabeth Goldman. Lincoln: University of Nebraska Press, 2004. 27–55. Print.

Petty, Leslie. "The 'Dual'-ing Images of La Malinche and La Virgen de Guadalupe in Cisneros's *The House on Mango Street*." *MELUS* 25.2 (2000): 119–132. Print.

Pizer, Donald. "Self-Censorship and the Editing of Late Nineteenth-Century Naturalistic Texts." *The Theory and Practice of American Literary Naturalism: Selected Essays and Reviews*. Carbondale: Southern Illinois University Press, 1993. 133–152. Print.

Plascencia, Salvador. *The People of Paper*. New York: Mariner Books, 2005. Print.

Poey, Delia. "Coming of Age in the Curriculum." *Americas Review* 24.3–4 (1996): 201–217. Print.

Portes, Alejandro, and Rubén G. Rumbaut. *Children of Immigrants Longitudinal Study, 1991–2006*. Ann Arbor, MI: Inter-university Consortium for Political and Social Research, 2007. Web. 11 June 2014.

Pratt, Mary Louise. *Imperial Eyes: Travel Writing and Transculturation*. 2nd ed. New York: Routledge, 2008. Print.

Rama, Angel. *Transculturación narrativa en América Latina*. Mexico City: Siglo Veintiuno, 1982. Print.

Ramirez, Pablo. "Resignifying Preservation: A Borderlands Response to American Eugenics in Jovita González's and Eve Raleigh's *Caballero*." *Canadian Review of American Studies* 39.1 (2009): 21–39. Web. 13 Oct. 2011.

Rebolledo, Tey Diana. "Foreword." *Puppet*. By Margarita Cota-Cárdenas. Albuquerque: University of New Mexico Press, 2000. Print.

Rechy, John. *City of Night*. 1963. Intro. John Rechy. New York: Grove Press, 1984. Print.

———. "*City of Night* Remembered." *Beneath the Skin: The Collected Essays of John Rechy*. New York: Carroll and Graf Publishers, 2004. Print.

———. *The Life and Adventures of Lyle Clemens*. New York: Grove Press, 2003.

Reitani, Luigi: "Face to Face: Hölderlin in a New Italian Bilingual Edition." *MLN* 117.3 (2002): 590–598. Print.

Rios, Herminio. "Letter from the Editor." *Estampas del valle y otras obras*. Berkeley, CA: Quinto Sol, 1973. Print.

Rivera, John-Michael. "Recovering Mexican America in the Classroom." *Recovering the U.S. Hispanic Literary Heritage*. Vol. 5. Ed. Kenya Dworkin y Méndez and Agnes Lugo-Ortiz. Houston: Arte Público Press, 2006. 92–106. Print.

Rivera, Tomás. *. . . y no se lo tragó la tierra / And the Earth Did Not Part*. Trans. Herminio Rios. Berkeley: Quinto Sol, 1971. Print.

Rodríguez, Jaime Javier. "*Caballero*'s Global Continuum: Time and Place in South Texas." *MELUS* 33.1 (2008): 117–138. Web. 24 Mar. 2013.

Rodriguez, Richard. *Hunger of Memory: The Education of Richard Rodriguez*. 1982. New York: Dial Press, 2005. Print.

Rosaldo, Renato. "Politics, Patriarchs, and Laughter." *Cultural Critique* 6 (1987): 65–86. Web. 5 Nov. 2009.

Rudin, Ernst. *Tender Accents of Sound: Spanish in the Chicano Novel in English*. Tempe, AZ: Bilingual Press, 1996. Print.

Ruiz de Burton, María Amparo (see also Loyal, C.). *Conflicts of Interest: The Letters of María Amparo Ruiz de Burton*. Ed. Rosaura Sánchez and Beatrice Pita. Houston: Arte Público Press, 2001. Print.

———. *The Squatter and the Don*. San Francisco: Samuel Carson & Co., 1885. Print.

———. *The Squatter and the Don*. 1885. Ed. Rosaura Sánchez and Beatrice Pita. Houston: Arte Público Press, 1992. Print.

———. *The Squatter and the Don*. 1885. Ed. Rosaura Sánchez and Beatrice Pita. 2nd ed. Houston: Arte Público Press, 1997. Print.

———. *The Squatter and the Don*. 1885. Ed. Jennifer M. Acker. New York: Modern Library Classics, 2004. Print.

Rumbaut, Rubén G., Douglas S. Massey, and Frank D. Bean. "Linguistic Life Expectancies: Immigrant Language Retention in Southern California." *Population and Development Review* 32.3 (2006): 447–460. Print.

Sadowski-Smith, Claudia. *Border Fictions: Globalization, Empire, and Writing at the Boundaries of the United States*. Charlottesville: University of Virginia Press, 2008. Print.

———. "Twenty-First-Century Chicana/o Border Writing." *South Atlantic Quarterly* 105.4 (2006): 717–737. Web. 13 June 2013.

Saeta, Elsa. "Ana Castillo's *Sapogonia*: Narrative Point of View as a Study in Perception." *Confluencia* 10.1 (1994): 67–72. Print.

Salazar, Carmen. "Margarita Cota-Cárdenas." In *Dictionary of Literary Biography. Chicano Writers, Second Series*. Ed. Francisco Lomelí and Carl R. Shirley. Vol. 122. Detroit: Gale, 1992. 82–87. Web. 6 Oct. 2009.

Saldívar, José David. "Chicano Border Narratives as Cultural Critique." *Dialectics of Our America: Genealogy, Cultural Critique, and Literary History*. Durham, NC: Duke University Press, 1991. Print.

Saldívar, Ramón. "Ideologies of the Self: Chicano Autobiography." *Diacritics* 15.3 (1985): 25–34. Print.

———. "Narrative, Ideology, and the Reconstruction of American Literary History." *Criticism in the Borderlands: Studies in Chicano Literature, Culture, and Ideology*. Ed. Héctor Calderón and José David Saldívar. Durham, NC: Duke University Press, 1991. 11–20. Print.

Saldívar-Hull, Sonia. *Feminism on the Border: Chicana Gender Politics and Literature*. Berkeley: University of California Press, 2000. Print.

Sánchez, Rosaura, and Beatrice Pita. "Introduction." *The Squatter and the Don*. By María Amparo Ruiz de Burton. Ed. Sánchez and Pita. 2nd ed. Houston: Arte Público Press, 1997. Print.

Sandoval, Chela. "Chicana/o Artivism: Judy Baca's Digital Work with Youth of Color." *Learning Race and Ethnicity: Youth and Digital Media*. Ed. Anne Everett. Cambridge, MA: MIT Press, 2008. 81–108. Web. 20 Aug. 2015.

Sedlmeier, Florian. "Rereading Literary Form: Paratexts, Transpositions, and Postethnic Literature around 2000." *Journal of Literary Theory* 6.1 (2012): 213–233. Web. 1 Aug. 2015.

Seuling, Barbara. *How to Write a Children's Book and Get It Published*. Hoboken, NJ: John Wiley & Sons, 2005. Print.

Shillingsburg, Peter. "A Slight Conflict of Aims: Scholarly vs. Academic Editing." *Editors, Scholars, and the Social Text*. Ed. Darcy Cullen. Toronto: University of Toronto Press, 2012. 35–43. Print.

Shirley, Paula. "*Memories of the Alhambra* by Nash Candelaria." *MELUS* 6.2 (1979): 100–103. Print.

Short, Kayann. "Coming to the Table: The Differential Politics of *This Bridge Called My Back*." *Eroticism and Containment: Notes from the Flood Plain*. New York: New York University Press, 1994. Print.

Shuru, Xochitl Estrada. "Poetics of Hysteria: Political Consciousness and Insanity in *Puppet* by Margarita Cota-Cárdenas." *CEA Critic* 67.3 (2005): 1–15. Print.

Socolovsky, Maya. "Borrowed Homes, Homesickness, and Memory in Ana Castillo's *Sapogonia*." *Aztlan* 24.2 (1999): 73–94. Print.

Soja, Edward. *Thirdspace: Journeys to Los Angeles and Other Real-and-Imagined Places*. Hoboken, NJ: Wiley-Blackwell, 1996. Print.

Sommer, Doris. *Proceed with Caution, When Engaged by Minority Writing in the Americas*. Cambridge, MA: Harvard University Press, 1999. Print.

Sorsoli, Lynn. "'I Remember,' 'I Thought,' 'I Know I Didn't Say': Silence and Memory in Trauma Narratives." *Memory* 18.2 (2010): 129–141. Web. 27 July 2014.

Spurgeon, Sara L. *Ana Castillo*. Boise: Boise State University Press, 2004. Print.

Saint John, Rachel. *Line in the Sand: A History of the Western U.S.-Mexico Border*. Princeton, NJ: Princeton University Press, 2012. Print.

Stavans, Ilan. "Introduction to the 40th Anniversary Edition." *Barrio Boy*. By Ernesto Galarza. South Bend, IN: Notre Dame University Press, 2011. ix-xxiii. Print.

Suarez, Michael F. "Historiographical Problems and Possibilities in Book History and National Histories of the Book." *Studies in Bibliography* 56 (2003–2004): 141–170. Print.

Taylor, Gary. "In Media Res: From Jerome through Greg to Jerome (McGann)." *Textual Cultures: Texts, Contexts, Interpretation* 4.2 (2009): 88–101. Print.

Tokarczyk, Michelle. *Class Definitions: On the Lives and Writings of Maxine Hong Kingston, Sandra Cisneros, and Dorothy Allison*. Cranbury, NJ: Associated University Presses, 2008. Print.

Torres, Héctor. "Discourse and Plot in Rolando Hinojosa's *The Valley*: Narrativity and the Recovery of Chicano Heritage." *Confluencia: Revista Hispanica de Cultura and Literatura* 2.1 (1986): 84–93. Print.

Torres, Lourdes. "In the Contact Zone: Code-Switching Strategies by Latino/a Writers." *MELUS* 32.1 (2007): 75–96. Web. 6 May 2009.

Truett, Samuel. *Fugitive Landscapes: The Forgotten History of the U.S.-Mexico Borderlands*. New Haven, CT: Yale University Press, 2008. Print.

Truss, Lynn. *Eats, Shoots & Leaves: The Zero Tolerance Approach to Punctuation*. New York: Penguin, 2004. Print.

Tuan, Yi-Fu. *Space and Place: The Perspective of Experience*. Minneapolis: University of Minnesota Press, 1977. Print.

Tuttle, Jennifer S. "The Symptoms of Conquest: Race, Class, and the Nervous Body in *The Squatter and the Don*." *María Amparo Ruiz de Burton: Critical and Pedagogical Perspectives*. Ed. Amelia María de la Luz Montes and Anne Elizabeth Goldman. Lincoln: University of Nebraska Press, 2004. 56–71. Print.

Valdés, Maria Elena de. "In Search of Identity in Cisneros's *The House on Mango Street*." *In Sandra Cisneros's* The House on Mango Street. *Bloom's Modern Critical Interpretations*. 1992. New York: Infobase Publishing, 2010. 3–18. Print.

Van Dyke, Charles. *Books and How to Use Them: Some Hints to Readers and Students.* New York: Fords, Howard, and Hulbert, 1883. Web. 26 Aug. 2015.

Van Hooft, Karen. "Re: Candelaria Editorial Questions." Message to the author. 21 July 2015. Email.

———. "Re: Castillo Editorial Questions." Message to the author. 12 Aug. 2015. Email.

Vasquez, Librado Keno, and Mari Enriqueta Vasquez. *Regional Dictionary of Chicano Slang.* Austin, TX: Jenkins, 1975. Print.

Velasco, Juan. "Automitografías: The Border Paradigm in Chicana/o Autobiography." *Biography* 27.2 (2004): 313–338. Web. 13 Sept. 2011.

Venegas, Daniel. *Las aventuras de don Chipote o cuando los pericos mamen.* 1928. Mexico City: Secretaría de Educación Pública and Centro de Estudios de la Frontera Norte, 1985. Print.

———. *The Adventures of Don Chipote; or, When Parrots Breast-Feed.* Trans. Ethriam Cash Brammer. Houston: Arte Público Press, 2000. Print.

Villar Raso, Manuel, and María Herrera-Sobek. "A Spanish Novelist's Perspective on Chicano/a Literature." *Journal of Modern Literature* 2.1 (2005): 17–34. Web. 18 Nov. 2009.

Walter, Roland. "The Cultural Politics of Dislocation and Relocation in the Novels of Ana Castillo." *MELUS* 23.1 (1998): 81–97. Print.

Weldt-Basson, Helene. "Silence as Narrative Strategy in Sandra Cisneros's *The House on Mango Street.*" *Cuadernos de Aldeeu* 16.1 (2000): 201–209. Print.

Wellisch, Hans. *The Conversion of Scripts, Its Nature, History, and Utilization.* New York: Wiley, 1978. Print.

Wiggins, Alison. "What Did Renaissance Readers Write in Their Printed Copies of Chaucer?" *Library: The Transactions of the Bibliographical Society* 9.1 (2008): 3–36. Web. 3 Oct. 2010.

Wolfe, Joanna, and Christine Neuwirth. "From the Margins to the Center: The Future of Annotation." *Journal of Business and Technical Communication* 15.3 (2001): 333–371. Web. 21 July 2013.

Yañez, Richard. "Desert Vista." *El Paso del Norte: Stories on the Border.* Reno: University of Nevada Press, 2003. 1–17. Print.

———. "Re: Questions about 'Desert Vista.'" Message to the author. 3 July 2015. Email.

Yarbro-Bejarano, Yvonne. "The Multiple Subject in the Writing of Ana Castillo." *Americas Review* 20.1 (1992): 65–72. Print.

Young, John K. *Black Writers, White Publishers: Marketplace Politics in Twentieth-Century African American Literature.* Jackson: University Press of Mississippi, 2006. Print.

Zilles, Klaus. *Rolando Hinojosa: A Reader's Guide.* Albuquerque: University of New Mexico Press, 2001. Print.

"Zoot Suit: The Time and Its Temper." New York: Playbill, 1972. Print.

Index

Note: page numbers in italics refer to figures.

About the Author

ALLISON E. FAGAN is an assistant professor of English at James Madison University in Harrisonburg, Virginia, where she teaches contemporary ethnic American literatures. She has essays on Chicana/o and Latina/o print culture published or forthcoming in *MELUS*, *College Literature*, the *Routledge Companion to Latino/a Literature*, and the *Journal of Modern Literature*.

Available titles in the Latinidad: Transnational Cultures in the United States series:

María Acosta Cruz, *Dream Nation: Puerto Rican Culture and the Fictions of Independence*

Rodolfo F. Acuña, *The Making of Chicana/o Studies: In the Trenches of Academe*

Xóchitl Bada, *Mexican Hometown Associations in Chicagoacán: From Local to Transnational Civic Engagement*

Adriana Cruz-Manjarrez, *Zapotecs on the Move: Cultural, Social, and Political Processes in Transnational Perspective*

Marivel T. Danielson, *Homecoming Queers: Desire and Difference in Chicana Latina Cultural Production*

Allison E. Fagan, *From the Edge: Chicana/o Border Literature and the Politics of Print*

Rudy P. Guevarra Jr., *Becoming Mexipino: Multiethnic Identities and Communities in San Diego*

Colin Gunckel, *Mexico on Main Street: Transnational Film Culture in Los Angeles before World War II*

Marie-Theresa Hernández, *The Virgin of Guadalupe and the Conversos: Uncovering Hidden Influences from Spain to Mexico*

Lisa Jarvinen, *The Rise of Spanish-Language Filmmaking: Out from Hollywood's Shadow, 1929–1939*

Regina M. Marchi, *Day of the Dead in the USA: The Migration and Transformation of a Cultural Phenomenon*

Desirée A. Martín, *Borderlands Saints: Secular Sanctity in Chicano/a and Mexican Culture*

Marci R. McMahon, *Domestic Negotiations: Gender, Nation, and Self-Fashioning in US Mexicana and Chicana Literature and Art*

A. Gabriel Meléndez, *Hidden Chicano Cinema: Film Dramas in the Borderlands*

Priscilla Peña Ovalle, *Dance and the Hollywood Latina: Race, Sex, and Stardom*

Amalia Pallares, *Family Activism: Immigrant Struggles and the Politics of Noncitizenship*

Luis F. B. Plascencia, *Disenchanting Citizenship: Mexican Migrants and the Boundaries of Belonging*

Cecilia M. Rivas, *Salvadoran Imaginaries: Mediated Identities and Cultures of Consumption*

Jayson Gonzales Sae-Saue, *Southwest Asia: The Transpacific Geographies of Chicana/o Literature*

Mario Jimenez Sifuentez, *Of Forest and Fields: Mexican Labor in the Pacific Northwest*

Maya Socolovsky, *Troubling Nationhood in U.S. Latina Literature: Explorations of Place and Belonging*

CPSIA information can be obtained
at www.ICGtesting.com
Printed in the USA
LVOW04s1428190716
496919LV00020B/160/P

9 780813 583792